TELLING THE TRUTH

The Theory and Practice of Documentary Fiction

Barbara Foley

Cornell University Press   Ithaca and London

CORNELL UNIVERSITY PRESS GRATEFULLY ACKNOWLEDGES
A GRANT FROM THE ANDREW W. MELLON FOUNDATION
THAT AIDED IN BRINGING THIS BOOK TO PUBLICATION.

First published 1986 by Cornell University Press.

International Standard Book Number 0–8014–1877–1
Library of Congress Catalog Card Number 85–48198
Printed in the United States of America
Librarians: Library of Congress cataloging information
appears on the last page of the book.

The paper in this book is acid-free and meets the guidelines
for permanence and durability of the Committee on Production
Guidelines for Book Longevity of the Council on Library Resources.

TELLING THE TRUTH

To Houston, Adam, and Margaret

Contents

Preface

There is a regime language that derives its strength from what we are supposed to be and a language of freedom whose power consists in what we threaten to become. And I'm justified in giving a political character to the nonfictive and fictive uses of language because there is a conflict between them. . . .

I could claim that history is a kind of fiction in which we live and hope to survive, and fiction is a kind of speculative history, perhaps a superhistory, by which the available data for the composition is seen to be greater and more various in its sources than the historian supposes. . . .

There is no fiction or nonfiction as we commonly understand the distinction: there is only narrative. . . .

We [novelists] have it in us to compose false documents more valid, more real, more truthful than the "true" documents of the politicians or the journalists or the psychologists. Novelists know explicitly that the world in which we live is still to be formed and that reality is amenable to any construction that is placed upon it. It is a world made for liars and we are born liars.

—E. L. Doctorow

If contemporary literary theory has anything of value to teach us, it is that all texts inevitably situate themselves with reference to other texts. The present text bears a polemical relation to its context. When I argue that the documentary novel engages in dramatically different representational practices in different eras, but constitutes, nonetheless, a distinct species of fiction and moreover renders cognition of its referent, I am not simply describing a literary genre; I am taking a position within central literary debates of our time.

In E. L. Doctorow's words I find three propositions that point to important issues in these debates.[1] First, Doctorow says that the borderline between fictional and nonfictional narrative can and should be abolished: "There is no fiction or nonfiction . . . : there is only narrative." Fiction is a kind of history, history a kind of fiction; they differ only in the kinds of human potentiality that they portray. Second, however, Doctorow argues that fiction is "more valid, more real, more truthful" than nonfiction because, as a "false document," the fictional work openly admits that "reality is amenable to any construction that is placed upon it." Curiously, then, fiction is both identical with and superior to nonfiction; I shall comment below on the logical problem involved here. Third, Doctorow attaches an urgent political agenda to his distinction between fiction and nonfiction. The former, associated with a "regime language," is disciplinary; the latter, associated with a "language of freedom," is liberatory. Presumably, then, narrative eradicates the borderline between the two by an admission of the fictionality of reality. This is an emancipatory act, for it asserts the superior explanatory power of "lies" over "facts." Doctorow's comments illuminate his own novelistic practice, to be sure, but they signify much more than a theory of discourse applicable simply to his own work. Doctorow's remarks set forth the main premises that guide, I believe, a good deal of contemporary writing and theorizing about writing. This book largely grows out of my response to these premises.

Let me address first the notion that the borderline between nonfictional and fictive discourse is an arbitrary boundary, setting up a false discrimination between fact and imagination, when the truth is that "reality is amenable to any construction that is placed upon it." This is Doctorow's way of expressing an idea that has become highly influential and popular among both literary theorists and novelists— namely, that reality is itself a fiction, a text, a linguistic convention. Thus Mas'ud Zavarzadeh, setting forth his poetics of the nonfiction novel, argues that the "'fictuality' of current experience escapes the monoreferential narratives which require an unequivocal pledge to fact or fiction. . . . [The nonfiction novel] is a narrative which is simultaneously self-referential and out-referential, factual and fictional, and thus well equipped to deal with the elusive fusion of fact and fic-

[1]E. L. Doctorow, "False Documents," *American Review*, 26 (November 1977): 217, 229–30, 231, 232.

tion which has become the matrix of today's experience."[2] Robert Scholes declares that "it is because reality cannot be recorded that realism is dead. All writing, all composition, is construction. We do not imitate the world, we construct versions of it. There is no mimesis, only poesis. No recording. Only constructing."[3] Raymond Federman holds that "SURFICTION is the only fiction that still means something today, . . . because it exposes the fictionality of reality."[4] Jerome Klinkowitz, in his recent *The Self-Apparent Word,* argues that only writing that he calls "self-apparent" can be an antidote to the "mimetic poison" of inherited fictional modes. "To practice writing is not to parody signifying, it is to destroy the very practice of signifying itself," he declares. And the superiority of self-apparent writing derives from its superior epistemology. "We know reality only through our fictions," he concludes. "Reminding readers that fictions are provisional realities and not bedrock truth is the essence of self-apparent writing."[5]

Many contemporary writers of fiction and journalism add their voices to the chorus, proclaiming the unreality of reality and the undecidability of discourse. Norman Mailer, in *The Armies of the Night,* writes that history inhabits a "crazy-house" and that the "mystery of the events at the Pentagon," even when reconstructed by means of newspaper reports and eyewitness accounts, can be only a "collective novel."[6] Philip Roth declares that American reality "stupefies, . . . sickens, . . . infuriates, and finally . . . is even a kind of embarrassment to one's own meager imagination. [It] is continually outdoing our talents, and the culture tosses up figures almost daily that are the envy of any novelist."[7] Ronald Sukenick, whose polemical statements sometimes verge on self-parody, exclaims, "Reality doesn't exist, time doesn't exist, personality doesn't exist. . . . In view of

---

[2]Mas'ud Zavarzadeh, *The Mythopoeic Reality: The Postwar American Nonfiction Novel* (Urbana: University of Illinois Press, 1976), 56–57.

[3]Robert Scholes, *Structural Fabulation: An Essay on the Fiction of the Future* (Notre Dame: University of Notre Dame Press, 1975), 7.

[4]Raymond Federman, *SURFICTION: Fiction Now . . . and Tomorrow* (Chicago: Swallow, 1975), 7.

[5]Jerome Klinkowitz, *The Self-Apparent Word: Fiction as Language/Language as Fiction* (Carbondale: Southern Illinois University Press, 1984), 40, 59, 135.

[6]Norman Mailer, *The Armies of the Night: History as a Novel, the Novel as History* (New York: New American Library, 1968), 284.

[7]Philip Roth, "Writing American Fiction," *Commentary,* 31 (March 1961): 224.

these annihilations, it will be no surprise that literature, also, does not exist—how could it?"[8] "There is," he concludes elsewhere, "no such thing as fiction. Instead there is a continuing fictive discourse which continually redefines itself."[9]

These writers and theorists differ, of course, in their diagnoses of the reasons for this ontological collapse. Some, taking an apocalyptic view of the post–World War II era, argue that the fictionality of reality is a product of recent historical developments. Thus Zavarzadeh proposes that the "bizarre" and "fictual" nature of contemporary reality is a result of "runaway contemporary technologies."[10] John Hollowell suggests that the apocalyptic mood of the sixties, with the political protests, televised assassinations, and hippie counterculture, resulted in a "blur . . . of the comfortable distinctions between reality and unreality, fantasy and fact."[11] John Hellmann states that, in the sixties, "long-buried forces in the American psyche were coming to the surface with an almost eerie simultaneity in politics, in national and individual violence, in subcultures, in urban slums, in technology, in the young." Because of the "added force" of "mass-media journalism," the individual American "found himself daily confronted by realities that were as actual as they seemed fictive."[12]

Other writers and critics suggest that the experience of the Holocaust has permanently dislocated both reality and our consciousness of reality. Lawrence Langer, for example, states, "The existence of Dachau and Auschwitz as historical phenomena has altered not only our conception of reality, but its very nature."[13] Edward Alexander notes, "The nature and magnitude of the Holocaust were such as to mark almost certainly the end of one era of consciousness and the be-

[8]Ronald Sukenick, "Fiction in the Seventies: Ten Digressions on Ten Digressions," *Studies in American Fiction*, 5 (Spring 1977): 107–8.

[9]Quoted from a tape recording by Jerome Klinkowitz, in *The Life of Fiction* (Urbana: University of Illinois Press, 1977), 18.

[10]Zavarzadeh, 21.

[11]John Hollowell, *Fact and Fiction: The New Journalism and the Nonfiction Novel* (Chapel Hill: University of North Carolina Press, 1977), 5.

[12]John Hellmann, *Fables of Fact: The New Journalism as New Fiction* (Urbana: University of Illinois Press, 1981), 2.

[13]Lawrence Langer, *The Holocaust and the Literary Imagination* (New Haven: Yale University Press, 1975), xii. See also Alfred Alvarez, "The Literature of the Holocaust," *Commentary*, 5 (November 1964): 65–69, and Alvin Rosenfeld, "The Problematics of Holocaust Literature," in *Confronting the Holocaust: The Impact of Elie Wiesel*, ed. Rosenfeld and Irving Greenburg (Bloomington: Indiana University Press, 1978), 1–30.

ginning of another. . . . The human imagination after Auschwitz is simply not the same as it was before."[14]

I should point out, of course, that contemporary writers and literary theorists do not always say that inherited distinctions between fiction and nonfiction need to be collapsed because of some especially horrific quality attaching to the reality of the postwar era. More programmatic advocates of the reality-as-fiction thesis would declare that what we commonly accept as reality has in fact always been a construct. Jacques Derrida, I am sure, would chide Scholes for his naively logocentric belief that reality could ever be recorded, advocating that the critic instead "affirm . . . a world of signs" that "determines the non-center otherwise than as the loss of the center."[15] The binary opposition fiction/nonfiction, Derrida reminds us, is part of a "hierarchical axiology" that has perpetuated the repressive dualisms of Western metaphysics for centuries.[16] Michel Foucault insists that all explanatory paradigms are essentially fictional. Referring to his own work on the history of sexuality, he notes, "I am well aware that I have never written anything but fictions. . . . One 'fictions' history on the basis of a political reality that makes it true, one 'fictions' a politics not yet in existence on the basis of a historical truth."[17] Lennard J. Davis, using Foucault's methodology in his recent exploration of the origins of the English novel, concludes that "novels are framed works . . . whose attitude toward fact and fiction is constitutively ambivalent." Throughout its history, Davis maintains, the novel "is a factual fiction that is both factual and factitious."[18] Where the apocalyptic critics endorse a kind of peculiar reflectionism—a distorted reality produces a distorted discourse—the poststructuralist critics argue that the crisis in reference is an abiding feature of discourse itself. Both schools of critics agree, however, in their convic-

[14]Edward Alexander, *The Resonance of Dust: Essays on Holocaust Literature* (Columbus: Ohio State University Press, 1979), 1-2.

[15]Jacques Derrida, "Structure, Sign, and Play," in *The Languages of Criticism and the Sciences of Man*, ed. Richard Macksey and Eugenio Donato (Baltimore: Johns Hopkins University Press, 1972), 264.

[16]Jacques Derrida, "Limited Inc abc," in *Glyph: Johns Hopkins Textual Studies 2* (Baltimore: Johns Hopkins University Press, 1977), 236.

[17]Michel Foucault, *Power/Knowledge: Selected Interviews and Other Writings, 1972-77*, ed. Colin Gordon, trans. Gordon, Leo Marshall, John Mepham, and Kate Saper (New York: Pantheon, 1980), 193.

[18]Lennard J. Davis, *Factual Fictions: The Origins of the English Novel* (New York: Columbia University Press, 1983), 212.

tion that referentiality is dead—if it ever was alive—and that the task of writers and critics is to get on with the business of living in, and talking about, a fictional world.

I encountered various versions of these polemics when I was fresh from writing a (largely neo-Aristotelian) dissertation on John Dos Passos's *U.S.A.* trilogy, and they struck me as provocative but also profoundly unsatisfactory. On the one hand, such pronouncements gave the final drubbing to the myths of empiricist and positivist objectivism. These straw men, of course, have been dead for some time, but a few more licks can never do any harm. As I surveyed the works of Dos Passos's descendants, I could readily see that contemporary writers interested in the relation between fact and fiction were even more disturbed by the bizarre opacity of social reality than were Dos Passos and his modernist contemporaries. On the other hand, I also became convinced that, despite their bold proclamations about the dissolution of boundaries, contemporary novelists and journalists were continuing in their own works to invoke discursive contracts that were decidedly fictional or nonfictional. As Christine Brooke-Rose laconically notes, "the very statement that the ontological fact is itself without significance is a signifying statement, imposing a view of reality as non-significant, imposing, that is, the significance of non-significance."[19] Doctorow, for all his free play with the felt verifiability of the "facts" included in *Ragtime*—did Freud and Jung go through the Tunnel of Love together when they visited Coney Island?—treats his major characters and major actions as fictive constructs. As in more traditional historical novels, data drawn from presumably extratextual sources enter the text primarily to corroborate the text's thematic design and are incorporated into a fictive totality. Mailer, by contrast, projects throughout *The Armies of the Night* a third-person autobiographical presence remarkably similar to that created by Henry Adams in his *Education*. When, in part 2 of *Armies*, Mailer switches gears to give a novelistic account of events he did not witness, he tells us in no uncertain terms that he is doing so. Turning to what I could learn about the responses of other readers to contemporary works of journalism and fiction, I found my own reactions provisionally confirmed. None of the reviewers of *Ragtime* com-

[19]Christine Brooke-Rose, *A Rhetoric of the Unreal: Studies in Narrative and Structure, Especially of the Fantastic* (Cambridge: Cambridge University Press, 1981), 4.

plained that Doctorow had distorted the historical record; they may have quarreled with him on various scores, but they appear to have acceded to his play with facts on the grounds that he was simply writing a novel. By contrast, many readers of works such as *In Cold Blood*, *The Executioner's Song*, and *Roots* have stated that the credibility of the narrative collapsed for them when they discovered that certain details had been invented or significantly changed to enhance the thematic patterning of the text.[20] Clearly these readers did not feel that the writers' disregard for information existing in the historical record represented support for the proposition that contemporary reality is weird and unknowable; they simply felt that they had been deceived. I found, in other words, that even in works asserting the "significance of non-significance," the idea that history is a fiction has been asserted in conventionally novelistic, journalistic, and autobiographical ways.

As I pondered these questions, I became less interested in contemporary documentary writers themselves—whose solipsism I found generally irritating and barren—and more interested in the literary-historical and theoretical questions that their writings raised. Was Doctorow correct in his assertion that the novel has always pretended to be a false document? If I was correct in my feeling that fictional and nonfictional discourse are qualitatively distinguished in our time, could I assume that this has always been the case? To answer these questions, I embarked upon an examination of the shifting borderline between fiction and its counterparts in historical, journalistic, biographical, and autobiographical writing. I discovered—and here is one of the central problems explored in this book—that literary kinds are constitutively historical to a degree that, in my Chicago

---

[20]For an attack on Alex Haley's veracity in *Roots: The Saga of an American Family*, see Mark Ottoway, "Tangled Roots," *Times* (London), April 10, 1977, pp. 17, 21. Phillip K. Tompkins questions Capote's claim to have invented none of his materials in "In Cold Fact," reprinted in Irving Malin, ed., *Truman Capote's "In Cold Blood": A Casebook* (Belmont, Calif.: Wadsworth, 1968), 45–59. John Hersey attacks both Tom Wolfe's *The Right Stuff* and Mailer's *The Executioner's Song* for specious claims to be telling the truth, in "The Legend on the License," *Yale Review*, 70 (Autumn 1980): 1–25. Mailer's veracity in *Armies* is more difficult to assess. Alfred Kazin asserts that Mailer's account of the Pentagon march has been "scornfully rejected by those who marched with him," but Dwight MacDonald, who marched with Mailer, maintains that he and Robert Lowell cannot dispute Mailer's accuracy. See Kazin, "The Imagination of Fact," in *Bright Book of Life: American Novelists and Storytellers from Hemingway to Mailer* (Boston: Little, Brown, 1973), 228, and Macdonald, "Politics," *Esquire*, May 1968, 44.

School naïveté, I had never imagined. Authors signaled fictional intentions by widely varying conventions; if mimesis had any continuous essence, this seemed to consist simply in its being a contractual agreement to understand reality by means of certain analogizing procedures. Even the documentary novel, which I had originally supposed to practice a more or less constant strategy of testimonial corroboration, turned out to alter dramatically its modes of empirical authentication as it moved from the eighteenth century to the twentieth. Writers maintained at all times, I could see, some kind of borderline between fictional discourse and its various counterparts—between analogizing and directly propositional assertion—but this borderline was in no way fixed or permanent.

The current debates about factual and fictive discourse turned me in the direction of literary history, but they also motivated me to reformulate some of my ideas about mimesis as a mode of cognition. I became increasingly disquieted by the realization that, in proclaiming the fictiveness of all reality and all textuality, what seemed to appeal to writers and theorists about fiction was its presumed reluctance to make assertions about the historical world. The "power of freedom," it appeared, consisted in fiction's release from any obligation to offer determinate statements about reality. The "power of the regime," of determinate reference, was the province of the bad guys. This struck me as a peculiarly backhanded compliment: fiction's claim to privileged status was said to reside in its impotence. The antiassertionist view of mimesis contradicted my own experience: I had learned a tremendous amount from fictional works, not only about how novelists construed their reality, but also (do I dare to say it?) about the reality itself. Certainly Dos Passos had introduced me to a view of American history in the first three decades of the century that I had yet to relinquish, though it might be supplemented or corrected. And yet these new pronouncements cautioned me, and rightly so, about the necessarily ideological encoding of that knowledge—especially, indeed, when it purported to buttress itself with unmediated extratextual documentation. Perhaps my hero Dos Passos, with his newsreels and biographies, was a villain after all, bent upon epistemological deceit and political obfuscation.

Accordingly—here is the second of the principal theses explored in this book—I decided to examine the constitutive features of the mimetic contract and the distinctive qualities of the mimetic mode of cognition. If the referent of the mimetic text was not an inert and self-evident set of facts, what was it? If authorial perspective did not entirely close off cognition of the referent, how did it determine the conditions of knowledge? By what procedure, in other words, did the concrete particulars of character and event represented in a novel mediate and reconcretize actual people, occurrences, and situations? In seeking a way to answer these questions, I found that, once again, the genre of the documentary novel would furnish a useful test case. For, through its various postures of inviolable reliability, the documentary novel was especially vulnerable to the charge of ideological distortion and, indeed, fiction-making, in the negative sense of the word. I was not interested in updating Sidney's *Defence* to cover the cases of *Lost in the Funhouse* or *Tell Me a Riddle*, though clearly my argument would encompass these texts as well. Rather, I wished to describe the cognitive powers and limitations of such texts as Behn's *Oroonoko*, Defoe's *Moll Flanders*, Cooper's *The Spy*, Eliot's *Romola*, Isherwood's *Goodbye to Berlin*, Woolf's *Orlando*, Dos Passos's *U.S.A.*, and even—resist as its author might—*Ragtime*. Advocates of fictional assertion are in a peculiar situation these days. If they wish to demonstrate that fictional texts convey knowledge about historical actuality, they are constrained to show that the writer's adducement of a testimonial apparatus does not pose too formidable a barrier to the projection of cognition.

The literary-historical and theoretical aspects of the problem I was addressing piqued my curiosity, but its political implications invested it with a particular urgency for me. Doctorow is not alone in saying that the eradication of borders constitutes a radical praxis. The whole poststructuralist project of displacing, rupturing, subverting, and overturning the dualisms of Western metaphysics is characterized by a similar panache. Domination consists in the imposition of homogeneity, determinacy, and boundaries; liberation consists in heterogeneity, indeterminacy, and dispersal. My own political commitments —which were distinctly Marxist—made me wary of such pronouncements, particularly when they adopted a radical posture, claiming to pose a greater threat to bourgeois hegemony than any revolutionary praxis locked into a logocentric paradigm. No doubt the attack on the binary opposition fiction/nonfiction is intended to help us break free from those fetishized conceptions of reality that legitimate and rationalize the status quo. But it seems to me that the poststructuralist project deepens the writer's implication in the reification of advanced monopoly capitalism, insofar as the fetishization of textuality mediates the extreme abstraction of a society in which all human functions are rendered equivalent by the universal market. The authorial subject had been banished from the domain of politicized literary studies; he or she demanded reentry. I felt that a defense of documentary mimesis as assertive discourse, continuous with other kinds of writing in its claim to cognition but distinct and different in its mode of cognition, would help to reorient Marxist literary studies in some helpful ways.

To approach the question of the documentary novel from a Marxist perspective has proved no mean challenge, however. It is no longer possible—and in any event was never correct—to argue that the documentary novel replicates a self-evident reality with greater or lesser degrees of historical accuracy, which it is then the task of the critic to assess and evaluate. The reflectionist model of mimesis inherited from the later Lukács cannot accurately describe the mode of cognition embodied in the documentary novel, for it leaves insufficient theoretical space for a consideration of the extent to which the reality represented in the text is a construction of consciousness. Yet it is a highly questionable practice to argue, as do critics in the Althusserian school, that mimesis is primarily a signifying gesture, revealing a good deal about the ideologies that it exposes but nothing determinate about the reality to which the text "alludes." My indebtedness to these different tendencies in Marxist criticism is present throughout this book, but so also is my uneasiness with their theoretical premises. In outlining, then, a Marxist approach to the problem of documentary representation—the third, and synthesizing, concern of this study—I have kept a critical distance from most Marxist literary theory, preferring instead to turn to the pages of Marx and Lenin for a politics and an epistemology with which to reexamine the knotty problems of representation and mediation.

The inadequacy of existing paradigms in Marxist literary theory is further evinced by these paradigms' inability to account for the kinds of mimetic contracts proffered by writers who are, in any era, excluded from participation in certain mainstream ideological assumptions—such as black American writers. The reflectionist model cannot account for the tensions accompanying black writers' acts of fictional communication, because it presumes too ready an assimilation of the subject to dominant epistemological paradigms. The Althusserian model succeeds no better at this task, however, because it too glibly asserts that texts distance themselves from the ideological viewpoints that they express. My inclusion of a closing chapter on the uses of documentation in Afro-American fiction thus constitutes an attempt to redress several literary-historical and theoretical imbalances. In the first place, a scrutiny of Afro-American documentary novels reveals the need for the major tendencies in Marxist criticism to adjust themselves—the Lukácsian school to a greater stress upon subjective displacement in mimetic representation, the Althusserian school to a greater stress upon objective replication of the referent. Second, since Afro-American writers from the start have attached a particular urgency to their program of telling the truth, their writings contain an implicit challenge to much of the contemporary critical theory I discussed earlier. It is difficult to argue that reality is in any meaningful sense fictional for William Wells Brown or Margaret Walker. Finally, Afro-American literature has too often been construed as oppositional to dominant ideology merely through its explicit assertions about its referent. By incorporating documentary works by black writers into the theoretical framework I set forth here, I have tried to show how these works resist hegemony through the very conventions they assume and the generic contracts they hold out to the reader.

It is a commonplace for authors to use their prefaces to apologize for possible shortcomings of their books, and I am as eager as any to avail myself of the opportunity. I have three main reservations about this book. First, my investigation has taken me into many historical areas where I do not have a specialist's knowledge, and I am aware that some of my textual readings—as well as some of my generalizations about periods and genres—may be vulnerable to criticism from experts in these fields. Second, my attempt to relate vast social forces to the particularities of individual literary works has required me to treat the problem of mediation at a level of considerable generality. I introduce substantial analyses of philosophy and historiography to flesh out the relation between novels and contemporaneous ideological developments, but these materials reinforce my argument logically rather than empirically. In defense of this speculative methodology, I can only affirm that I do not envision the actual, lived relation between base and superstructure as abstract and schematic, even though requirements of brevity have compelled me to describe this relation in a somewhat schematic manner. Third, I recognize that my inquiry has required me to cut a wide swath of historical and theoretical materials. Had I limited myself to a single period or a single theoretical issue, I might have produced a more modest book, but it would not, I think, have been a better one. It is in my broad claims about the nature of fictional assertion and mediation that I hope to make my contribution to literary study, and it is on the basis of these claims that I wish primarily to be judged.

I am indebted to several colleagues and friends for their help and advice. Robert Streeter and the late Sheldon Sacks, who directed my dissertation, taught me to ask certain kinds of questions about literary works and literary developments and not to settle for easy answers. Robert Jones, William Andrews, L. S. Dembo, and Walter Rideout, all former colleagues at the University of Wisconsin at Madison, read portions of the book in its early stages and offered useful suggestions. John Michael Lennon and John Hellmann helped me to refine my argument in the theoretical section. Several colleagues at Northwestern University—Elizabeth Dipple, Martin Mueller, Paul Breslin, and Gayle Pemberton—commented on various chapters and aided me in shaping the argument of the parts and the whole. Various friends and colleagues in the InterNational Committee against Racism—Bonnie Blustein, Gregory Meyerson, Houston Stevens, Russell Reising, Finley Campbell, and Val Woodward—contributed to my knowledge of Marxism in invaluable ways. Gerald Graff read the entire manuscript at a crucial stage and made highly constructive suggestions about substance, organization, and style; those familiar with Graff's work will see its imprint on many of my pages.

Harry Shaw of Cornell University gave a careful and comprehensive reader's report that helped me to streamline my argument. Richard Ohmann provided an incisive critique of an early version of the theory section and later offered some valuable caveats when he read the entire manuscript for Cornell University Press. Marjorie Weiner painstakingly typed a version of the text in the days before I had access to a word processor. I am very grateful to these individuals for their generosity with their time, energy, and expertise.

My greatest debt is to my husband, Houston Stevens, and my children, Adam and Margaret, whose love and patience have enabled me to be a scholar, teacher, political activist, wife, and mother. I dedicate this book to them.

BARBARA FOLEY

Evanston, Illinois

PART I

THEORY

The Documentary Novel and
the Problem of Borders

Belief in fiction cannot be a matter of degree. We either accept the incidents of a story as if they were true, or we are aware of them as fiction.
There can be no halfway house, no keeping an open mind, no sus-
pending our judgement until further evidence is available.

—Vivienne Mylne

In this book I shall be arguing that the documentary novel
constitutes a distinct fictional kind. It locates itself near the border between factual discourse and fictive discourse, but it does not propose
an eradication of that border. Rather, it purports to represent reality
by means of agreed-upon conventions of fictionality, while grafting
onto its fictive pact some kind of additional claim to empirical validation. Historically, this claim has taken various forms. The pseudofactual novel of the seventeenth and eighteenth centuries simulates or
imitates the authentic testimony of a "real life" person; its documentary effect derives from the assertion of veracity. The historical novel
of the nineteenth century takes as its referent a phase of the historical
process; its documentary effect derives from the assertion of extratextual verification. The documentary novel in the modernist era bifur-
cates into two distinct genres. The fictional autobiography represents
an artist-hero who assumes the status of a real person inhabiting an
invented situation; its documentary effect derives from the assertion
of the artist's claim to privileged cognition. The metahistorical novel
takes as its referent a historical process that evades rational formulation; its documentary effect derives from the assertion of the very indeterminacy of factual verification. Finally, the Afro-American documentary novel represents a reality submitting human subjects to
racist objectification; its documentary effect derives from the presen-

tation of facts that subvert commonplace constructions of reality. In all its phases, then, the documentary novel aspires to tell the truth, and it associates this truth with claims to empirical validation. If it increasingly calls into question the possibility of truth-telling, this skepticism is directed more toward the ideological assumptions undergirding empiricism than toward the capacity of fictive discourse to interpret and represent its referent.

Clearly the documentary novel, as I define it in this book, is not a minor subgenre that can be readily relegated to the margins of novelistic production in any given era. On the contrary: in the seventeenth and eighteenth centuries, the documentary novel is closely aligned with writing that Lennard J. Davis calls the "news/novel discourse";[1] in the nineteenth century, the documentary novel intersects with the major tradition of realism; in the early decades of the twentieth century, it participates in the principal concerns of modernism. Much writing in the entire domain of Afro-American prose fiction has a pronounced documentary quality. Thus central texts from each phase in the history of the novel (for example, *Moll Flanders, Pamela, Waverley, Henry Esmond, Orlando, A Portrait of the Artist as a Young Man, Native Son*) can be adjudged to be documentary novels. But while the documentary novel overlaps with the mainstream tradition of the novel, it is not identical with this tradition. Rather, the documentary novel is distinguished by its insistence that it contains some kind of specific and verifiable link to the historical world. (Whether or not this link succeeds in being "extratextual" in a larger sense remains to be seen.) It implicitly claims to replicate certain features of actuality in a relatively direct and unmediated fashion; it invokes familiar novelistic conventions, but it requires the reader to accept certain textual elements—characters, incidents, or actual documents—as possessing referents in the world of the reader. The documentary novel is not superior to other modes of fictional discourse in its capacity for assertion—all fictions assert their propositional content with equal force and sincerity, I believe—but it does raise the problem of reference for explicit consideration. To investigate the truth-telling claims of the documentary novel is thus to illuminate the assertive capacities of fiction in general.

[1] Lennard J. Davis, *Factual Fictions: The Origins of the English Novel* (New York: Columbia University Press, 1983).

As we shall see in the literary-historical portions of this book, the documentary novel's shift in representational strategy reveals the inevitable historicity of generic definitions. Factual and fictive discourses are not immutable essences but are historically varying types of writing, signaled by, and embodied in, changing literary conventions and generated by the changing structures of historically specific relations of production and intercourse. As M. M. Bakhtin has remarked, "The boundaries between fiction and nonfiction, between literature and nonliterature and so forth are not laid up in heaven. Every specific situation is historical. And the growth of literature is not merely development and change within the fixed boundaries of any definition; the boundaries themselves are constantly changing."[2] In examining the documentary novel's protean identity, I have had to abandon many prior conceptions about what constitutes fiction, the novel, history, and the elusive quality that I am terming the "documentary" effect. Modes of discourse do not remain within "fixed boundaries"; they change as much as do the modes of social and political representation in the worlds that they take as their referents.

I have discovered, nonetheless, that the distinction between fictional discourse and its various nonfictional counterparts—history, journalism, biography, autobiography—has remained a qualitative one. The need to distinguish between narratives held to be imaginary and those held to be directly representational would seem to be not a post-Cartesian phenomenon, testifying to the alienation of subject from object, but an abiding feature of discursive production. Even in the seventeenth and eighteenth centuries, when the documentary novel possessed its most ambiguous generic identity, the issue was not that prose fiction simply blended into purportedly veracious kinds of writing but that its primary locus, the romance, could not effectively assert the kind of truth that the early pseudofactual novelists wanted to tell. The pseudofactual novel's ambiguous generic status does not mean that writers and readers of the time inhabited an ontological haze but that they felt obliged to simulate veracious discourses if they hoped to appear credible to their readers. To say, as Bakhtin does, that the borderline between fiction and nonfiction is "constantly changing" does not mean that writers have not routinely respected such a borderline; it means, on the contrary, that writers have

[2]M. M. Bakhtin, *The Dialogic Imagination: Four Essays*, ed. Michael Holquist, trans. Caryl Emerson and Holquist (Austin: University of Texas Press, 1981), 33.

composed their fictions in contradistinction to one or more acknowledged forms of nonfictional writing. Fiction, I would propose, is intrinsically part of a binary opposition; it is what it is by virtue of what
it is not.

To some, this argument will seem trivial or self-evident. As I indicated in my prefatory remarks, however, recent years have witnessed
a wholesale assault upon the idea that fictional and nonfictional writing can—or should—be qualitatively differentiated. The theoretical
arguments for the nonqualitative position come mainly from poststructuralism, but many writers and critics have added their voices.
In this prolegomenon to my central theoretical and historical discussions, I shall confront the principal claims of my adversaries by arguing on logical grounds for the superiority of a qualitative view of
mimesis. (By "qualitative" I mean different in kind rather than in degree.) In so doing, I run the risk of appearing to endorse an ahistorical
or essentialist view of mimesis. Certainly it is true, as we shall see,
that many defenses of the uniqueness of mimesis do in fact reify the
realms of fictional and nonfictional discourse and deny their continually altering character. I believe, however, that a qualitative approach
to the matter of defining fictionality is consonant with the premises
of a materialist literary theory, so long as we remember that binary
oppositions are dialectical oppositions as well. In order to counter the
objection that my entire analysis of the theoretical and historical features of documentary mimesis is based on a fallacious premise about
the distinctness of discursive kinds, I shall defend my procedure here,
trusting that the full validation of my argument will emerge in the
chapters that follow.[3]

[3]In Chapters 1 to 4, I shall frequently be citing—and disputing—the views of critics
who use the term "literature" or "poetry" where I use the term "fiction" or "mimesis." I am
aware that this procedure may appear imprecise. The term "poetry," of course, often refers
to verse; the term "literature" can be taken either as an honorific term denoting the quality
of a text or as a highly general term denoting the whole province of "imaginative" writing
—thus including a good deal of history, biography, autobiography, and journalism. In the
discussions that follow, I have tried to adhere as closely as possible to the intentions of the
critics cited: I have not adduced in support of my argument an opposition between "literature" and "nonliterature," for example, when its author means a distinction between "serious" and "popular" writing. It would have been incorrect, however, to confine my debates
to those critics who use the terms "fiction" and "nonfiction," since critics often do mean
"fictionality" when they discuss the essential feature(s) of "literary" or "poetic" discourse.
For more on the definition of "literature," see the various essays in Paul Hernadi's collection What Is Literature? (Bloomington: Indiana University Press, 1978); Raymond Wil-

The view that fictional and nonfictional discourse cannot be qualitatively distinguished ordinarily rests on one of three arguments. The first of these, which I shall term the "spectrum" argument, centers on the claim that the significant qualities of factuality and fictionality inhere in separate facets of a literary work, rather than in any informing paradigm, and that the task of criticism is to assess the impact of these upon the work's rhetorical effect. Thus Paul Hernadi advocates a "microstructural theory of poetic discourse," which holds that any given literary work possesses aspects of various discourses and should be analyzed not as a text unified by a single generic frame but as a unity of multiple components reflecting the richness of literary discourse in general. Hernadi repudiates the investigation of "generic conventions as reflections of historically conditioned preferences of writers and readers." Instead, he asserts, "The finest generic classifications of our time make us look beyond their immediate concerns and focus on the order of literature, not on borders between literary genres."[4] Scholes and Kellogg, in *The Nature of Narrative*, reach a similar conclusion from the opposite direction, for they insist that it is such "historically conditioned preferences" that furnish the logical basis for a nonqualitative definition of mimesis. The novel has historically synthesized two narrative impulses, they argue, one directed toward the "empirical," or historical, and the other directed toward the "fictional," or imaginary. Empirical and fictional are blended tendencies, rather than distinctive kinds; history and fantasy stand as the poles of a narrative spectrum, with different narrative forms such as autobiography, realism, and romance occupying positions at various points along the scale. The "recording of specific fact, the representation of what resembles specific fact, and the representation of generalized types of actuality," declare Scholes and Kellogg, are all to be aligned along the empirical part of the narrative spectrum.[5]

---

liams, *Marxism and Literature* (Oxford: Oxford University Press, 1977), 45–54; and Tzvetan Todorov, "The Notion of Literature," *New Literary History*, 5 (Autumn 1973): 5–16. Note, also, that I use the term "mimesis" interchangeably with "fiction." Some theorists would include under the rubric of mimesis any discourse purporting to represent reality (that is, history, biography, autobiography, and so forth) but would exclude fictions of the more romantic or fantastic variety.

[4]Paul Hernadi, *Beyond Genre: New Directions in Literary Classification* (Ithaca: Cornell University Press, 1972), 184.

[5]Robert Scholes and Robert Kellogg, *The Nature of Narrative* (New York: Oxford University Press, 1969), 86–87.

A second type of nonqualitative argument, which I shall term the "family resemblance" argument, is based upon an invocation—albeit somewhat simplified—of Ludwig Wittgenstein's theory of linguistic reference. In his discussion of the definitive characteristics of concepts such as games, Wittgenstein points out the difficulties involved in the attempt to delineate a limited set of criteria that descriptively include all activities commonly held to be games and exclude all other activities: "Consider for example the proceedings we call 'games.' . . . What is common to them all?—Don't say, there *must* be something common, or they would not be called '*games*'—but *look* and *see* whether there is anything common to all. For if you look at them you will not see something that is common to *all*, but similarities, relationships, and a whole series at that." Drawing an analogy between games and the physical traits shared by the members of the same family, Wittgenstein concludes, "We see a complicated network of similarities overlapping and crisscrossing; sometimes overall similarities, sometimes similarities of detail."[6] For Wittgenstein, no fixed set of properties defines the term "game," just as no fixed set of physical characteristics is shared by all members of the same family. For Wittgenstein, language seduces us into believing that certain words denote actually existing sets of relations, when all that these words really denote is concepts used to order the world of things.

Applied to the problem of defining mimesis, the "family resemblance" argument proposes that qualitative distinctions between factual and fictional discourse are founded upon fallacious logic. Morris Weitz, for example, invokes Wittgenstein when he asserts that all aesthetic categories, including the theory of literary kinds, are concepts with blurred edges and that it is therefore impossible to formulate a clear description of mimetic discourse. Asking himself whether an experimental fiction utilizing new kinds of referential procedures can be classified as a "novel," he observes, "What is at stake here is no factual analysis concerning necessary and sufficient properties but a decision as to whether the work under examination is similar in certain respects to other works, already called 'novels,' and consequently warrants the extension of the concept to cover the new case." Every such classificatory decision is, however, necessarily an ad hoc decision:

[6]Ludwig Wittgenstein, *Philosophical Investigations,* 3d ed., trans. G. E. M. Anscombe (New York: Macmillan, 1956), 1, secs. 66–69.

"Art," itself, is an open concept. New conditions (cases) have constantly arisen and will undoubtedly constantly arise; new art forms, new movements will emerge, which will demand decisions on the part of those interested, usually professional critics, as to whether the concept should be extended or not. . . . Art, as the logic of the concept shows, has no set of necessary and sufficient properties, hence a theory of it is logically impossible and not merely factually difficult.[7]

Charles Stevenson, also invoking Wittgenstein, introduces a mathematical model to solve the problem of fictional classification. Since fictionality is signaled by a multiplicity of possibly relevant textual properties, he argues, and since no fictional work will possess all the traits associated with mimesis, fictional representation consists of a "weighted average" of mimetic elements.[8] According to Stevenson, an arithmetical computation of discernible features will yield the basis for a definitive decision about a text's qualification for membership in the class of fictions. The "family resemblance" argument claims for itself the virtues of both historicity and empirical precision: to posit a fixed set of fictional features violates not only the course of literary-historical development but also the diversity of features present in any given fictional text.

Proponents of the spectrum and family resemblance approaches to generic definition quite correctly alert us to the danger of taking fictionality to reside in an immutable set of textual properties. But their arguments are only superficially empirical and historicist. The spectrum argument conflates the necessary recognition of historical shifts in the mimetic contract with the impossibility of logical classification, thereby precluding any inquiry into the historically varying

[7]Morris Weitz, "The Role of Theory in Aesthetics," *Journal of Aesthetics and Art Criticism,* 15 (September 1956): 28, 32.

[8]Charles Stevenson, "On 'What Is a Poem?'" *Philosophical Review,* 66 (July 1957): 329–62. Also see N. W. Visser, "The Generic Identity of the Novel," *Novel,* 11 (Winter 1978): 101–14. For a persuasive critique of the application of the "family resemblance" concept to logical problems in aesthetic theory, see Maurice Mandelbaum, "Family Resemblances and Generalization Concerning the Arts," in *Problems in Aesthetics: An Introductory Book of Readings,* ed. Morris Weitz, 2d ed. (London: Macmillan, 1970), 181–98. Mandelbaum argues that "family resemblance" theorists err in their focus upon "manifest features" rather than upon "relational attributes," which would require the critic to "consider specific art objects as having been created by someone for some actual or possible audience" (187). In mathematics, as Stevenson observes, the quantitative approach to generic definition entails a repudiation of set theory. See Abraham Kaplan and H. F. Schott, "A Calculus for Empirical Classes," *Methodos,* 3 (1951): 165–90.

31

epistemological bases of generic distinctions. Scholes and Kellogg quite rightly point out that the various modes of fictional, historical, and autobiographical discourse have adopted conventions signaled by widely varying textual features, and they convincingly demonstrate that certain markers of generic identity have even reversed their functions: the unwitnessed monologue, now a sure indicator of an author's fictional intentions, was once, they show, an accepted convention of heroic history. But a recognition of the relative—that is, historically variable—nature of the fact/fiction opposition does not mean that this opposition is denied absolute status at any given historical juncture. A spectrum of empirical possibilities is not the same thing as a spectrum of discursive kinds. As Barbara Herrnstein Smith puts it, "There is no principle of relative differentiation that could allow us to speak of any given composition as 'more' or 'less' fictive . . . and thereby assign it its proper place on the continuum. The distinction between natural and fictive is absolute."[9] The spectrum argument ends up treating generic categorization as a framework imposed a posteriori by literary critics, ruling out the possibility that it may constitute a necessary basis for the contracts formed between actual writers and readers.

The central problem with the family resemblance argument is that it treats all textual elements as having an equal claim upon the reader's attention, with no single trait being privileged by convention or authorial intention to exercise a dominant influence in the reader's apprehension of the text's generic identity. The text is, quite simply, the sum of its parts; if these parts cannot add up to a sufficient total, then the text is not recognizable as a member of the family of fictions. But to maintain that separate elements in factual or fictive works signal a certain family resemblance does not imply that qualitatively defined sets of relations among these elements cannot also be uncovered. Concepts with blurred edges are not necessarily concepts that lack a principle of unity; indeed, as Wittgenstein himself pointed out, concepts such as "games," while not readily definable in descriptive

[9]Barbara Herrnstein Smith, "On the Margins of Discourse," *Critical Inquiry*, I (June 1975): 774. For a penetrating discussion of the changing boundary between autobiography and the novel, a distinction that is "dependent on distinctions between fiction and nonfiction, between rhetorical and empirical first-person narrative," see Elizabeth Bruss, *Autobiographical Acts: The Changing Situation of a Literary Genre* (Baltimore: Johns Hopkins University Press, 1976), 5–18.

terms, are easily definable in practice, since clearly people know when they are playing games and when they are not. Wittgenstein's "insight into the looseness of our concepts, and its attendant jargon of 'family resemblance,'" remarks John Searle, "should not lead us into a rejection of the very enterprise of philosophical analysis."[10]

The third type of nonqualitative argument—the one developed recently with the most vehemence—has come from poststructuralist critics, who, invoking Nietzsche, propose that all our discourses about the material world, both factual and fictive, are circumscribed by the texts we construe in relation to that world. The very act of formulating an explanatory scheme is, for Barthes and Derrida, an enterprise inevitably shaped by language and ideology and is therefore fictive, in effect if not in intent. The project of criticism should not be to perpetuate the metaphysical dualisms of Western thought —among which the opposition of fiction and nonfiction figures centrally—but to reveal the inadequacy of reductive binary oppositions that privilege the products of the "creative" imagination, relegate (non)fiction to the margins of discourse, and ignore the textuality of all writing. Thus Roland Barthes has argued that

> the only feature which distinguishes historical discourse from other kinds is a paradox: the "fact" can exist linguistically only as a term in a discourse, yet we behave as if it were a simple reproduction of something on another plane of existence altogether, some extra-structural "reality." Historical discourse is presumably the only kind which aims at a referent "outside" itself that can in fact never be reached.

Historical discourse is, therefore, a "fake performative, in which what claims to be the descriptive element is in fact only the expres-

[10]John R. Searle, *Speech Acts: An Essay in the Philosophy of Language* (Cambridge: Cambridge University Press, 1970), 55. According to John M. Ellis, Wittgenstein's theory of language, properly understood, leads to the conclusion that literature can be qualitatively described by means of a "functional" definition. "When we seek a definition," he argues, "what we are seeking is not a statement of the features held in common by the members of the category, but the appropriate circumstances for the use of the word and the features of those circumstances that determine the willingness or unwillingness of the speakers of the language to use the word" (*The Theory of Literary Criticism: A Logical Analysis* [Berkeley: University of California Press, 1974], 34). Weitz is a crude Wittgensteinian, Ellis implies, for Weitz takes the impossibility of definition as the alternative to referential definition. The value of Ellis's theory is diminished, however, by his adherence to a nonassertive view of mimesis: the functionality of literary works, it turns out, consists in their being "used by society in such a way that the text is not taken as specifically relevant to the immediate context of its origin" (43).

sion of the authoritarian nature of that particular speech-act."[11] For Barthes, the insistence upon a referent beyond textuality is not simply a gesture of epistemological naïveté: it is an act of political repression.

Derrida develops the militantly antigeneric implications of Barthes's argument. The formulation of the binary opposition fiction/nonfiction produces, for Derrida, a "hierarchical axiology" that presupposes "an origin or . . . a 'priority' held to be simple, intact, normal, pure, standard, self-identical."[12] One aspect of the opposition (in this case, fiction) is implicitly valorized, and the other (nonfiction) is defined by subordination or exclusion—that is, by nonidentity. A deconstruction of such metaphysical categories reveals that what is excluded constitutes much more than nonidentity and that identity itself—as a pure essence beyond difference—is a specious category. When brought to bear upon the theory of discursive genres, the deconstructive project therefore reveals that

> the law of the law of genre . . . is a principle of contamination. . . . The trait that marks membership inevitably divides; the boundary of the set comes to form . . . an internal pocket larger than the whole; and the outcome of this division and of this overflowing remains as singular as it is limitless. . . . The principle of genre is unclassifiable, it tolls the knell of the . . . classicum, of what permits one to call out orders and to order, the manifold without a nomenclature. . . . [Genre designation] gathers together the corpus and, at the same time . . . keeps it from closing, from identifying itself with itself. This axiom of non-closure or non-fulfillment enfolds within itself the condition for the possibility and the impossibility of taxonomy.[13]

[11]Roland Barthes, "Historical Discourse," in *Introduction to Structuralism*, ed. Michael Lane (New York: Basic, 1970), 153, 154–55. For an instance of the political rhetoric that critics sympathetic with poststructuralism frequently attach to their discussions of the fact/fiction distinction, compare Suzanne Gearhart: "[All theories of literature and all theories of history] have consistently sought to fix the boundary between them and to establish once and for all the specificity of the fields in one of two ways: democratically, in that each accepts a mutually agreed on boundary which grants to each its own identity and integrity; or, just as often, imperialistically, in that each tries to extend its own boundary and to invade, engulf, or encompass the other. . . . In the second [case, the other genre] is overcome, cannibalized, incorporated into the sameness of the imperializing field" (*The Open Boundary of History and Fiction: A Critical Approach to the French Enlightenment* [Princeton: Princeton University Press, 1984], 4).

[12]Jacques Derrida, "Limited Inc abc," in *Glyph: Johns Hopkins Textual Studies* 2 (Baltimore: Johns Hopkins University Press, 1977), 236. See also *Positions*, trans. Alan Bass (Chicago: University of Chicago Press, 1981), 39–47.

[13]Derrida, "The Law of Genre," quoted in Michael Ryan, *Marxism and Deconstruction: A Critical Articulation* (Baltimore: Johns Hopkins University Press, 1982), 19.

For Derrida, the very attempt to formulate genre distinctions is un-
dermined by the subversive nature of writing, which interpenetrates
among the epistemological categories that ideology sets up to delineate its terrain.

We may be grateful to Derridean deconstruction for calling our attention to the ideological agenda that is inevitably attached to the binary opposition fiction/nonfiction. As I shall argue in the following
chapter, the common valorization of "creative" or "imaginative"
writing does frequently imply a fetishization of mimetic discourse
and a positivist reduction of nonfictional discourse to the unmediated
reportage of "what is." But, while I would certainly agree with
Barthes that historical discourse is in its way as saturated in ideology
as is mimetic discourse, I would not therefore conclude that historical
and mimetic discourse adopt equivalent representational procedures
or constitute equivalent modes of cognition. And while I would grant
Derrida's point that Western philosophy is pervaded by abstract and
ahistorical oppositions that, in the guise of reflecting transcendent essences, naturalize dominant ideology, I would not therefore conclude
that all inherited cognitive oppositions are equally ideological and
equally fallacious. Some oppositions—between fact and fiction, for
instance—describe very real (and, I believe, necessary) cognitive operations, in which actual historical people engage and have engaged.
Indeed, the Derridean project itself is hardly exempt from the practice
of binary opposition. Its universe is unremittingly dualistic, with the
forces of logocentrism, homogeneity, and repression locked in combat with those of differance, heterogeneity, and dispersal. If we recognize, as surely we must, that certain binary oppositions have been
used to legitimate a hierarchical social order, the solution is not to jet-
tison binary opposition altogether but to formulate a binary opposition to class dominance that will carry political force. In this effort, it
is not helpful to argue that all discourses are fictions or that the goal
of criticism is to formulate, in Derrida's words, "undecidables" that
"can no longer be included within philosophical (binary) opposition,
but which, however, inhabit philosophical opposition, resisting and
disorganizing it, *without ever* constituting a third term."[14] The refusal
to constitute a third term cannot go very far toward dislodging the
"hierarchical axiology."

[14]Derrida, *Positions*, 43. See also my "The Politics of Deconstruction," in the special issue "Deconstruction at Yale," *Genre*, 17 (Spring–Summer 1984): 113–34.

It should be apparent that, when one argues for a qualitative definition of fictionality, much more than the classification of discourse is involved: at stake, ultimately, is a whole debate about the relation between—and the context of—perception and cognition. I have no wish here to extend this debate. To support my assertion that fictional and nonfictional discourses are distinguishable not in degree but in kind, however, I would point out that most twentieth-century theories of cognition—in fields from psychology to the philosophy of science to linguistics—have found it necessary to postulate that the human mind characteristically uses polarity as an essential device in gaining understanding. Any given particular must be understood as part of a larger scheme, these theories tell us, if it is to be considered at all. The possible relevance of such theories to the problem of defining fictionality should be clear: the genres of fictional discourse engage informing paradigms qualitatively different from those of the various genres of nonfictional discourse, and even a presumably verifiable fact must be framed and contextualized before its signification can be determined.

From the field of Gestalt psychology, for example, we learn that perception ordinarily operates within qualitative and totalizing frames of reference. The rabbit-duck drawing, Gestalt psychologists would tell us, has two possible, and mutually exclusive, interpretations—it is either a rabbit or a duck. The viewer can readily enough grasp both perceptual possibilities but can process only one scheme at any particular instant. Any given detail in the drawing makes sense as part of either ordering scheme, but it demands wholly different interpretations when it is "read" from each perspective. Only a prior conventional context, external to the object of perception, can provide decisive criteria for adjudging the correctiness of one or another interpretation. It is impossible, concludes E. H. Gombrich of this notorious example, to see "what is 'really there,' to see the shape apart from its interpretation."[15] There are no innocent perceptions: if perception is to produce cognition, it must invoke a framework of prior assumptions about what is being seen.

Gregory Bateson and Erving Goffman have argued that a great variety of human behaviors can be explained by means of the Gestalt model. Bateson proposes that, in activities such as play, fantasy, and

[15]E. H. Gombrich, *Art and Illusion: A Study in the Psychology of Pictorial Representation* (Princeton: Princeton University Press, 1960), 5.

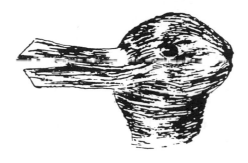

psychotherapy, the participants agree upon "psychological frames" that perform a "metacommunicative function," giving the receiver "instructions or aids in his attempt to understand the messages included within the frame."[16] Psychological frames are, moreover, both exclusive and inclusive, excluding certain messages by including others and vice versa: according to Bateson, Gestalt paradigms are necessary for the unambiguous signaling of complex and overdetermined meanings. Goffman examines the operations of all sorts of social codes—from body language to advertising—in terms of what he calls "primary frameworks": "Each primary framework allows its user to locate, perceive, identify and label a seemingly infinite number of concrete occurrences defined in its terms. [The user] is likely to be unaware of such organized features as the framework has and unable to describe the framework with any completeness if asked, yet these handicaps are no bar to his easily and fully applying it."[17] Primary frameworks can also be transformed, or "keyed," in such a way that almost all the elements in the original activity signal an entirely new meaning when incorporated into a keyed context. Keying involves an agreement among the parties involved to bracket the keyed activity, pretending to follow the rules of the primary framework but actually following a set of very different rules. For Bateson and Goffman, then, the entire range of human behavior, serious and playful, is regulated by conventions that bear a "metacommunicative" re-

---

[16]Gregory Bateson, "A Theory of Play and Fantasy," in his *Steps to an Ecology of Mind: Collected Essays in Anthropology, Psychiatry, Evolution, and Epistemology* (San Francisco: Chandler, 1972), 187–88. For more on the relations among Gestalt frames, play and fantasy, and fictionality, see Kendall L. Walton, "Fearing Fictions," *Journal of Philosophy*, 75 (January 1978): 5–27.

[17]Erving Goffman, *Frame Analysis: An Essay on the Organization of Experience* (Cambridge: Harvard University Press, 1976), 21.

lation to any given activity. An activity is understood as a *kind of thing*, and it is defined largely by contradistinction to what it is not.

Turning to the field of the philosophy of science, we may note that it has become axiomatic that scientists ordinarily hypothesize generalizations and then seek out the evidence that would validate, qualify, or refute those generalizations. Early bourgeois science proposed that human beings characteristically construct conceptual categories on the basis of inductively accumulated experience—a procedure that results, in Hume's words, in "that *perfect* habit, which makes us conclude in general, that instances, of which we have no experience, must necessarily resemble those of which we have."[18] T. S. Kuhn, by contrast, cautions that "no natural history can be interpreted in the absence of at least some implicit body of intertwined theoretical and methodological belief that permits selection, evaluation, and criticism."[19] Karl Popper, who sees the growth of scientific knowledge as a process of "conjecture and refutation," holds that the mind intrinsically possesses the "expectation of finding a regularity."[20] Michael Polanyi, rejecting those versions of Gestalt psychology that describe the perceiver as a passive receiver of preformed paradigms, declares, "I am looking at Gestalt . . . as the outcome of . . . an active shaping of experience performed in the pursuit of knowledge."[21] For these theorists, the scientific method consists in the constant evaluation of explanatory frames. Particulars do not yield up their meaning; they need to be located within a qualitatively defined larger scheme if they are to possess value as evidence.

Finally, it bears noting that such concepts as "tacit knowledge" and "primary frameworks" bear a distinct resemblance to Noam

[18]David Hume, *Treatise of Human Nature*, ed. L. A. Selby-Bigge (Oxford: Clarendon, 1907), 135. For more on Hume's inductive argument, see also I, 3, vi and I, 3, xii.

[19]T. S. Kuhn, *The Structure of Scientific Revolutions*, 2d ed. (Chicago: University of Chicago Press, 1970), 16–17.

[20]Karl Popper, *Conjectures and Refutations: The Growth of Scientific Knowledge* (New York: Basic, 1962), 47.

[21]Michael Polanyi, *The Tacit Dimension* (Garden City: Doubleday, 1966), 6. In citing Polanyi, Kuhn, and Popper, I do not mean to imply that I endorse the particular theories of scientific method and development that these philosophers have evolved. I am simply noting the fact that modern philosophers of science of widely varying ideological orientations, neopositivist to intuitionist, have all found it necessary to posit that thought cannot take place in the absence of informing paradigms into which data—even anomalous data —must be incorporated. For a critique of both Popper's rationalism and Kuhn's irrationalism, see Larry Laudan, *Progress and Its Problems: Toward a Theory of Scientific Growth* (Berkeley: University of California Press, 1977).

Chomsky's theory of linguistic competence, which posits that native speakers of a language are governed by an "abstract system underlying behavior, a system constituted by rules that interact to determine the form and intrinsic meaning of a potentially infinite number of sentences."[22] The process of acquiring language therefore means that "a child must devise a hypothesis compatible with presented data —he must select from the store of potential grammars a specific one that is appropriate to the data available to him."[23] Whenever a speaker utters a statement, then, he or she is invoking a "deep structure" that is the basis for the statement's being coherent and comprehensible (even if the statement is new to the listener). The goal of the study of the "universal grammar" of language, Chomsky concludes, is not simply to illuminate the procedures of language acquisition and communication; it is nothing less than the discovery of the general properties of human intelligence.[24]

These various descriptions of the relation of perception to cognition could, I suppose, be taken as evidence that human intelligence can never know reality, but that it merely imposes its fictions on what it encounters. In my view, however, their implication is quite different. There is no reason to suppose that facts are created by interpretations if they are bound to them. We are free to see a duck or a rabbit, but not a giraffe; the Gestalt figure is not a Rorschach inkblot. The Copernican view of the solar system did not construct the data that rendered it a more powerful explanatory model than the Ptolemaic system. Nor is there any reason to conclude that any given "primary framework" or "tacit knowledge" or "deep structure" constitutes innate or transhistorical knowledge of a Kantian or Jungian kind. The human mind may have certain innate proclivities, but these are necessarily enacted through cognitive frames that are preeminently social constructs: the manifold variations in past and present human behavior testify to the embeddedness of any given conceptualization in a highly changeable social reality. These theories of cognition and language simply suggest that human intelligence characteris-

---

[22]Noam Chomsky, *Language and Mind* (New York: Harcourt, Brace & World, 1968), 62.

[23]Chomsky, *Aspects of the Theory of Syntax* (Cambridge: MIT Press, 1965), 36.

[24]Chomsky, *Language and Mind*, 24. For an applicaiton of Chomsky's theory of "deep structure" to the problem of mobilizing and perceiving generic distinction in imaginative literature, see Sheldon Sacks, "The Psychological Implicaitons of Generic Distinctions," *Genre*, 1 (1968): 106–15.

tically operates in a configurational and—indeed—binary manner. Particulars must be grasped as functional components in qualitatively defined totalities—and excluded from other possible totalities—if they are to be grasped at all.

In this book I shall argue that both fictional discourse and nonfictional discourse make use of totalizing frames analogous to those explicitly formulated by psychology, linguistics, and the philosophy of science. Any given element in a narrative, I shall suggest, must be scanned and interpreted as either factual or fictive in order to be read and understood. There is no specifically linguistic essence of fictionality that is immediately perceptible in the particulars of a text. As Victor Lange aptly puts it,

> Whether or not we are in the presence of a fictional field is . . . a matter of contextual analysis; it cannot be recognized unless we examine the specific aesthetic and logical uses to which the facts that sustain it have been put. The quality of the fact itself, whether it is related to any presumed actuality or is fanciful and non-realistic, is of little concern for the determination of the fictional mode. The invented speeches in Tacitus are clearly part of a non-fictional intention; the actual letter which Rilke incorporated in *Malte Laurids Brigge* assumes, within the purposes of the novel, a distinctly fictional character.[25]

The writer assumes that the reader will possess the "competence" to know how to understand each particular, and that the "tacit knowledge" undergirding this competence is the knowledge of generic conventions shared by writer and reader alike. The nonfictional and fictional Gestalts employed by Tacitus and Rilke, respectively, are a function of the primary frameworks shared by readers of modern novels and ancient histories. I am arguing, in short, for a definition of mimesis as a contract, wherein writer and reader share an agreement about the conditions under which texts can be composed and comprehended. Even when writers take quantitative steps toward altering

[25]Victor Lange, "The Fact in Fiction," *Comparative Literature Studies*, 6 (September 1969): 260. For other theories of fictional discourse explicitly invoking the concept of Gestalt, see Smith, 775–76; Ralph W. Rader, "The Concept of Genre in Eighteenth-Century Studies," in *New Approaches to Eighteenth-Century Literature: Selected Papers from the English Institute* (New York: Columbia University Press, 1974), 84–86; and Norman Friedman, *Form and Meaning in Fiction* (Athens: University of Georgia Press, 1975), 196–97.

the terms of this agreement, they do so in the context of qualitatively defined discursive conventions. And the essence of mimesis—for it has an essence, pace Derrida and company—is that it is a social practice, whereby authors impart cognition of a particular kind to their readers.

The documentary novel, accordingly, is a species of fiction distinctly characterized by its adherence to referential strategies associated with nonfictional modes of discourse but also demanding to be read within a fictional Gestalt familiar to contemporaneous readers. Its dramatically altering strategies of representation do not mean that fictional discourse and nonfictional discourse are indistinguishable; they point instead to the changing terms of the fictional contract in different social formations. But to assert that the documentary novel does not inhabit some epistemologically hazy realm is merely to render a negative definition of its features and capacities. I turn now to examine the nature of the mimetic contract and then to specify the mode of cognition that is distinctly characteristic of mimetic discourse. We cannot appreciate the problem of asserting reference that confronts particularly the documentary novelist without a fuller understanding of the assertive capacities of mimesis in general. We shall now examine those capacities.

2

The Mimetic Contract and
the Problem of Assertion

The naive reader or critic who claims certain novels are dishonest is
sometimes not quite so naive as are theoreticians who have assured him
that fiction . . . cannot lie . . . because it cannot assert.
—Thomas J. Roberts

Most modern literary theorists would grant fictional discourse a status distinct from that of nonfictional discourse. The oppo-
nents to the qualitative definition of mimesis, although vociferous,
are still in the minority. When we examine the various criteria that
have been adduced as the basis for fiction's claim to an autonomous
identity, however, we frequently encounter a curious anomaly. Fiction is uniformly praised for its power: it uses language in a concentrated manner prohibited to nonfiction; it arouses the emotions and
liberates consciousness from the constraints of ideology; it carries the
reader into another world; it offers none of the commitments of statement and all of the joys of pseudostatement. None of these formulations, however, offers a satisfactory account of fiction as a mode of
cognition; indeed, what the great majority routinely state or imply is
that fiction cannot assert propositions that are to be taken as seriously as those conveyed through other modes of discourse. Fiction's
impotence is therefore a peculiar correlative to its power.

In Chapters 3 and 4, I shall set forth my own theory of fictional reference and shall argue that mimesis is *constitutively* a social and historical phenomenon. In the present chapter I intend to refute the principal formalistic theories of fiction that enjoy popularity at present and
to argue for the necessity of viewing mimesis as an intentionally defined contract. I make no pretension here to offer a full critique of either the individual critics I cite or the schools to which I assign them.
My aim is simply to schematize the main alternative approaches to

mimesis and to associate these approaches with familiar critical figures. I have three reasons for undertaking this excursus into the realm
of opposing theory. First, I hope to show that the inadequacy of the
commonly accepted views of mimesis stems from their refusal to
view it as a social contract. The hypostatization of elements such as
linguistic texture, ontology, and affective response results from a textual fetishism that insists upon fragmenting mimetic communication
into its component parts and divesting it of social significance. We
will grasp the Gestalt by means of which fictional discourse conveys
cognition, I believe, only if we see the fictional work as a contract
designed by an intending author who invites his or her audience to
adopt certain paradigms for understanding reality. Second, however,
I wish to demonstrate that even those modern theories of mimesis
that acknowledge the central role of the author—such as the speech-
act theories that I discuss in the last portion of this chapter—fail to
give a full account of authorial intention. It is only when the authorial
subject is viewed as a social subject rooted in a specific historical
context—a perspective most effectively developed in Marxist literary
theory—that the propositional content and assertive force of the text
can be fully appreciated. The argument in this chapter thus sets the
stage for my formulations in Chapters 3 and 4, insofar as it prepares
us to see that Marxism is not merely one among a plurality of possible methodologies. Finally, I wish to ground my discussion of the
documentary novel in a theory of mimesis that dispels conclusively
the notion that fictional works do not assert their propositional contents. A critique of antiassertionist theories of mimesis is an essential
precondition to the investigation of any type of fictional discourse, I
believe, but especially so to the study of the documentary novel,
which posits that its reference to actual people and events empowers
it to tell a particularly compelling truth. Accordingly, the following
critique of formalist theories of fiction should be recalled when we
examine the historically varying modes of fictional assertion presented in Part 2 of this book. These modes of fictional assertion are
meant seriously, I shall argue, and therefore must be taken seriously.

Textual Definitions

Many modern theorists seeking the differentia of factual and fictive
discourse have looked to the text itself to discover the distinguishing

features of mimesis. For the textual theorist, extratextual concerns —conventions, the needs of authors and audiences, social forces of broader kinds—may illuminate the text, but they are irrelevant to the definition of mimesis as such: mimesis is intrinsic to texts that employ elements of language or structure in certain ways. Despite their diversity, these approaches share a tendency to isolate a feature found in many mimetic texts and to identify this feature as the defining quality of all fictive discourse.

The Language of Mimesis

Language is in the foreground of much twentieth-century literary theory, so it is no accident that many theorists have discovered the essence of fictional discourse to consist in its unique use of language. There are three main versions of the linguistic criterion. The first posits that fiction is distinguished by its characteristic linguistic texture. Monroe Beardsley, for example, maintains that much of the "implicit meaning" of literature derives from the "opacity" of its linguistic texture.[1] Similarly, René Wellek and Austin Warren argue that "literary" language (that of prose fiction and of poetry) is characteristically connotative, while that of science is denotative.[2] The second linguistic criterion for defining mimesis rests on the contention that fictional language is nonparaphrasable. J. M. Cameron states, "I could not give an alternative poetic description, for there could be no criterion (as there would be in the case of a real description) for deciding whether or not the alternative description has succeeded. The poetic description has the form of a description; but it exists only as *this* description, these words, in this order."[3] The third linguistic criterion rests upon the premise that, as Margaret MacDonald says, in a fictional work language is used "to originate, not to report." A storyteller, she declares, "performs [and] does not—or not primarily—

[1]Monroe C. Beardsley, *Aesthetics: Problems in the Philosophy of Criticism* (New York: Harcourt, Brace & World, 1958), esp. 126–28.

[2]René Wellek and Austin Warren, *Theory of Literature*, 3d ed. (New York: Harcourt, Brace & World, Harvest, 1956), 22–23.

[3]J. M. Cameron, "Poetry and Dialectic," in *The Night Battle: Essays* (London: Burns & Oates, 1962), 137. For further development of the nonparaphrasability theory, see also David Lodge, *The Language of Fiction: Essays in Criticism and Verbal Analysis of the English Novel* (London: Routledge & Kegan Paul, 1966).

inform or misinform."[4] The definitive quality of fictive language thus becomes its lack of referentiality. Roman Jakobson found a sharp distinction between the "poetic" and the "communicative" or "referential" functions of language: "The supremacy of the poetic function over the referential function does not obliterate the reference," he concludes, "but makes it ambiguous."[5]

It should be apparent that these different linguistic criteria are quite closely related to one another. Language that is used in a connotative way cannot be said to possess the same power of reference as language that is denotative, and its force would seem to reside in its inimitable construction. It should also be apparent that each of these criteria poses severe logical and practical drawbacks to developing a comprehensive theory of fictionality. The criterion of linguistic texture is arbitrary and inexact: the highly colored, ironic language of Marx's *Eighteenth Brumaire* poses a sharp contrast to the flat, reportorial prose of *Studs Lonigan*, but I would not want to conclude that Marx is therefore a novelist, and Farrell a sociologist. Features such as "semantic density," remarks Stein Haugom Olsen, are "noticed only when they serve an independently defined funciton"; in order to identify such a feature and to see it as "artistically relevant," the decision "must already have been reached that the text is a literary work."[6] The criterion of fictional nonparaphrasability encounters comparable difficulties. Writers frequently rewrite their texts, which suggests some prelinguistic formulation in the author's mind to which the various stylistic formulations in some way correspond. "Though fictional worlds emerge from words," states James Phelan, "and though sometimes the particular words an author chooses are extremely important for creating a fictional world effectively, these worlds are finally not worlds of words, but worlds of characters, actions, emotions, and thoughts."[7] While stylistic theorists claim to discern the

[4]Margaret MacDonald, "The Language of Fiction," reprinted in *Perspectives on Fiction*, ed. James L. Calderwood and Harold Toliver (New York: Oxford University Press, 1968), 64.

[5]Roman Jakobson, "Closing Statement: Linguistics and Poetics," in *Style in Language*, ed. Thomas Sebeok (Cambridge: Technology Press of MIT, 1960), 371.

[6]Stein Haugom Olsen, "Defining a Literary Work," *Journal of Aesthetics and Art Criticism*, 35 (Winter 1976): 137.

[7]James Phelan, *Worlds from Words: A Theory of Language in Fiction* (Chicago: University of Chicago Press, 1981), 149. Recent work in linguistics indicates that, while the style may be the man, it does not constitute the work. Studies of the reading activity reveal that, in

distinctive feature of mimesis in its unique appropriation of language, their argument has a paradoxical premise. "The idea of style," remarks Richard Ohmann, "implies that words on a page might have been different, or differently arranged, without a corresponding difference in substance." To fault an author on the grounds that a sentence is ill-phrased—as critics often do—is to contend that the sentence might have been better phrased and thus to imply that the sentence can be a more or less effective tool for getting at a peculiarly solid—and prelinguistic—referent. Ohmann continues, "Another writer would have said *it* another *way*."[8]

The nonreferentiality criterion at first appears to be a more formidable adversary. We must conclude, after all, that the name "Bigger Thomas" does not denote an actual inhabitant of Chicago. But—and this point is crucial to an understanding of referentiality in the documentary novel—certain words appearing in fictional discourse do carry a power of direct historical reference. As we shall see below, *Waverly* would not persuade its readers to take a certain view of his-

---

confronting both fictional and nonfictional narratives of sustained duration, people characteristically forget the specific linguistic (syntactical) formulations of texts and instead formulate abbreviated and schematized versions of their conceptual content. Teun A. Van Dijk remarks, "Recall, comparison and other mental operations with sentences are based on semantic representations. Syntactic structures appear to be immediately erased from memory, which points at their 'superficial' character." This discovery suggests that a reader's experience of both fictional and nonfictional texts hinges not primarily upon stylistic effects, however powerfully these may register in the short-term memory, but upon a generalized apprehension of propositional content, which is lodged in the long-term memory. Indeed, as Gerald Graff has argued, our reliance upon the interpretive schemes carried in the long-term memory gives aesthetic power to stylistic materials noted in the short-term memory. See Van Dijk, *Some Aspects of Text Grammars: A Study in Theoretical Linguistics and Poetics* (The Hague: Mouton, 1972), 324–25, and Graff, "Literature as Assertions," in *American Criticism in the Poststructuralist Age*, ed. Ira Konigsberg, Michigan Studies in the Humanities (Ann Arbor: University of Michigan Press, 1981), 152–56.

[8]Richard Ohmann, "Generative Grammars and the Concept of Literary Style," *Word*, 20 (December 1964): 427. For the argument that any alteration in "surface structure" is an alteration in substance, see Stanley Fish, "Affective Stylistics: Literature in the Reader," *New Literary History*, 2 (Autumn 1970): 123–62. Fish asserts, "We comprehend not in terms of the deep structure alone, but in terms of a *relationship* between the unfolding, in time, of the surface structure and a continual checking of it against our projection (always in terms of surface structure) of what the deep structure will reveal itself to be, and when the final discovery has been made and *the* deep structure is perceived, all the 'mistakes,' the positing, on the basis of incomplete evidence, of deep structures that failed to materialize, will not be cancelled out. They have been experienced; they have existed in the mental life of the reader; they *mean*" (144).

torical process if its Bonnie Prince Charlie did not signify the real Pretender; the J. P. Morgan who appears in Dos Passos's *U.S.A.* is not merely a fictional character who comments in a general way upon the depredations of capital. Moreover—and I shall treat this point at considerable length in the next chapter—it is important to recognize that a fictional text's propositional relation to the historical world cannot be simply equated with the referential capacities of its individual sentences. Michael Scriven observes:

> Generally speaking . . . the sentences in a story cannot be said to be true or false, as could the statements in a sermon. But the story as a whole can certainly be said to paint a true (or false) picture of its subject. D. H. Lawrence on the Midland mining towns, Arthur Koestler on Communist interrogation proceedings, Alan Paton on conditions in the Union of South Africa, can be praised for the versimilitude of their account or criticized for its inaccuracy.[9]

Most discussions of fictional reference are muddled by the assumption that truth attaches exclusively to separate sentences and entities, rather than to things-in-relation. Indeed, a positivist epistemology lurks not far beneath the surface of the nonreferentiality criterion: the only realities, it seems, are palpable "facts," and if a discourse cannot refer to these, it has no referent at all.

The Ontology of Mimesis

A second textual definition of mimesis distinguishes factual and fictive discourse on the basis of textual ontology. Taking as their premise Husserl's distinction between the realm of "essential universality" and the factitious sphere of "spatio-temporal facts,"[10] a number of phenomenological critics have attempted to locate the differentia of mimesis in one or more textual features that signal the presence of a realm ontologically discontinuous with that of ordinary experience. One argument centers on the status of the narrator in factual and fictive discourse: presumably the author of a factual work *is* the narrator and is therefore wholly responsible for the statements in the narra-

[9]Michael Scriven, "The Language of Fiction," *Proceedings of the Aristotelian Society*, supp. vol. 28 (1954): 187.

[10]Edmund Husserl, *Ideas: General Introduction to a Pure Phenomenology*, trans. W. R. Boyce Gibson (London: Allen & Unwin, 1931), 54 and passim.

47

tive, whereas the narrator of a novel is not necessarily to be identified with the author in propria persona, alike as the two may be in outlook. Thus Laurent Stern, for example, suggests that the narrators in fictions are themselves fictive characters: "We must make-believe that the stories told within the literary work of art are told by fictional characters."[11] Kate Hamburger, who repudiates the notion that mimesis consists exclusively in the fictiveness of the narrator, asserts that the novel's "lack of an 'I-Origo'" is nonetheless one among several important indicators of the text's removal from the ontological sphere of the reader.[12]

Other phenomenological critics focus their attention on the perceived status of the narrative's spatiotemporal realm. Disjunction between the spatiotemporal realm of the text and that of the reader signals the presence of fictionality; conjunction between the two spheres reveals the presence of factuality. Thus Robert Champigny states, "I interpret a narrative in a novelistic perspective if . . . I do not situate the event of my reading in relation to the narrated event." Hence there is an unbridgeable gap between the "realities" of text and reader: "Events in a spatio-temporal field can be historical for me only if they are spatially and temporally related to me: I must posit myself as an event or process among others."[13] Roman Ingarden, perhaps the most rigorous—at least the most sonorous—of the phenomenological critics, articulates the formalism latent in the ontological approach to mimesis. "We remain in the realm of the work itself," he states, "without taking an interest in extraliterary reality." The "concretization of aesthetically valent qualities" is thus the goal of the literary work: "In their opalescent dual meaning, the semantic units, clothed in particular sound materials, project an intuitive material permeated with special materially colored qualities, which allows the reader to apprehend just that qualitative cluster of values which arises as a necessary phenomenon from such intuitive material."[14] If

[11]Laurent Stern, "Fictional Characters, Places, and Events," *Philosophy and Phenomenological Research*, 26 (December 1965): 210.

[12]Kate Hamburger, *The Logic of Literature*, 2d rev. ed., trans. Marilyn J. Rose (Bloomington: Indiana University Press, 1933), 73–74.

[13]See Robert Champigny, *Ontology of the Narrative: An Analysis* (The Hague: Mouton, 1972), 17, and "Implicitness in Narrative Fiction," *PMLA*, 85 (October 1970): 990.

[14]Roman Ingarden, *The Cognition of the Literary Work of Art*, trans. Ruth Ann Crowley and Kenneth R. Olsen (Evanston: Northwestern University Press, 1973), 37, 68. For further instances of the phenomenological approach to mimesis, see Knut Hanneborg, *The*

we can penetrate through the "opalescent . . . meaning" of this statement, it seems to be saying that the presence of fictionality is signaled by the reader's loss of interest in the historical world—a loss that is presumably compensated by the semantic resonance of the text.

The stipulation that fiction involves ontological displacement reminds us, lest we forget, that even the most transparently realistic fictive works do not routinely depict real persons and events. But the view of fiction as ontologically discontinuous does not prove particularly useful in accounting for the phenomenon of the documentary novel, which explicitly attempts to break down ontological barriers by incorporating presumably unmediated elements of actuality into the fictional work. Moreover, unless the ontological definition of mimesis is understood simply as a restatement of the truism that fiction involves invention, it frequently takes us in circles, for it fails to locate identifiable textual features conventionally signaling fictionality and ends up simply conflating reader response and authorial intention with the "text itself." How is spatiotemporal disjunction a textual property in the absence of a responding reader? How is the presence or absence of an "I-Origo" inferable from the particulars of the text, without some prior or external conception of the signaled intentions of the author? How can intuitive material—an odd blend of subjective and objective features—be signaled by "materially colored qualities" (whatever they may be)?[15] The very fixation upon individual textual features renders ontological definitions incapable of specifying any precise relation between the fictive text and historical actuality. As Kendall Walton has complained, "The ordinary concept of 'fictional worlds'—worlds that are different from the real one, but

---

Study of Literature: A Contribution to the Phenomenology of the Humane Sciences (Oslo: Universitetsforlaget, 1967), and Felix Martinez-Bonati, *Fictive Discourse and the Structure of Literature: A Phenomenological Approach*, trans. Philip W. Silver (Ithaca: Cornell University Press, 1981).

[15]Unlike the other phenomenological theorists, Hamburger cannot be charged with simply transferring reader response to the text. Indeed, she spots this type of circularity as a pitfall of phenomenological criticism and attacks Ingarden on logical grounds: "The designation of the sentences in a novel or in a drama as quasi-judgments implies nothing but the tautological fact that whenever we read a novel or a play we know we are reading a novel or a play" (*The Logic of Literature*, 20). Hamburger develops an elaborate set of textual markers of fictionality. Her criteria are, however, bound by the conventions of the nineteenth-century realistic novel. And she remains open to the criticism posed to the quantitative and family resemblance theorists in Chapter 1: How does one determine the necessary and sufficient properties that define a work of fiction?

worlds nonetheless—is a device to paper over our confusion about whether or not fictions are real; it is an attempt to have it both ways."[16] And if "fictional worlds" have no relation to the real world —for this is finally what spatiotemporal disjunction means, at least for Husserl—then what kind of knowledge can they yield? What is the referent of mimesis—if indeed there is one?

The Structure of Mimesis

Of the various textual definitions of mimesis, those focusing on structure possess the greatest value. Most trace their lineage to Aristotle, who viewed the salient feature of poetry (in the broad sense) as formal unity. Although the materials of history possess no inherent structure, he claimed, focusing as they do upon "not one action but one period of time," those of poetry are selected in accordance with their capacity to elucidate the power of a work as a structurally unified whole.[17] Critics who discover the differentia of fictionality in structure argue that fictional works possess a cohering principle of unity, while nonfictional works are characterized by a certain formal incompleteness derived from the intractability of their raw materials. Thus the Russian Formalists, who undertook a rewriting of Aristotelian poetics in the early decades of the twentieth century, declared that the structural transformation of "story" into "plot" constitutes the essence of fiction-making. "Real incidents, not fictionalized by an author, may make a story," states Boris Tomashevsky. "The plot," by contrast, in which "events are *arranged* and connected according to the order of sequence in which they are presented in the work," is "wholly an artistic creation."[18] Murray Krieger has chosen "teleology" as the trait distinguishing the novel from the factual report: "Teleology is precisely what poetic form boasts as its essential charac-

[16]Kendall L. Walton, "How Remote Are Fictional Worlds from the Real World?" *Journal of Aesthetics and Art Criticism*, 37 (Fall 1978): 19.

[17]Aristotle, *Aristotle's Poetics: A Translation and Commentary for Students of Literature*, trans. Leon Golden (Englewood Cliffs: Prentice-Hall, 1968), chap. 23, p. 42. Hardison, in the commentary section of the volume, stresses the point that, in his distinction between poetry and history, Aristotle does not assert that poetry reveals some sort of higher truth, as Sidney supposed. See also Friedman, *Form and Meaning in Fiction* (Athens: University of Georgia Press, 1975), 5–6.

[18]Boris Tomashevsky, "Thematics," in *Russian Formalist Criticism: Four Essays*, ed. Lee T. Lemon and Marion J. Reis (Norman: University of Oklahoma Press, 1964), 68.

teristic. It is just the poet's freedom to put teleology where his object of imitation had none that distinguishes him from even the most arrogant historian who would fashion the past in the shapes of his private fancy."[19] Ralph W. Rader concludes that "in fiction, the form must totally subsume the whole matter of the work. In most factual works, even when there is literary intent, a good deal of material must necessarily remain only passively adjusted to the form."[20]

As we shall see in the next chapter, the reader's perception of a high degree of internal coherence in fact is essential to the functioning of the mimetic contract, for the configuration of the text as a whole does conventionally signal mimetic intentions. But, I shall argue, the text's structural Gestalt is inseparable from its cognitive praxis: structure per se, isolated from function, is meaningless as a criterion of fictionality, for one could readily argue—as Louis Mink has done—that all conceptualization operates in the configurational mode and that many forms of nonfictional writing are indeed highly structured.[21] The recent historiographical theory of scholars such as W. B. Gallie and Hayden White may have gone too far in the direction of fictionalizing history, but it has convincingly demonstrated that many of the structural features ordinarily associated with the novel also characterize the conventions of nineteenth- and twentieth-century historical narration.[22] Factual discourse, they suggest, involves not the absence of Gestalt but the invocation of a different Gestalt. I return to my central contention: mimesis entails a social contract; the textual features that signal its different conventions indicate that the fictional contract is being invoked, but they do not in themselves constitute the essence of fictional discourse.

The main problem besetting the various textual theories of mimesis briefly described here is that they attempt to locate the essence of

[19]Murray Krieger, "Fiction, History, and Empirical Reality," *Critical Inquiry*, 1 (December 1974): 342.

[20]Ralph W. Rader, "Literary Form in Fictional Narrative: The Example of Boswell's *Johnson*," in *Essays in Eighteenth-Century Biography*, ed. Philip B. Daghlian (Bloomington: Indiana University Press, 1968), 39.

[21]Louis O. Mink, "History and Fiction as Modes of Comprehension," *New Literary History*, 1 (Spring 1970): 541–58.

[22]See W. B. Gallie, *Philosophy and the Historical Understanding* (1964; New York: Schocken, 1968), chaps. 1 and 2; Hayden White, *Metahistory: The Historical Imagination in Nineteenth-Century Europe* (Baltimore: Johns Hopkins University Press, 1973).

mimesis solely in isolated textual features, without reference to the author/reader contracts within which these elements function. Textual theories divorce the fictional work from its social and historical context—from its referent on the one hand, from its producer and consumer on the other. The text therefore emerges as a reified entity presumably containing within itself all meaning and value, rather than as a field of force generating constantly varying relations between the author's intentions and the audience's assumptions, expectations, and needs. Indeed, the text undergoes a process similar to the phenomenon that Marx labeled "commodity fetishism," whereby, as Georg Lukács summarizes it, "a relation between people takes on the character of a thing and thus acquires a 'phantom objectivity,' an autonomy that seems so strictly rational and all-embracing as to conceal every trace of its fundamental nature: the relation between people."[23] Countering the conception popular among contemporaneous political economists that capital is a "thing," Marx pointed out that capital is a social relation, though mediated by the instrumentality of things. Literary theorists should take a cue from Marx and recognize that the fictional text is likewise a social relation, mediated through the instrumentality of objectifiable textual features.

Mentalist Definitions

Mentalist definitions of mimesis—that is, definitions seeking the differentia of fictionality in the kinds of responses a text evokes—would seem to pose a welcome alternative to the false objectivism of textual theories, in that they bring the question of explaining fictionality into the realm of social experience. But most mentalist theories of mimesis consider only the response of the reader to textual signals, thereby denying the functional importance of the text as a meeting ground between writer and audience.

Affective Theories

Some mentalist critics have identified fiction by its characteristic power to evoke an emotional response in the reader. Fiction is here

---

[23]Georg Lukács, *History and Class Consciousness: Studies in Marxist Dialectics*, trans. Rodney Livingstone (Cambridge: MIT Press, 1971), 83.

definable by its effects: we know that a discourse is fictional if it creates certain kinds of psychic reactions. Norman Holland maintains that fiction arouses the emotions of readers because it does not call upon them to engage in the "reality-testing" that customarily accompanies nonfiction and thus permits their feelings greater freedom.[24] Helmut Gauss argues that the reading of fictions is "an important control mechanism in our emotional housekeeping," in that "the experience of the fictional tension is an attempt at alleviating the existential tension."[25] Simon Lesser proposes that "fiction gives us compromise formations whereby repressed and repressing forces obtain expression in one and the same product . . . it provides a forum in which the positions of the id, the ego and the superego all receive a hearing."[26]

The difficulties posed by the affective argument should be fairly apparent. To begin with, factual and fictive discourse can hardly be distinguished by any difference in their ability to evoke emotion. True accounts such as *The Algiers Motel Incident* or *The Diary of Anne Frank* arouse more powerful feelings of indignation and pity than do many fictional narratives; novels such as *The Jungle* or *The Castle*, in their different ways, in fact compel readers to test the reality and confront the tension of their own experience. Similar problems exist for the notion that fictional texts intrinsically provide "compromise formations" reconciling the conflicts within ego-structure. *Moby Dick* may or may not project and resolve a clash of forces analogous to the conflict of superego and id, but *Barchester Towers* could hardly be said to accomplish a similar therapeutic task. As I shall argue below, fictions do indeed attempt to resolve contradictions that are experienced subjectively; but these contradictions can become part of a shared public discourse only if they mediate more general social contradictions. Affective definitions of fictionality rest upon a fundamental division of emotion from intellect and of the self from the social. By the very procedure of isolating emotive response as the differentia of mi-

---

[24]Norman Holland, *The Dynamics of Literary Response* (New York: Oxford University Press, 1961). See also his "Prose and Minds: A Psychoanalytic Approach to Nonfiction," in *The Art of Victorian Prose*, ed. George Levine and William Madden (New York: Oxford University Press, 1968), 314–37.

[25]Helmut Gaus, *The Function of Fiction: The Function of Written Fiction in the Social Process: An Investigation into the Relation between the Reader's Real World and the Fictional World of His Reading* (Ghent: E. Story–Scientia, 1979), 107, 131.

[26]Simon Lesser, *Fiction and the Unconscious* (Boston: Beacon, 1957), 78.

mesis, affective theories mechanize the very realm of subjective experience that they would invest with privileged value. As Christopher Caudwell remarked of subjectivist aesthetics, "Beauty and all related values become physiological activity."[27] The isolation of the reader's reactions from their genesis in author or text thus implies a curiously impoverished concepton of mind, in which feelings are defined with no relation to their stimuli.

Reader-Response Theories

A second species of mentalist theory, associated with the label "reader-response criticism," holds that subjective judgment (not necessarily emotionally charged) is the determinant of a text's essential qualities, including its generic identity. For David Bleich, who advocates that criticism base itself on the "subjective paradigm," textual determinacy of any kind is a logical impossibility, for readers create not only their own texts but also their own conditions for reading texts.[28] For Wolfgang Iser, who appears eager to avoid the solipsism implied by the more radical reader-response theory of Bleich, textual indeterminacy coincides with the very essence of fictional discourse itself. The fictional text "by its very nature must call into question the validity of familiar norms," declares Iser. Mimesis "represents a reaction to the thought system which it has chosen and incorporated into its repertoire. This reacton is triggered by the system's limited ability to cope with the multifariousness of reality, thus drawing attention to its deficiencies." The essence of fictionality thus involves the juxtaposition of questions and perspectives, rather than the promulgation or endorsement of any single (or for that matter, contradictory) view: "[Fiction] questions or recodes the signals of external reality in such a way that the reader himself is to find the motives underlying the question, and in doing so he participates in producing the meaning."[29] You may discover one meaning, and I another, Iser con-

[27]Christopher Caudwell, *Studies and Further Studies in a Dying Culture* (New York: Monthly Review, 1971), 80–81.

[28]David Bleich, *Subjective Criticism* (Baltimore: Johns Hopkins University Press, 1978), 11.

[29]Wolfgang Iser, *The Act of Reading: A Theory of Aesthetic Response* (Baltimore: Johns Hopkins University Press, 1978), 87, 72, 74. Iser attempts to qualify his stance by noting that some fictions—he cites chivalric romances and socialist realist novels as instances— shore up "unstable" systems of ideas: their propositionality is thus presumably an inverse

cludes, not because reality evades determinate formulation, but simply because mimesis does.

Iser, it must be conceded, at least admits that the fictionality of a text is not determined by its audience. Where Bleich removes the intending author from the scene entirely, positing that readers, and readers alone, set the terms of the mimetic contract, Iser holds that authorial intention is coterminous with textual undecidability. But we are left with an unconvincing version of the New Critical criterion of opacity: individual sentences may not project linguistic ambiguity, but the text as a whole does—indeed, must. Mimesis is antagonistic to the propositions it seems to contain: it presents them for consideration only to deny them any power of assertion. If authors intend to propose views of the world that they want their readers to take seriously, they are ill-advised to do so by means of fictional discourse.

Intentionalist Definitions

Textual definitions of mimesis fetishize language, and mentalist definitions fetishize subjective reader response. We sense progress, however, when we turn to intentionalist definitions of mimesis, which view the literary work as "a goal-directed effort made by a creating intellect"; literary theory must therefore "deal with the role of intention and assign it a proper place in literary understanding."[30] Applied to the problem of defining fictionality, this principle, following Thomas Roberts, means that "fiction is make-believe and let's pretend and let's suppose and let's assume. It is not pretending or be-

---

function of the plausibility of the ideas they contain. This argument strikes me as heavily loaded, since Iser clearly regards works of these kinds as inferior; the bourgeois novel is for him both the model and the type of the fictional contract. For a more effective sort of reader-response criticism, see Peter J. Rabinowitz, "Assertion and Assumption: Fictional Patterns and the External World," *PMLA*, 96 (May 1981): 408–19. Rabinowitz is interested in working back from the response of the reader to the manipulations and assumptions of the author, and he establishes useful distinctions among what he calls "actual," "authorial," "narrative," and "ideal" audiences in order to analyze the various levels of response that are actuated in the process of reading a fiction. See "Truth in Fiction: A Reexamination of Audiences," *Critical Inquiry*, 4 (Autumn 1973): 121–41.

[30]Stein Haugom Olsen, "What Is Poetics?" *Philosophical Quarterly*, 26 (October 1976): 351.

lieving or supposing or assuming: it is what follows an invitation to others to share in a pretending."[31] Mimesis is therefore a species of intentionally defined contract. Roberts summarizes, "A work of fiction by intention is a small or large body of propositions the author thinks true—even in many cases factually true—framed by a small or large body of propositions the author thinks false."[32] Mimesis originates historically in the writer and conveys itself to the reader by means of textual signals that invite reader participation: "I'll pretend" is an invalid declaration if it cannot be assumed to mean "let's pretend."

The intentionalist argument currently enjoying the greatest popularity draws its theoretical framework from speech-act theory. Speech-act theorists of fiction follow J. L. Austin's analysis of any given utterance as comprehending three separate speech acts: the locutionary act (that is, the physical act of uttering words); the illocutionary act (that is, the speaker's goal in making the utterance, such as stating, asking, ordering); and the perlocutionary act (that is, the speaker's effect upon the audience, such as arousing curiosity, confusing, threatening).[33] The illocutionary act is seen as the crucial act that defines the fictionality or factuality of a given discourse. "There is no textual property, syntactical or semantic, that will identify a text as a work of fiction," argues Searle. "What makes it a work of fiction is, so to speak, the illocutionary stance that the author takes toward it, and that stance is a matter of the complex illocutionary intentions that the author has when he writes or otherwise composes it." These "complex illocutionary intentions" are signaled to the reader by appeal to a "set of horizontal conventions that break the conventions established by the vertical rules of factual discourse."[34]

Barbara Herrnstein Smith, who constructs an entire theory of fictionality based upon speech-act theory, posits that

> the essential fictiveness of novels . . ., as of all literary artworks, is not
> to be discovered in the unreality of the characters, objects, and events

---

[31]Thomas J. Roberts, "Fiction outside Literature," *Literary Review*, 22 (Fall 1978): 9.

[32]Roberts, *When Is Something Fiction?* (Carbondale: Southern Illinois University Press, 1972), 94–108.

[33]J. L. Austin, *How to Do Things with Words* (1955; Oxford: Clarendon, 1975), 94–108.

[34]John R. Searle, "The Logical Status of Fictional Discourse," *New Literary History*, 6 (Winter 1975): 325, 326.

alluded to, but in the unreality of the *alludings* themselves. In other words, in a novel or tale, it is the *act* of reporting events, the *act* of describing persons and referring to places, that is fictive. The novel *represents* the verbal action of a man reporting, describing, and referring.[35]

For Smith, all "poetry" (meaning fictional discourse) is "fiction" in the sense that it takes as its object of imitation one or another species of "natural" discourse. It is by its very nature a pseudostatement. Robert L. Brown and Martin Steinmann, Jr., point out that the differentia of fictional discourse—which they call the "pretense-of-reporting rule"—is not a grammatical rule constituted by textual features but a "genre-rule" constituted by social practice. "A discourse *is* fictional," they argue, "because its speaker or writer intends it to be so. But it is *taken as* fictional only because the hearer or reader *decides* to take it so. . . . The decision to read a discourse as fictional or nonfictional is a decision to use one set of constitutive rules rather than another, and we really can't read it—interpret it—at all until we have made this decision."[36] In the various speech-act approaches to the definition of fictionality, the differentia is based, we should note, on the intention of the author: mimetic conventions are enacted because the author, as determinate historical agent, wishes to enact them.

Intentionalism furnishes grounds for a productive inquiry into the nature of the mimetic contract. First, it provides theoretical grounding for the notion that factual and fictive disocurse are to be qualitatively distinguished. If mimesis involves an invitation on the part of the author and a decision on the part of the reader to follow certain rules that preclude other rules, then it follows that—to reinvoke Wittgenstein—different rules imply different games. One cannot simultaneously engage in "let's pretend" and take literally the content

[35]Barbara Herrnstein Smith, "Poetry as Fiction," *New Literary History*, 2 (Winter 1971): 272. In its logical extension, Smith's view of fiction as the imitation of nonfictional, or "natural," discourse is indistinguishable from Johathan Culler's contention that "whenever a work seems to be referring to the world one can argue that this supposed reference is in fact a comment on other texts and postpone the referentiality of the fiction to another moment or another level" ("Presupposition and Intertextuality," *Modern Language Notes*, 91 [December 1976]: 1383). Such postponement can go on indefinitely, of course, and the "referent" becomes, in essence, textuality itself.

[36]Robert L. Brown and Martin Steinmann, Jr., "Native Readers of Fiction: A Speech-Act and Genre-Rule Approach to Defining Literature," in *What Is Literature?* ed. Hernadi (Bloomington: Indiana University Press, 1978), 149–50.

of the pretense; recognizing the rabbit of fictionality necessarily rules out seeing the duck of factual discourse. Second, intentionalism requires us to see mimesis as a mode of social praxis. As Olsen puts it, "Authors and readers possess a common institutional framework which allows authors to intend texts as literary works and the reader to interpret them as intended to be taken as literary works. . . . [To identify a text as a literary work] is to assign a role to the text in an institution of which one knows the rules."[37] Where mentalist theories are only superficially social (they conflate meaning with reader response and lose track of the author altogether), intentionalist theories see the author as the originating point of a contractual activity that is realized in the reader's response through the invocation of a "common institutional framework." Third, intentionalism rescues what is valid in textual and mentalist theories at the same time that it offers a superior ground for argument. As Ohmann notes,

> If the work of literature is mimetic of speech-acts, then it is in a sense *exhibiting* both quasi-speech-acts and the sentences that purportedly help to bring about these acts. To exhibit them is to direct attention to them, and, among other things, to their intricacy of meaning and their formal regularity. Similarly, since the quasi-speech-acts of literature are not carrying on the world's business—describing, urging, contracting, etc.—the reader may well attend to them in a non-pragmatic way, and thus allow them to realize their emotive potential. In other words, the suspension of normal illocutionary force tends to shift a reader's attention to the locutionary acts themselves and to their perlocutionary effects.[38]

Intentionalism clarifies textual and mentalist theories, showing how the "formal regularity" and the "emotive potential" of the mimetic work are highlighted through the writer's decision to invoke the mimetic contract.

Despite its usefulness to a contractual view of mimesis, however, the intentionalist position—particularly its speech-act variant—encounters certain difficulties. The intentionalist critic does not ordinarily specify *how* the genre-signifying intentions of the author are communicated to the reader, nor, for that matter, *why* this signaling

[37]Olsen, "Defining a Literary Work," 138.
[38]Ohmann, "Speech Acts and the Definiton of Literature," *Philosophy and Rhetoric*, 4 (Winter 1971): 17

should take place at all. Roberts does not explain the procedure whereby the "framing" propositions that the author thinks to be false are acknowledged as false by the reader. Ohmann does not tell us how we know that the illocutionary force of a fiction has been suspended. Searle grants that an investigation into the syntactic and semantic conventions governing the writing and reading of fictions is necessary to determine how the reader knows when the author has invoked a set of fictive "horizontal conventions." Yet, in his well-known comparison of the opening chapter of an Iris Murdoch novel with a news story from the *New York Times*, he also makes the contradictory claim that the fictional text is semantically and syntactically indistinguishable from the journalistic one.[39] Along similar lines, Smith argues that Clarendon's description of John Hampden in *The History of Rebellion* is generically indistinguishable from the first paragraph of Tolstoy's "The Death of Ivan Ilyitch"—a difficult point to square with her view that the difference between factual and fictive discourse is absolute.

The solution is not, however, to return to "text" or "reader" and to travel the hermeneutical circle once again. For the abstraction accompanying these definitions derives not from any logical deficiencies inherent in intentionalism as such but from the unduly atomistic conception of the text and the unduly narrow conception of writer and reader that accompany the particular theories we have examined. These theories fail to view the fictional contract as a fully social phenomenon; they fragment the act of mimetic representation and dehistoricize the people engaging in the text's communicative contract. Richard Gale's version of "suspended illocutionary force," for instance, entails the quite absurd dissolution of individual sentences into assertive and nonassertive components: "The effect of a fictive illocutionary act is to drain of illocutionary force every verb that oc-

---

[39]Because Searle omits discussing the actual conventions that are invoked in the novel and the journalistic report, he leaves himself open to "intentional fallacy" accusations, even though he purports to carry the discussion beyond this level. As Lubomír Dolozel has remarked of Searle's theory of fictionality, "When ascribing a certain illocutionary intention to the author, we do so a posteriori, after having determined—intuitively or empirically—the fictional or nonfictional status of his utterance. This is a general weakness of intentional fallacy: first we decide what are the properties of a text and then we ascribe the properties to the author's intentions (or the failure of these intentions). The intention itself is not independently testable, at least not by logical procedures." See his "Commentary," *New Literary History*, 6 (Winter 1975): 468.

curs within its space."[40] On a somewhat broader scale, Searle's and Smith's isolation of the opening paragraphs from realistic novels as proof of semantic and syntactic ambiguity is equally fallacious. The passages themselves, to be sure, may contain no telltale signs of their fictionality, but the title pages that precede, as well as the dialogue, the interiorizing, the development of character, and the construction of plot line that follow, are—at least for readers in the past two centuries—unequivocal indicators of Murdoch's or Tolstoy's fictional intentions. The novelist's incorporation of elements associated with familiar models in journalism or history simply requires the reader to be alert to the text's empirical claims. Presumably a fiction that invokes the aura of recognized modes of factual discourse will ask to be read as a realistic—as opposed to a fantastic—rendition of the configuration of social reality. Even Roberts's apparently more flexible formulation of an opposition between "framing" and "framed" statements in fiction divides the text along false lines. I shall be arguing quite a different point: most sentences in a fictional text simultaneously testify to a nonexistent state of affairs while implying propositional claims about the historical world. It is the configuration of the text as a whole, not the presence of isolable elements, that signals to the reader the author's fictive or nonfictional intentions. Even when these elements are documentary particulars presumably making an unmediated reference to historical actuality (Scott's historical footnotes, for example), they are subordinated to the terms of a generic contract that guides the reader's comprehension of the text as a whole.

The tendency of intentionalist critics to locate fictionality in atomized components of the text implies a correspondingly atomized and ahistorical conception of author and reader. Apparently Searle's readers approach Murdoch's novel and the *New York Times* with no prior conceptions of what they are doing, responding to each text in pristine innocence. But writers obviously do not issue generic contracts in social vacuums, and readers do not inhabit the Garden of Eden. Writers are perfectly well acquainted with the primary frameworks that they share with their readers and with the ways that their readers are likely to perceive the relation that any part of a text bears to the whole. Even when authors choose to disrupt or alter these frame-

---

[40]Richard Gale, "The Fictive Use of Language," *Philosophy*, 46 (October 1971): 336.

works, they do so ordinarily by conventional discursive institutions. We may therefore find it useful, as Robert Weimann urges, to substitute some such term as "genesis" for "intention," insofar as genesis encompasses not merely the subjective wills of authors as individuals but the "total context of which the individual 'generative intention' is only a factor."[41] By contrast, the author and reader to whom Searle and Smith refer bear an uncanny resemblance to the abstract *Homo economicus* of early bourgeois political theory, who approaches epistemological questions with a tabula rasa and contractual relations with an assumption of unfettered autonomy.

In addition to the tendency to fragment texts and to isolate authors from their historical worlds, most intentionalist definitions of mimesis have an even more serious drawback, namely, a tendency to argue that mimesis necessarily suspends illocutionary force and, above all, makes no assertions. The intentionalist definitions discussed here do imply a functionalist approach to literary categories, for they state that literary kinds are constituted by the actual uses that people make of them. These arguments usually carry the paradoxical claim, however, that mimesis is that species of discourse that is socially agreed upon to have no funciton. Smith claims that "the context of a fictive utterance . . . is *historically indeterminate.*"[42] Roberts contends that authors do not attribute propositional significance to their "framing" statements.[43] Brown and Steinmann contend that "all . . . truth conditions are suspended" in mimesis.[44] Olsen, who understands so well the institutional context of the mimetic contract, concludes that "when statements occur in literary works, they . . . are etiolated."[45] Even Ohmann, who throughout his criticism exhibits an acute awareness of the ideological effects of literature as "performance," concludes that mimesis possesses "suspended" illocutionary force.[46] Mimesis is thus defined by absence, or negation; it is a gesture without a referent, and it is marked as a species of discourse by its in-

---

[41]Robert Weimann, *Structure and Society in Literary History: Studies in the History and Theory of Historical Criticism* (Charlottesville: University of Virginia Press, 1976), 6.

[42]Smith, "Poetry as Fiction," 275.

[43]Despite his ponderous and unhelpful differentiation between the "framing" and the "framed," Roberts does not make the error of positing that fictions are nonassertive. See the epigraph to this chapter.

[44]Brown and Steinmann, 149–50.

[45]Olsen, "Defining a Literary Work," 141.

[46]Ohmann, "Speech Acts and the Definition of Literature."

tended refusal to make serious interpretive statements about the world. If fictive discourse is indeed defined by the etiolation or suspension of illocutionary force, then no fictive mode of cognition exists, but simply a conventional disclaimer implicitly attached to all mimetic texts that reads, "Do not take any of this seriously."

The view of fiction as nonassertive discourse enjoys virtually unquestioned status these days. But sometimes our unexamined assumptions are those that require the closest scrutiny. Certainly a brief look at the history of criticism indicates that the contemporary conception of mimesis is in fact a fairly recent phenomenon. Plato wished to expel poets from his republic because they were liars; Pascal called the poetic imagination "man's ruling faculty, queen of lies and error"; Hume stated that "poets themselves, tho' liars by profession, always endeavor to give an air of truth to their fictions."[47] I am not advocating that we reinstate the old view of poets as liars; I am simply saying that one can argue for fiction's distinct status as a mode of discourse without conceding that it consists of nonassertive discourse. Indeed, I shall suggest that quite the opposite is the case: mimesis possesses what Graff calls "hyper-assertive" capacities,[48] and it performs highly significant social funcitons when it mobilizes these capacities.

Twentieth-century literary theory has clearly made major advances in the definition of fictionality. Instead of assuming separate essences for fictive and factual discourse, it has called upon us to scrutinize the logical bases for the distinctions that we ordinarily erect between the two. Instead of proclaiming the correspondence of the mimetic text to some a priori aesthetic universal, it has required us to focus our attention upon actual linguistic, structural, and ontological properties routinely found in fictional works. Instead of viewing author and reader as figures governed by preordained responsibilities or limita-

---

[47]Plato, *The Republic*, trans. Francis MacDonald Cornford (Oxford: Clarendon, 1941), 329–33; Blaise Pascal, *Pensées*, trans. H. F. Stewart (New York: Pantheon, 1950), no. 75, p. 39; David Hume, *Treatise of Human Nature*, ed. L. A. Selby-Bigge (Oxford: Clarendon, 1907), 121.

[48]Graff, "Literature as Assertions," 146. Those who are familiar with Graff's work on propositionality and assertion will recognize the extent of my indebtedness to his ideas throughout this chapter. For an incisive critique of the antiassertive stance of speech-act theory, see Martha Woodmansee, "Speech-Act Theory and the Perpetuation of the Dogma of Literary Autonomy," *Centrum*, 6 (Fall 1978): 75–89.

tions, it has compelled us to examine their varying contributions to the mimetic contract. Despite these theoretical advances, however, many recent discussions of mimesis have been flawed by the tendency to dissolve the mimetic contract into its component parts and to minimize its embeddedness in material reality. The text is fetishized, the author and reader are dehistoricized, and mimesis is divested of the capacity to make assertions. We must demonstrate that the mimetic contract involves a commitment to take seriously the text's propositional claims. We shall now therefore discuss the mode of cognition that is distinctly characteristic of the mimetic contract.

3

Mimesis, Cognition, and
the Problem of the Referent

Art is "knowledge" in a nonconceptual form and shares with science the fact of being bound to the laws of social processes, of being an "essential phenomenon." . . . Art is distinguished from science by the *mode* of its appropriation of reality. . . . The object of artistic appropriation is "the total content of our existence" (Hegel), the "whole wealth of the world"; the "total social object" (Lenin). Aesthetic reflection, that is, refers to the totality of economic, social, cultural and ideological processes.

—Thomas Metscher

The main problem besetting the twentieth-century theories of fictionality discussed in the preceding chapter is that they take as their premise one or another version of the Kantian view of the aesthetic as "purposive nonpurposiveness." Assuming that the "purposive" features of mimetic discourse are directed toward the "nonpurposive" ends of linguistic reflexivity, emotive release, or pseudo-statement, they define a work as fictional to the extent that it divests itself of the power to refer and to assert. The logic of the formalist argument is unremittingly circular.

If we wish to argue that fiction constitutes a distinct mode of discourse, we need not concede that it relinquishes the prerogative to tell the truth; on the contrary, we need to examine its characteristic strategies for conveying knowledge. Mimesis is, I propose, first and foremost a *mode of cognition,* enacted through a generic contract of which the purpose is to interpret and evaluate past or present historical actuality. In the realm of prose fiction, its principal strategy of representation is the construction of sets of characters and events that, through their relations with one another, suggest to the reader that the reality he or she inhabits possesses an *analogous configuration*. Mimesis inherently generalizes, as do all analogies; through this process of generalization it formulates explanations of, and judgments upon, various forms of social existence. Although fiction portrays concrete persons and events, it operates by means of a process of abstraction, since the particular persons and events represented in the fictional text possess their generalizing resonance only because they are reconcretizations of broader thematic principles. According to Lenin,

> The universal exists only in the individual and through the individual. Every individual is (in one way or another) a universal. Every universal is (a fragment, or an aspect, or the essence of) an individual. Every universal only approximately embraces all the individual objects. Every individual enters incompletely into the universal. . . . Every individual is connected by thousands of transitions with other *kinds* of individuals (things, phenomena, processes).[1]

Because of these "thousands of transitions," mimesis as a mode of cognition is especially empowered to render knowledge. The mimetic text takes as its referent the world of *actual* "things, phenomena, processes"; and in its characters, actions, and settings it represents *particular* "things, phenomena, processes." But the procedure whereby the latter convey cognition of the former involves an operation of abstraction and generalization. Analogous configuration is therefore a process of mediation, through which the universal aspects of the referent are replicated in the individual features of the mimetic text.

As I shall argue in the next chapter, to proffer and to enter into a mimetic contract are ineluctably ideological acts. "Aesthetic representation," remarks Thomas Metscher, "is never the merely neutral transformation of empirical reality into the beautiful appearance of the art world, but implies the interpretation of this reality and the adoption of an attitude towards it: aesthetic reflection implies *the interpretation and evaluation of reality in the act of its aesthetic formation*."[2] Fictional representation is, among other things, an activity of persua-

---

[1]V. I. Lenin, *Collected Works*, trans. George H. Hanna, ed. Robert Daglish (Moscow: Progress, 1967), 38:359.

[2]Thomas Metscher, "Literature and Art as Ideological Form," *New Literary History*, 9 (Autumn 1979): 30; emphases are his. I quote below from p. 23.

sion, for it undertakes the representation of people and events that do not exist or have not existed in order to propose evaluative attitudes toward people and events that do exist or have existed. The invention of characters and events possessing differential ontological status thus engages the text in representational procedures that are simultaneously referential and judgmental. The mimetic work proposes ethical values and historical beliefs that readers may be assumed to share, and on the basis of these, the work attempts to move its readers to accept values and beliefs more or less consciously endorsed by the author, with which they may well not agree. Mimesis is therefore interpretive, persuasive, judgmental, and evaluative, at the same time that it deals cognitively with its referent. But—and here is my main contention—rather than retreating from the task of formulating propositions about the historical world, mimesis possesses, if anything, an intensified propositional power. "The author articulates an act of cognition in the process of creating the work," maintains Metscher. "He produces cognition *in the work* and the recipient acquires cognition through the work." As we shall see, the propositions of the fictional text in no way lose their status as assertive gestures, even when they are filled with contradions.

I am arguing, in short, that as a mode of cognition, mimesis affords knowledge of both the referent and the subject. In this chapter and the one following, I shall attempt to consider each of these entities separately. In so doing, it might appear that I am perpetuating the dualistic view of consciousness and actuality that sustains the antiassertionist view of mimesis I have been opposing, since formalist theories of fictionality, as we have seen, assume the autonomy of the perceiving (and of the creating) self. But there are two important reasons why an analytical distinction between subject and referent remains useful and necessary. First, Marxist criticism has to this point achieved only a rudimentary understanding of the ways in which —to borrow Lenin's terms—the "known object" of the fictional representation reproduces the "real object" of historical actuality. Theorists working in the Lukácsian tradition emphasize the text's replication of its referent—almost, at times, to the exclusion of any consideration of the specific ideological vantage point of the authorial subject. The world, in other words, writes the text. Theorists working in the Althusserian tradition, by contrast, contend that the fictional text's referential claims are severely compromised by its necessary entrapment within the network of assumptions and paradigms that its author takes as a point of origin. Ideology, in other words, writes the text. I believe both that worlds constitute authors and that authors constitute worlds; my consideration of the mimetic text as both reflection and appropriation is an attempt to map out the phenomenon of mediation in a way that may prove fruitful for further Marxist inquiry.

Second, it is important to keep in mind the distinction between referent and subject when we consider the genre of the documentary novel. For, as we shall see, the documentary novel, in its various modes, buttresses its claims to generalized cognition by invoking a seemingly unmediated reference to an extratextual reality. Whether this invocation of factual authority is relatively naive, as in Cooper, or self-critical, as in Dos Passos, the problem of cognitive adequacy remains an urgent one. To what extent can a factual reference—either veracious or verisimilitudinous—reinforce the text's generalizing propositions about the world it represents? To what extent does the summoning of extratextual testimony simply deepen the text's implication in ideology? And how does the author's proclamation of extra-authorial authority ("author-ity"—a term laden with signification) affect the terms of the mimetic contract in the documentary novel? By maintaining an analytical separation between subject and referent—at least in the initial stages of our inquiry—we remind ourselves that the project of mimetic truth-telling may be more problematic than it first appears. A truth is being told, with "facts" to back it up, but a teller constructs that truth and chooses those facts.

Analogous Configuration and Representational Modes

Analogous configuration projects propositions about the text's referent by establishing relations among separate elements in the text. Mimetic truth clearly cannot hinge upon the reference of single characters or events in the text to real persons or happenings, since most of its particulars are invented. Rather, the mutual interactions of different textual features—characters, events, social conditions, philosophical debates—determine the text's reference to the world of the reader. According to the terms of the mimetic contract, the reader agrees to view the structures and processes represented in the text as

67

equivalent to structures and processes existing in historical actuality. An equivalence of function establishes the analogy between world and text: whether naturalistic, realistic, romantic, or fantastic, the textual particulars signal that their roles within the fictional totality correspond to roles assumed by (possibly) quite different particulars in the world of the reader. Thus, despite its characteristic projection of a dense specificity, the mimetic text produces cognition through generalization. "Novelistic fictions are," Roy Pascal notes, "abstractions, projections of actual relationships isolated from some of the associations with which in real life they are bound, and which are thought by the novelist to be irrelevant to his immediate purpose."[3] Paradoxically, illusion resides in the peculiar concreteness of detail; "reality" is conveyed by relationality.

All fictions, I propose, operate according to the strategy of analogous configuration; they vary considerably, however, in the kinds of contracts they call upon the reader to endorse. Part 2 of this study will be devoted to an examination of the historically altering terms of the mimetic contract accompanying the genre I am calling the documentary novel. Invoking here a fictional typology more familiar to my readers, I would suggest that the so-called major modes of fictional narrative—sometimes described as naturalism, realism, romance, and fantasy—are simply variations on the basic form of the mimetic contract. In each of these modes, authors set up different sorts of expectations about the kinds of evidence that can be adduced to support the analogies they are asserting. The point could be schematized as follows. In a naturalistic novel such as *Studs Lonigan,* the analogy tends toward a high degree of sociological precision.

Studs : Catholic Irish-American worker possessing false consciousness : : *Danny* : Ex–Catholic Irish-American proletarian intellectual possessing class consciousness.

In a more realistic novel such as *Bleak House,* by contrast, the analogy tends to be more general, although it still signifies a particular historical time and place.

[3]Roy Pascal, "Narrative Fictions and Reality: A Comment on Frank Kermode's *The Sense of an Ending,*" *Novel,* 11 (Fall 1977): 49.

Jo : The poor and oppressed in England of the Industrial Revolution : : *Lady Dedlock* : The wealthy and powerful in England of the Industrial Revolution.

A romance such as *The Scarlet Letter* proposes an analogy of increasingly remote historical reference, although it still relies upon a certain degree of social and historical specificity.

Hester : Female exemplar of acknowledged sin in Puritan New England : : *Dimmesdale* : Male exemplar of hidden sin in Puritan New England.

A fantasy such as *Slaughterhouse-Five* rests upon an analogy that moves away from quotidian reality and toward ethical schematism.

Billy Pilgrim : Alienated modern man : : *Tralfamadorians* : The appeal of amoral determinism.

Analogous configuration is an ineluctably totalizing procedure. As in the Gestalt model, each textual particular must be understood in relation to the configuration of the whole if it is to be understood at all.

Each of the analogies cited above posits, moreover, that the text's relation to its referent is diachronic rather than synchronic. That is, the plot articulates what the author sees as the underlying *dynamis* of essential social realities. Thus the divergent fates of Studs and Danny suggest Farrell's judgment of the tragic effects of false consciousness in the American working class; Lady Dedlock is morally implicated in the diseased body politic that eventually destroys Jo; Hester's triumph over the forces that wear down Dimmesdale poses an ironic commentary on the moral assessments routinely attached to gender and social position in colonial Boston and reveals the purgative effects of admitting membership in the community of sin; Billy Pilgrim's calm prediction of his own absurd death valorizes the Tralfamadorians' ethical passivity. The felt inevitability of the fictional text's narrative teleology conveys the author's sense of the moral or historical tendency embedded in his or her materials. As Henry James remarked, the novelist must "find [for characters] the right relations, those that would most bring them out; [he must] imagine, . . . invent

and select and piece together the situations most useful and favour-
able in the sense of the creatures themselves, the complications they
would be most likely to feel."[4] "Situations" and "complications" are
a necessary correlative of "relations": configuration implies motion,
and analogy implies destiny.

In the various modes of the mimetic contract, the fictional work
thus proposes cognition by asserting that its configuration is analogous to an existing state of historical or moral affairs. The reader's
perception of the particular produces cognition of the general. Even
though that rendition of the general is inevitably framed from the author's ideological standpoint, the analogizing strategy of the text
tends to efface the reader's conscious awareness of the informing
authorial perspective. Since the particulars of the text furnish the only
available data by which historical actuality is known and judged, appearance is, in mimesis, presented as equivalent to essence. Even
if—to anticipate my argument in Chapters 5 through 8—some textual details possess presumably unmediated referents in historical actuality, the text's analogizing procedures still enforce the illusion of
equivalence. Documentation supplements rather than supersedes the
assertion of generalized correspondence.

In naturalistic and realistic novels, however, the felt precision of
separate data is integrally related to the effectiveness of the text's proposed analogy with its referent. Since the author's rendition of elements in historical actuality involves a considerable amount of sociological specificity, the novelistic contract requires that the depiction
of the fictional figures—and of their environments—be apprehended
as commensurately accurate. Farrell must carefully relate speech patterns and demographical changes on Chicago's South Side that can be
readily corroborated, and his characters must engage in activities that
continually illustrate the foundations of consciousness in immediate,
felt social relations. *Studs Lonigan*'s relation to its referent is dictated
by a high degree of quotidian probability: Studs's relations with family, church, and gang convey general propositions about working-
class life, but these propositions are taken seriously only if the text
successfully replicates behaviors and actions that demonstrate sociological typicality. Dickens enjoys considerably more imaginative lati-
tude than does Farrell. Nonetheless, the novelistic contract of *Bleak*

---

[4]Henry James, *The Portrait of a Lady,* ed. Leon Edel (Boston: Houghton Mifflin, 1963), 5.

House places distinct limits upon the text's departure from the realm of familiar probability, and Dickens must keep careful rein on his affinity for supernatural occurrences such as the spontaneous combustion of Krook. Naturalistic and realistic novelists are therefore compelled to fulfill their contracts by adhering to fairly stringent conventions of plausibility. If they wish to tell a large truth about the general, they must tell us many smaller truths about the particular. Mary McCarthy remarks on novels in these traditions,

> We do really . . . expect a novel to be true, not only true to itself (like a poem or statue), but true to actual life, which is right around the corner. . . . The presence of fact in fiction, of dates and times and distances, is a kind of reassurance—a guarantee of credibility. If we read a novel, say, about conditions in post-war Germany, we expect it to be an accurate report of [these] conditions . . . ; if we find that it is not, the novel is discredited.[5]

McCarthy is not simply espousing a naive positivism here. Realism and naturalism create the expectation of empiricist overdetermination: the "guarantee of credibility" is an operational condition accompanying certain forms of the mimetic contract.

In romantic or fantastic fictions, by contrast, the quotidian plausibility of particular details figures a good deal less crucially in the novelistic contract. In *The Scarlet Letter,* Hawthorne replicates the history of Puritan Boston with considerable fidelity (there even was a real Mistress Hibbens, who was executed in 1656 for witchcraft), but these data are not required by the novelistic contract he invokes. His tale must be plausibily located in historical reality, but he must also be allowed a universe in which letters blaze in the heavens and bore their way into human flesh. The text takes as its referent a set of historically specific gender relations, but it constructs an analogous configuration around moral questions that are presumed to be largely timeless.[6] Vonnegut enjoys even greater license to wander from accepted

[5]Mary McCarthy, "The Fact in Fiction," *Partisan Review,* 27 (Summer 1960): 451.

[6]Recently the notions that much American fiction is "romance" and that "romance" involves a repudiation or avoidance of concretely historical reference have come under sharp attack. Much of this attack is warranted. Harry B. Henderson, one of the first to question the ahistorical underpinnings of the "romance" theory of American literature, noted that even Hawthorne, who dabbled with the supernatural more than many other American romancers, anchored his fictions in a carefully researched historical background (see *Versions*

canons of plausibility. He can make the Tralfamadorians look as bizarre as he wishes—the more so the better—so long as they voice philosophical views that effectively outline his moral framework. Everyday probabilities of chronology are abandoned, and "facts" about Earthlings—often recapitulated in stark concreteness—are juxtaposed with apparently equivalent "information" about Tralfamadorians. Indeed, documentary data enter the text to enhance its sense of irreality. Vonnegut's prefacing of his tale with a patently autobiographical reminiscence of the firebombing of Dresden—"All this happened, more or less"[7]—anchors the tale in actual historical events to stress all the more the strange dislocations Vonnegut sees at the core of contemporary historical actualities.

"Reality" is therefore as much present in *Slaughterhouse-Five* as it is in *Studs Lonigan,* insofar as both texts aim to render the shape and essential development of historical actuality, not primarily in its particulars, but in what the author sees as being its significant constitutive principles. The issue is not, then, that some fictional modes are more autotelic and others more referential; all are equally autotelic (configurational) and referential (analogous) at the same time. All are, moreover, equally assertive. Even if Vonnegut does not adhere to the sociological precision of a Farrell, he is as committed to representing reality as is Farrell. Neither text asserts that Studs or Billy Pilgrim ever lived, but neither suspends its illocutionary force. Each marshals every rhetorical resource available to the specific form of its contract to convince its reader of the validity of its general propositions about human life and destiny.

I can anticipate two objections to the theory I am setting forth here. First, it might be asserted that my analogies are themselves subjective

---

of the Past: The Historical Imagination in American Fiction [New York: Oxford University Press, 1974], esp. 114–26). I would argue, nonetheless, that the conventional signals accompanying the deployment of historical particulars in *The Scarlet Letter* are quite different from those accompanying particulars in, say, *The Pioneers* or "Benito Cereno." The procedure of reconcretization in *The Scarlet Letter* removes the world of the novel considerably from that of Puritan New England, since the essential principles shaping the novel's analogous configuration are conceived as pointing to a transhistorical realm of truth. For more on the argument that "romance" and "realism" characterize American and English fictions of the mid-nineteenth century, respectively, see Nicolaus Mills, *American and English Fiction in the Nineteenth Century: An Antigenre Critique and Comparison* (Bloomington: Indiana University Press, 1973).

[7]Kurt Vonnegut, *Slaughterhouse-Five; or The Children's Crusade: A Duty-Dance with Death* (New York: Delacorte, 1969), 1.

constructs, since not all readers would agree that the relations between the characters I cite are best described by the particular analogies I have framed. Indeed, it might be charged that I am simply
masking positivist assumptions by transposing my penchant for objectivism from facts to relations: my presumably self-evident analogies are in fact a highly personal—and ideological—interpretation of
the texts involved. To this objection I would respond that my analogies are not intended to be exhaustive or exclusionary descriptions or
interpretations of the novels cited. Certainly much more can be said
about the relation of Jo to Lady Dedlock than that it conveys a critique of class relations: their juxtaposition also moves us to consider
the relation of innocence to corruption, of youth to age, of the oppression of poverty to the oppression of gender, as well as to contemplate the interconnectedness of all human destinies. Similarly, Billy
Pilgrim's flight to Tralfamadore invites not only a meditation on
contemporary alienation but also an inquiry into the psychological
trauma specific to World War II and its aftermath. My point is quite
limited and modest: in considering these novels, we could formulate
none of these interpretive patterns and themes if we did not first
weigh the nature and extent of these characters' reference to historical
actuality. Jo and Lady Dedlock tell us nothing at all about the human
condition if they do not tell us about the peculiar intersection of human destinies in the era of the Industrial Revolution. The multiple interpretive analogies that can be derived from their relationship are
contingent upon a specifically referential analogy that affixes them in
a particular historical actuality. In the case of Billy Pilgrim and the
Tralfamadorians, by contrast, we would be hampered in our efforts
to construct derivative analogies if we sought too direct a reference in
historical actuality. The Tralfamadorians' mode of existence constitutes an interesting speculation on relativity theory, but these creatures are patently imaginative constructs nonetheless; while Billy Pilgrim, for all his grounding in the commodity fetishism of a distinctly
post–World War II American culture, is a cartoon caricature of contemporary anomie. Whatever grounding his psychological dilemma
may have in particular realities of World War II—and Vonnegut's
strongly felt autobiographical presence guarantees such a foundation
—his existential situation leads to further interpretation insofar as it is
seen as a fairly abstracted representation of the contemporary human
condition. When we seek to determine the strategy of analogous con-

figuration practiced in a given text, then, we are not trying to confine its meaning to its reference. Rather, we are attempting to establish its reference in such a way that its meaning can be more fully understood.

As a second possible objection, some readers may still disagree that analogous configuration implies assertion. Fictional works presumably may contain propositions about the world and may even render cognition of the world, yet they do not necessarily *assert* their view of things. To this objection I would reply that analogous configuration, while indirect in its method of representation, is a quintessentially assertive strategy of representation. A is to B as C is to D; this formulation contains two *is*'s to one *as*. The fact that *is* does not occupy the central position of *as* (which constitutes a kind of equal sign, connecting the world of the novel and that of the reader) does not diminish the explanatory force of the analogy. The novel poses a complex, ethically charged, and determinate relation between Jo and Lady Dedlock, or between Arthur Dimmesdale and Hester Prynne. If, as I have argued above, analogous configuration necessarily involves reference, then the *is* connecting Jo and Lady Dedlock or Hester Prynne and Arthur Dimmesdale carries as much force as does an *is* in a work of anthropology or history, since it requires the reader to search out the companion *is* in historical actuality. The fictional *is*, of course, represents a different kind of *is* than that discoverable in much nonfictional discourse, for it conveys cognition of a generalized kind: we cannot expect a novel to offer a direct representation of an actual state of affairs. As we shall see in Part 2 of this book, even when a text draws verifiable historical particulars into its assertions about the world, these particulars must first be framed by the relevant novelistic conventions. Nonetheless, the two linking verbs connected by the conjunction do constitute a complete thought—and do possess a formidable capacity to tell the truth.

The Problem of the Referent

The theory of analogous configuration I am outlining bears a certain resemblance to familiar theories of mimesis—New Critical, Aristotelian, Lukácsian, Althusserian—but differs from each of these in one or more crucial respects.

New Critical theories of fictional representation (at least those that do not construe mimesis as consisting completely in linguistic opacity) hold that the fictional work possesses a highly ordered configuration but that this configuration has little to do with reference. Wimsatt and Brooks differentiate fictive from factual discourse on the basis that the former aims at "coherence," the latter at "correspondence"; Northrop Frye posits that the "final direction of meaning" in imaginative literature is inward, while that in "descriptive or assertive writing" is outward.[8] These criteria of coherence and inwardness clearly bear a certain affinity to my stipulation that mimesis refers to historical actuality through its projection of relationality, rather than of verifiable particularity. But for these theorists, the stress upon configuration leads to one or another version of the formalist claim that mimetic texts cannot make assertions. Presumably, the greater the coherence or internal direction of the text, the lesser its obligation to make verifiable statements about the historical world. Beauty and Truth exist in inverse proportion to one another. My concept of analogous configuration leads to quite a different conclusion. The text's coherence signals the explanatory abstractions by which the author interprets the historical actuality to which the text analogously corresponds. Its inwardness is constituted by its abstraction of a pattern of configuration from the external reality that furnishes its referent. Analogous configuration is thus not a retreat from reference; it is a means to reference.

My notion of analogous configuration clearly has a good deal more in common with Aristotelian poetics than with modern formalism. My discussion of analogy is quite close to Aristotle's notion of the poetic universal (that is, "what sort of man turns out to say or do what sort of thing according to probability or necessity").[9] Moreover, my analysis of narrative as the assertion of a moral teleology places my discussion of mimesis in clear alignment with Aristotle's insistence upon viewing the poetic text as a coherent whole shaped by an informing power, or dynamis. Finally, my view that the fictional

---

[8]William K. Wimsatt and Cleanth Brooks, *Literary Criticism: A Short History* (New York: Knopf, 1957); Northrop Frye, *The Anatomy of Criticism: Four Essays* (Princeton: Princeton University Press, 1957), 74.

[9]Aristotle, *Aristotle's Poetics: A Translation and Commentary for Students of Literature,* trans. Leon Golden (Englewood Cliffs: Prentice-Hall, 1968), chap. 9, p. 17. Below I refer to chap. 25, p. 46.

text asserts its appropriation of its referent also accords with his conception of mimesis as a means of conveying truth. Aristotle may have stipulated that poetry and history aim at different kinds of propositionality, but he never held that poetry's "persuasive impossibilities" do not seek to persuade, or that the poet's essential (as opposed to accidental) errors do not detract from the adequacy of his representation.

Nonetheless, my theory departs significantly from Aristotle's in its conception of the way that the referent is reconcretized in the mimetic work. Aristotle assumes that the poet can directly and unproblematically render the essential configuration of the social world and that the "sort of man" portrayed in the text replicates a universal that simply and unquestionably exists. He does not consider the possibility that authorial presuppositions might in some way determine the conditions of access to the universal, or, indeed, that the universal itself might be the product of social experience, susceptible to challenge and change. The problem of selection and construction is therefore, for Aristotle, socially uncomplicated. The definition of "such a man" implicitly entails property and citizenship, and the perspective from which judgments are framed is restricted to deviations from an ethical norm located firmly within that definition. The universal is confined to the range of moral imperatives accessible to the ruling class; Aristotle simple was not obliged to construct a theoretical model accounting for a discursive situation where, for example, both *Gone with the Wind* and *Jubilee* might purport to be treating the "same" referent, and (adjusting for gender) Scarlett O'Hara and Vyry might embody the "kind of man" who enables us to grasp the essence of that referent. As Alfred Sohn-Rethel has pointed out, the very activity of conceptual abstraction was, in Aristotle's time, relegated to a realm of contemplation only tangentially linked to material activity.[10] While signaling the complexity of a society increasingly penetrated by the exchange relation, the process of conceptual abstraction was sealed off from production; philosophical ideas enjoyed virtual autonomy in relation to practice. Accordingly, the issue of mediation did not arise

---

[10]Alfred Sohn-Rethel, *Intellectual and Manual Labor: A Critique of Epistemology*, trans. Martin Sohn-Rethel (Atlantic Highlands, N.J.: Humanities, 1978). See also Herbert Marcuse, "The Affirmative Character of Culture," in *Negations: Essays in Critical Theory*, trans. Jeremy J. Shapiro (Boston: Beacon, 1968), 88–133.

as a relevant question in Aristotle's poetics, and the relation between mimetic abstraction and historical actuality was reduced to a problem of form.

My argument clearly situates itself in the Marxist tradition. But here it encounters significant opposition from the schools of both Lukács and Althusser. Invoking Aristotle and Lenin, Lukács says that the goal of all great art is "to provide a picture of reality in which the contradiction between appearance and reality, the particular and the general, the immediate and the conceptual, etc., is so resolved that the two converge into a spontaneous integrity in the direct impression of the work of art and provide a sense of an inseparable integrity."[11] He argues that "the totality of the work of art is intensive, and that the self-containment of a work of art is therefore the reflection of the process of life in motion and in concrete context." The realistic novel is especially suited to this task, declares Lukács, for it delineates typical characters who, in their intersecting fates, epitomize the essential dialectic of history in their time. Where for Aristotle the referent was the unfolding of an individual destiny within a fixed universe, for Lukács the referent becomes historical process itself; indeed, "the aesthetic illusion is only possible," declares Lukács, "when the work of art reflects the total objective process of life with *objective accuracy.*" Mimetic representation thus necessitates, by definition, the penetration beneath appearance to essence—actually, to essence-in-motion—and its criterion for value is political: only works that replicate the trajectory of history can be said to possess genuine aesthetic value. Lukács's argument thus provides consistent grounds for determining the superiority of *Jubilee* over *Gone with the Wind* on the

[11]Lukács, "Art and Objective Truth," in *Writer and Critic and Other Essays,* ed. and trans. Arthur D. Kahn (New York: Grosset & Dunlap, Universal Library, 1971), 34. The passages that I quote below appear on pp. 38, 37, and 41. Some readers unfamiliar with the canon of Lukács's work may be puzzled by the discrepancy between my relatively harsh treatment of him here and my approving citation of him in Chapter 7. The reason for my different responses to Lukács's work is that Lukács himself changes substantially over the years: the revolutionary repudiation of reification in *History and Class Consciousness* (1923) has become ossified into a reflectionist—and in many ways conservative—advocacy of critical realism by the mid-1930s. Lukacs's later position boxes him into several corners. How, for example, can a writer be condemned for creating reified representations of a reified world if fiction reproduces the essential dynamics of reality? For an acute discussion of the contradictions in the later Lukács, see the last chapter of Carolyn Porter's *Seeing and Being: The Plight of the Participant Observer in Emerson, James, Adams, and Faulkner* (Middletown: Wesleyan University Press, 1981).

basis of something other than the purely formalistic criterion of internal coherence.

The great value of Lukács's theory of mimesis is that it effectively demonstrates how mimesis takes as its referent neither inert particulars nor timeless universals but specific historical processes. But Lukács's theory also suffers from a somewhat mechanistic reflectionism, for it ends up conflating a normative description of fiction with a prescriptive one. I am not quarreling with Lukács's stipulation that the critic should evaluate the author's implied politics, or with his judgment that these politics can frequently be said to produce superficial, inadequate, or incorrect representations of historical actuality. Marxists must hold that some descriptive interpretations of the social world are more valid than others and that a primary criterion for adjudication among them is political. But for Lukács to equate the representation of typical characters in Homer's epics, Shakespeare's plays, or the realistic novel with the definition of mimesis as such is faulty logic. By his definition, fiction delineates social tensions through the projection of imagined microcosms; to the extent that any work fails to perform this task, it is shallow and also, by extension, not fictional. Despite Lukács's protests against the positivism of the naturalists, his own reflectionism takes certain features of the referent as self-evident, with the difference that he asserts the referent to be essence, rather than epiphenomenon. And where Aristotle's objectivism is understandably linked to the epistemological and ideological limits informing the social synthesis of his time, in the case of Lukács such naive objectivism is less excusable. The evident multiplicity of ideological perspectives informing modern mimetic works should lead toward an increased recognition and a more thorough analysis of the function of ideological abstraction in fictional representation, rather than toward a reductionist definition of mimesis that would exclude whole schools of writers on what are, ultimately, formalistic rather than political grounds.

To the extent that partisanship enters the process of fictional production, for Lukács it occurs as a dialectic embedded within the referent, as "objective partisanship." The subjective perspective of the writer, therefore, need not enter the overall mimetic process; what matters, finally, is that historical actuality be neutrally reflected within the totality of the mimetic text. Lukács's discussion illuminates the process whereby analogous configuration renders knowledge of essential historical processes, but it encourages no investigation into mimesis as praxis. For all its attention to the dialectics of its referent, mimesis can never be more than a replication of that referent: there is no dialectic between author and world. Lukács's formulation thus prohibits inquiry into the possible meaning of Marx's rather enigmatic remark that literature is one of "the acquired *forces* of production"[12] (italics added)—in other words, a phenomenon that shapes, and is not merely shaped by, social reality. Paradoxically, then, Lukács's insistence that mimesis provides knowledge of the referent ends up reducing the significance of that knowledge: fiction tells us nothing that history cannot, for there is no specifically fictional mode of cognition.

Where Lukács errs in the direction of objectivism, critics working in the Althusserian paradigm err in the opposite direction by repudiating the notion of reflection altogether. Fredric Jameson, for example, argues that the mimetic text is grounded in a "historical or ideological subtext." The "paradox of the subtext," he remarks, is that the

> literary work or cultural object, as though for the first time, brings into being that very situation to which it is also, at one and the same time, a reaction. It articulates its own situation and textualizes it, thereby encouraging and perpetuating the illusion that the situation itself did not exist before it, that there is nothing but a text, that there never was an extra- or con-textual reality before the text generated it in the form of a mirage.[13]

[12]Marx, quoted in Cliff Slaughter, *Marxism, Ideology, and Literature* (Atlantic Highlands, N.J.: Humanities, 1980), 205. The conception of literature as a "productive force" has not yet been adequately explored within Marxist criticism. Brecht spoke of a "production aesthetic" but did not give it a clear theoretical formulation. Fredric Jameson justly observes: "One cannot without intellectual dishonesty assimilate the 'production' of texts . . . to the production of goods by factory workers: writing and thinking are not alienated labor in that sense, and it is surely fatuous for intellectuals to seek to glamorize their tasks—which can for the most part be subsumed under the rubric of the elaboration, reproduction, or critique of ideology—by assimilating them to real work on the assembly line and to the experience of the resistance of matter in genuine manual labor" (*The Political Unconscious: Narrative as a Socially Symbolic Act* [Ithaca: Cornell University Press, 1981], 45). Nonetheless, if we are to avoid a passively reflectionist model of mimetic discourse, it is crucial to see literature as in some sense "producing" consciousness in its readers. This need not imply, of course, that writers do not mediate ideology—dominant or otherwise—in the process of producing consciousness: what is produced need not be new, even if its specific articulation is unique.

[13]Jameson, 82.

Jameson thus maintains that a "Real" exists beyond the bounds of textuality. In his formulation, however, it becomes difficult indeed to distinguish the text's "situation" as discourse from its "situation" in historical actuality, or, even, to determine how the Real is not a mirage or simply another text (what Julia Kristeva calls the "géno-texte").[14] Jameson is clearly anxious to retain some sort of referential power for mimesis and to avoid the solipsistic conclusion that "because history is a text, the 'referent' does not exist." But he is very uneasy with the notion of mediation, which, he says, "aims to demonstrate . . . that *the same* essence is at work in the specific languages of culture as in the organization of the relations of production." History, as "absent cause," is "inaccessible to us except in textual form, and . . . our approach to it and to the Real itself necessarily passes through its prior textualization, its narrativization in the political unconscious."[15]

The problem with this formulation is that, once all reality and experience have been drawn, however hesitantly, under the rubric of textuality, it becomes virtually impossible to work back to the Real, which itself—as is suggested by Jameson's peculiar use of capitalization—becomes mystified and opaque. Textuality may not be all there is, but it is all that matters. The Real is reified as a realm of facticity existing prior to human intervention; once we fall into the world of textuality, the Real is irrecoverable. Jameson exhorts us to be materialists ("always historicize"), but he removes the epistemological grounds that would enable us to carry out his injunction.

Terry Eagleton, who does not share Jameson's divided allegiance between Hegelian and Althusserian Marxism, jettisons the category of mediation altogether. According to Eagleton, fiction embodies no representation of historical actuality but only the representation of the ideological paradigms whereby historical actuality is apprehended. "History . . . certainly 'enters' the text," Eagleton concludes, "but it enters it precisely *as ideology,* as a presence determined and distorted by its measurable absences."[16] The screening effect of ideology necessarily obscures the text's reference to historical actuality; indeed, Eagleton argues, "the literary text's lack of a direct referent consti-

---

[14]Julia Kristeva, *La révolution du language poétique* (Paris: Seuil, 1974), 339–40.

[15]Jameson, 35.

[16]Terry Eagleton, *Criticism and Ideology: A Study in Marxist Literary Theory* (1976; London: NLB, Verso, 1978), 72. The passages quoted below appear on pp. 78, 69, and 95.

tutes the most salient fact about it: its fictiveness." Mimesis thus invokes, for Eagleton, the illusion of referentiality: if there is a Real, it exists at the vanishing point of an infinite regress of textual codifications. Ideology, finally, not only constitutes historical actuality but also supplies the subject who tries to appropriate that actuality. "Ideology . . . so produces and constructs the real," remarks Eagleton, "as to cast the shadow of its absence over its presence. . . . Ideological space is curved like space itself, and history lies beyond it as only God could lie beyond the universe."

When the referent becomes absence, or even the mysterious Prime Mover of "absent cause," fiction retreats from offering explanations of historical actuality. "History" and "ideological space" become two incommensurable realms of experience, and fiction can represent only signifying practices, but never the material processes in relation to which these signifying practices are deployed. It is no accident, I think, that both Jameson and Eagleton present History, Ideology, and the Real in almost religious terms: materiality becomes that which is by definition inaccessible to representation, and even mimesis and cognition become hypostatized as incompatible—and antagonistic—kinds of activity.[17]

Thomas Lewis, another Althusserian critic, offers a more promising discussion of the conjunction of ideology and historical actuality in the mimetic referent, for he attempts to argue that mimesis does indeed posit a referent—a material object of representation, existing beyond authorial consciousness. Lewis remarks, "When most of us as critics want to determine the referent of the text—that is, what the text alludes to or talks about other than itself—we have cultural, social practices in mind (the *thing-for-us*) and not the inert, unsignifying (because untransformed by human labor) . . . realm of the *thing-in-*

---

[17]For much of my criticism of the Althusserians I am indebted to Tony Bennett's useful *Formalism and Marxism* (London: Methuen, 1979), 111–42. Bennett asserts: "Rather than conceiving of particular ideologies, particular works of literature and particular sciences which, according to their nature and the uses to which they are put, may be either progressive or regressive in their political implications, each being mapped out as an area of class struggle, Althusser's positions implied that class struggle takes place between the eternal verities of science, the eternal falsehoods of ideology and the eternal equivocations of literature. . . . Class struggle, that is, is displaced from the sphere of each of these practices and comes to occupy the epistemological spaces between them" (138). I have argued elsewhere, however, that Bennett himself remains wedded to the Althusserian paradigm, if reluctantly. See my review of *Formalism and Marxism* in *Modern Philology*, 80 (May 1983): 443–46.

itself."[18] He therefore describes the referent as the "cultural ideological unit," that is, an ideologically constructed set of relations. But Lewis does not argue that this thing-for-us forbids access to the thing-in-itself. He invokes Lenin's distinction between the real object and the known object, and he posits a dual referent: the raw materials of historical actuality and, simultaneously, the particular configuration imposed upon these materials by the author's favored ideological paradigm. Different "cultural ideological units" may therefore compete to cover the same conjunction of historical actualities. The artist makes choices among competing ideological conceptions that are, as he rather opaquely states, "rival formal organizations with a common content experience that itself embodies conflicting elements that may function in varying arrangements with differently graded valences." This conception of the referent as "cultural ideological unit" thus suggests how it is possible that both *Jubilee* and *Gone with the Wind,* with their "rival formal organizations," can claim to portray the "common content experience" of the Civil War South—and, moreover, to render knowledge of it.

Even Lewis's valuable discussion encounters a central difficulty that is, however, endemic to the Althusserian project; his analysis adopts the inevitable Althusserian opposition of Literature and Ideology. "The aesthetic effect," Lewis argues, "consists precisely in the work's disruptive relationship to the ideological materials (cultural units, the *stuff* of lived experience) that it seizes as its object and transforms." That is, something inherent in mimesis itself renders problematic its own procedures of mediation; mimesis is inherently disruptive of, and adversarial toward, the interpretive propositions it contains. The thing-for-us is invariably cast into an ironic light by the thing-in-itself, and the distinguishing feature of mimetic discourse, Lewis concludes, is its "privileged status in relation . . . to ideology, on the one hand, and to knowledge on the other." The referent in this context, while it may "constitute an object that lends itself to knowledge," is "itself neither a real object nor a knowledge." By disrupting ideology, then, the mimetic text also disrupts reference.

Situating mimesis in a kind of discursive limbo between Ideology and Science, Althusserian theory ends up stripping mimesis of its propositional status. In Althusser's words:

[18]Thomas E. Lewis, "Notes toward a Theory of the Referent," *PMLA,* 94 (May 1979): 463. The passage quoted below is from p. 471.

Art . . . does not give us a *knowledge* in the *strict sense,* it therefore does not replace knowledge (in the modern sense: scientific knowledge), but what it gives us does nevertheless maintain a certain *specific relationship* with knowledge. This relationship is not one of identity but one of difference. . . . The peculiarity of art is to 'make us see,' . . . 'make us perceive,' 'make us feel' something which *alludes* to reality.[19]

Although the Althusserians would no doubt deny the charge, it seems to me that this formulation distinctly resembles the antiassertionist stance that I criticized in the bourgeois theorists covered in the previous chapter. Iser's notion that fictional texts are distanced from their implied propositions and themes bears a kinship to Lewis's statement that mimesis disrupts ideology; Searle's stipulation that fiction suspends illocutionary force resembles in some ways Althusser's view that literature "alludes" to reality. By consigning all fictive discourse to an epistemological region midway between ideology and science, moreover, the Althusserian definition makes it impossible to judge whether one representation of historical actuality possesses more legitimacy than another. According to the Althusserian argument, *Gone with the Wind* is as disruptive of ideology as is *Jubliee,* and the texts offer no criteria for adducing the greater or lesser adequacy of each known object as an explanatory account of the real object that is the Civil War. If Marxist criticism considers itself to be politically committed, this is a peculiar place for it to end up.

The view of mimesis as analogous configuration enables us to see fiction as a qualitatively defined mode of discourse, characterized not by language, ontology, or reader response but by its own distinct mode of conveying cognition. It enables us, moreover, to formulate the process by which the fictional text appropriates—and asserts its appropriation of—its referent. But the same referent can furnish the raw material for very different configurations and can suggest widely

[19]Louis Althusser, "A Letter on Art in Reply to André Daspre," in *Lenin and Philosophy and Other Essays,* trans. Ben Brewster (London: Monthly Review, 1971), 222. In his later *Essays in Self-Criticism,* trans. Grahame Lock (London: NLB, 1976), Althusser criticizes his own "theoretical tendency" in saying that the distinction between "Ideology" and "Science" differentiates bourgeois ideology from Marxism—which, he says, presents their antagonism in rationalist and idealist terms (119–25). This seems to me a valid self-criticism. I have not yet seen it applied to a reworking of the relation of "Literature" to "Science" and "Ideology" in Althusserian literary theory, however.

varying propositions about the analogous relation between text and world. This variability exists because analogous configuration is a procedure not only of replication but also of abstraction, and because abstraction is a quintessentially ideological activity.

4

Mimesis, Cognition, and the Problem of the Subject

The concrete totality is a totality of thoughts, concrete in thought, in fact a product of thinking and comprehending; but not in any way a product of the concept which thinks and generates itself outside or above observation and perception; a product, rather, of the working-up of observation and conception into concepts. The totality, as it appears in the head, as a totality of thoughts, is a product of a thinking head, which appropriates the world in the only way it can. . . . The subject retains its autonomous existence outside the head just as before; namely as long as the head's conduct is merely speculative, merely theoretical. Hence, in the theoretical method, the subject, society, must always be kept in mind as the presupposition.

—Karl Marx

The critical category of analogous configuration refers to the external thrust of mimesis, its appropriation of a world existing beyond the margins of the text. It has as its dialectical counterpart the critical category of ideological abstraction, which denotes the internal or subjective character of mimesis, its necessary interpretation of historical actuality from the perspective of an individual author's consciousness. For when the fictional work reconcretizes actual processes and structures in the historical world, it attempts to persuade the reader of the legitimacy of the author's specific conception of those processes and structures. The relations described among the analogized persons and occurrences are not evaluatively neutral, after all, but inherently interpretive, judgmental, and ideological. The process of generalization is a process of abstraction, and abstraction necessarily involves orders and hierarchies, elevations and demotions, all emanating from the authorial subject's conception of the nature of the totality of which the referent is a part. An author creates certain characters and circumstances and not others, and depicts them in a certain way and not another; the text's projection of certain qualities and relations as essential represents the author's view of the essential nature of things.

The acts of proposing and accepting the mimetic contract are therefore political acts. The mimetic contract requires that the reader suspend beliefs and preferences for the duration of reading and that, as Harold Osborne puts it, he or she "put into abeyance his own natural responses and accept those inherent in the art work. In this way a person enjoying aesthetically a piece of . . . fictional art can savour evaluative and emotional attitudes other than those which are natural to him in everyday life, putting himself for the time being under the direction of the literary work."[1] This statement does not mean, of course, that authors can impose upon their readers whole structures of feeling with which these readers do not agree. Writers may shape some expectations in their readers, but they also fulfill others: as Peter Rabinowitz has recently argued, authors routinely affirm many of their audience's assumptions at the same time that they assert attitudes or ideas that are new or unfamiliar.[2] Nor does this mean that readers passively accept the terms of the mimetic contract. Indeed, they may find themselves in Ohmann's situation: "I read *against* the author," he declares, "the refractory unseen audience, delivering bronx cheers as I go."[3] But to admit that we read against the author is to concede that the author is demanding from us a response. Ohmann concludes, "Literary mimesis implicates the reader in an imagined society by making him party to the acts that imply it. There is no ethically neutral way for him to fulfill his role. He must give consent to the ethos of the created society, or reserve his endorsement to one degree or another. Either way, the poem calls his political imagination into play, presses him into political choice."[4] The fact that this politi-

---

[1] Harold Osborne, "On Artistic Illusion (2)," *British Journal of Aesthetics,* 9 (July 1969): 221.

[2] Peter J. Rabinowitz, "Assertion and Assumption: Fictional Patterns and the External World," *PLMA,* 96 (May 1981): 408–19.

[3] Ohmann, personal communication, March 5, 1983.

[4] Ohmann, "Literature as Act," in *Approaches to Poetics: Selected Papers from the English Institute,* ed. Seymour Chatman (New York: Columbia University Press, 1973), 102. For another analysis of ideology and reader response that stresses resistance as well as participation on the part of the reader, see Manfred Neumann, "Literary Production and Reception," *New Literary History,* 8 (Autumn 1976): 107–26.

cal choice is embodied in our response to characters who never lived does not diminish its seriousness.

Theories of Ideology and Theories of Mimesis

To say that the mimetic text requires an act of political choice is to assert its embeddedness in ideology. But the term "ideology" is clearly one of the most vexed—and vexing—in current critical discourse. Let me first clarify my own definition of the term. "Ideology" denotes the nexus of concepts by which individuals represent to themselves their situation in the social world. These individuals perhaps do not construe this relation as political, but their conception of it nonetheless is political—both in its genesis and in its implication. Ideology signifies both false and true consciousness. Since the ruling class in any given form of class society possesses hegemony, it is inevitable that the prevalent guide for understanding reality should distort actual relations in such a way as to rationalize existing social inequalities. At the same time, even dominant ideology contains partial truth; it draws together the conceptual abstractions by which very real individuals explain their relation to the social totality. Moreover, not all ideology is dominant ideology. Residual and emergent modes of thinking are also ideological, and even those that propose a revolutionary overthrow of existing relations of production are ideological.

The debate about ideology is one of the most heated issues in Marxist cultural studies—and justifiably so, since much of what one says about the relation of base to superstructure is shaped by the way one construes the nature of ideology and ideological production. Unfortunately, the writings of Marx and Engels on this subject are self-contradictory and provide little help in adjudicating a "correct" definition.[5] At times they take ideology to signify simply the reference of

[5]For more on the different significations of "ideology" in the writings of Marx and Engels, see Raymond Williams, *Marxism and Literature* (Oxford: Oxford University Press, 1977), 55–71. Also see Bhikhu Parekh, *Marx's Theory of Ideology* (Baltimore: Johns Hopkins University Press, 1982). Parekh ably delineates the connections between idealism and apologia in Marx's discussion of ideology and defends Marx's own implicit claim to be "beyond" ideology. But Parekh's strongly anti-Leninist bias prevents him from seeing the nonantagonistic contradiction between proletarian class partisanship and intellectual objectivity. Parekh treats Marx almost exclusively as a philosophical critic of bourgeois society,

all thought to its social origins—that is, any conceptual form, "legal, political, religious, aesthetic, or philosophic," by which "men become conscious of [the] conflict [between forces and relations of production] and fight it out."[6] At other times, Marx and Engels imply that ideology necessarily entails idealism and apologia. Thus the Young Hegelians were "ideologists," as was a "base" and "vulgar" thinker such as Malthus, who was a "shameless sycophant of the ruling classes."[7] At still other times, Marx and Engels imply that ideology simply denotes false consciousness. "Ideology is a process accomplished by the so-called thinker consciously, it is true, but with a false consciousness," remarked Engels. "The real motive forces impelling him remain unknown to him; otherwise it simply would not be an ideological process."[8]

If we are to understand the strategies of propositionality in documentary novels purporting to tell the truth, we must have a clear and consistent understanding of the meaning of ideology and of its relation to fictional discourse. I shall briefly summarize the four principal definitions of ideology and explore the views of mimesis they imply.

In its most restricted and negative sense of "apologia," or deliberately imposed false consciousness, "ideology" refers to systems of ideas consciously promulgated by the ruling class to enforce their hegemony. Thus George Fredrickson, in his study of racist pseudoscience in the United States during the nineteenth century, designates craniologists and ethnologists such as Nott and Gliddon as "racist ideologists."[9] Nott and Gliddon, he convincingly demonstrates, were well aware of the usefulness of their work to the slavery cause: "ideology" here signifies a system of conceptual domination deliberately imposed from above. The view of ideology as apologia accu-

---

rather than as a philosophical radical engaged in a committed political praxis. Hence Parekh accuses Marx of falling back upon enlightened self-consciousness as the final arbiter of truth and wrongly concludes that "in conferring upon self-consciousness the power to transcend the deepest influences of class and society, [Marx] remained an idealist" (222).

[6]Marx, *A Contribution to the Critique of Political Economy,* in *Basic Writings of Marx and Engels,* ed. Lewis Feuer (Garden City: Doubleday, 1959), 44.

[7]Marx and Engels, *The German Ideology, Part I,* in *The Marx-Engels Reader,* 2d ed., ed. Robert Tucker (New York: Norton, 1978); Marx, *Theories of Surplus Value* (Moscow: Progress, 1968), 2:420.

[8]Engels to Mehring, July 14, 1893, in Tucker, ed., *The Marx-Engels Reader,* 766.

[9]George Fredrickson, *The Black Image in the White Mind: The Debate on Afro-American Character and Destiny, 1817–1914* (New York: Harper & Row, 1971), chap. 3.

rately enough pinpoints the motives of a novelist like Thomas Dixon, who willfully provoked white separatist hysteria through fictional representations such as *The Clansman* or *The Leopard's Spots*. But, despite its usefulness in describing situations in which ruling classes mobilize systems of ideas for explicitly propagandistic purposes (and novelists aid in this process), the view of ideology as apologia is clearly inappropriate for the analysis of fictions possessing little immediate instrumental value to ruling-class interests. Indeed, it exculpates most writers entirely: if they are not conscious propagandists —and most clearly are not—then they are not political agents at all.

In a somewhat looser definition, "ideology" can be taken to mean "false consciousness," or even "necessary false consciousness." Franz Jakubowski, for example, associates ideology with the necessary conceptual distortions derivative from any individual's class position. "Ideology as false, partial consciousness corresponds," he says, "to a particular position in class society from which a correct, total understanding is impossible."[10] This formulation has the advantage of avoiding the hypothesis of conspiracy that inevitably attaches to the view of ideology as apologia, while still identifying the class-coded values and assumptions that underlie even the most apparently apolitical and universalistic discourse. The definition of ideology as false consciousness, however, reduces the discursive operations of consciousness to the level of secondary epiphenomena, usually determined by a reified—and crudely "material"—base. Indeed, in some ways this formulation simply inverts the dualistic epistemological hierarchy for which Marx and Engels faulted the idealism of the Young Hegelians: ideas and social forces do not interpenetrate but inhabit differential realms, of which one always exercises complete hegemony over the other. The view of ideology as necessary false consciousness prohibits, moreover, any consideration of ideological contradiction: individuals simply reproduce the ideological paradigms prevailing in their social groups, and residual or emergent ideological tendencies can never pose a significant challenge to dominant ideology. Taken to its logical conclusion, indeed, the view of ideology as necessary false consciousness precludes the possibility that people can function as purposive agents of historical change.

[10]Franz Jakubowski, *Ideology and Superstructure in Historical Materialism,* trans. Anne Booth (London: Allison & Busby, 1976), 103.

Applied to the theory of fictionality, the view of ideology as false consciousness construes mimesis as a superstructural epiphenomenon that is interesting mainly for what it can reveal about class hegemony in the realm of thought. Lukács's later writings on modernism, in which writers are seen as inescapably bound by the reification of monopoly capitalism, exemplify a relatively mechanistic formulation of the relation between this conception of ideology and the production of fictional works. Lucien Goldmann's "genetic structuralism" offers a more sophisticated methodology, but its limitations point to the liabilities that inevitably accompany any theory of mimesis that assumes a model of passive reflection. The greatest literary works, for Goldmann, are those that most clearly express the worldview of the author's social class or social group. Defining this "world-vision" as the "whole complex of ideas, aspirations and feelings which links together the members of a social group," Goldmann argues that writers are "exceptional individuals who either actually achieve or who come very close to achieving a completely integrated and coherent view of what they and the social class to which they belong are trying to do."[11] The literary text, according to Goldmann, reproduces in its structural coherence the explanatory frameworks whereby an author and his or her social class attempt to account for their position in the order of things. The ideological and formal configuration of the text is thus "homologous" with the dominant structure of consciousness informing both the authorial subject and the social group.

The primary virtues of Goldmann's formulation are that it accounts for the intersection of individual and social consciousness within literary structures and it sees both reference and ideological abstraction as directed toward processes rather than inert particularities. Goldmann's concern with what Raymond Williams calls "structures of feeling"[12] thus enables us to grasp ideology as the lived expe-

[11]Lucien Goldmann, *The Hidden God: A Study in Tragic Vision in the Pensées of Pascal and the Tragedies of Racine,* trans. Philip Thody (London: Routledge & Kegan Paul, 1969), 17. The passage quoted below appears on p. 19. As will become clear in Chapter 6, Goldmann's conception of "homologous structures" is quite different from my conception of "homologous configuration," which I see as distinctly related to the realist project. For an additional critique of the notion that ruling classes maintain dominance by means of ideological hegemony, see Nicholas Abercrombie, Bryan S. Turner, et al., *The Dominant Ideology Thesis* (London: Allen & Unwin, 1979).

[12]Williams, 128–35. For an analysis of Goldmann's influence on Williams's assimilation of continental Marxism into the English tradition, see Edward Said, "Traveling Theory,"

rience of a particular social group. But Goldmann's argument suffers from a perilous apriorism. Presumably one need only investigate Jansenism to know the essential features of Racine's and Pascal's world outlooks, or vice versa; the ideological configuration of the text bears a homologous relation to mental structures in both the author and the group, and identity simply reproduces itself on various levels of structural replication. Apparently no distinct mode of cognition characterizes mimetic discourse: mimesis is simply a form of ideology. Moreover, we might query whether writers—"great" or otherwise—can be so readily assimilated to a "collective group consciousness" as Goldmann supposes. Ideological determination, I would argue, should apply less to the restriction of subjects to the world outlooks of their classes than to the process by which different classes and ideological perspectives are mutually positioned. Individuals, while likely to be ideologically aligned with the social groups of their origin, are capable of situating themselves at various places in this configuration. The range of conceptual abstractions accessible to a particular individual is limited more by the overall configuration of the mode of production than by the person's class positioning.

Furthermore, Goldmann's conception of mimesis as a mediation of unified and consistent ideology implies that the coherence of the text is homologous with the coherence of the group consciousness that it presumably mediates. Aesthetic structure reproduces the structure of ideology; coherence signals the supersession of contradiction. Any given ideology indeed attempts to eradicate contradiction and to provide a comprehensive—if not always rational—explanatory framework. But we cannot therefore assume that any person's perspective is wholly constituted by a single ideological stance and uninfluenced by opposing positions. Homology, for Goldmann, ultimately implies homeostasis; the text may include contradictions, but these can readily be synthesized into a unified world view. Goldmann's view of mimesis precludes cognition of contradiction, for the subject emerges as hopelessly enmeshed in ideological paradigms that are generated by, but can never anticipate changes in, the social relations of production. By a curious twist, then, Goldmann's conception of "homologous structures" precludes cognition of the subject. The very stress

in his *The World, the Text, and the Critic* (Cambridge: Harvard University Press, 1983), 226–47.

upon "world-vision" precludes attention to the individual author as viewer of the world.

Althusser, in the most significant reaction against the Hegelian Marxism of Lukács and Goldmann, has proposed that ideology is, instead, a "'Representation' of the Imaginary Relationship of Individuals to the Real Conditions of Existence";[13] it is "determined in the last instance" by the economic infrastructure and the political imperatives of the ruling class and masks the true nature of the social relations of production, but it is also inseparable from the infrastructure and indeed constitutes a form of social activity. Ideology thus simultaneously serves the interests of the ruling class and enjoys relative autonomy in its cognitive operations by *"interpellating the individual as a (free) subject in order that he shall submit freely to the commandments of the Subject i.e. in order that he shall freely accept his subjection."* Employing Lacan's conception of the political character of the unconscious, Althusser argues that ideology gives people the illusion that they are independent agents when they are not. Rather than consisting merely of false consciousness, however, ideology articulates the real conditions—the "Subject-ion"—of their existence.

The Althusserian formulation at first seems to offer distinct advantages to a theory of mimesis. First, it suggests that ideology is itself a form of representation, rather than a reflection of preexisting realities. The representational procedures of fiction thus reproduce not a passive or static referent but the actual procedures by which consciousness explains reality to itself. According to Pierre Macherey,

> In that evocative power, by which it denotes a specific reality, [literary discourse] imitates the everyday language which is the language of ideology. We could offer a provisional definition of literature as being characterised by this power of parody. Mingling the real uses of language in an endless confrontation, it concludes by *revealing* their truth. Experimenting with language rather than inventing it, the literary work is both the analogy of a knowledge and a caricature of customary ideology.[14]

---

[13]Althusser, "Ideology and Ideological State Apparatuses (Notes toward an Investigation)," in *Lenin and Philosophy and Other Essays,* trans. Ben Brewster (London: NLB, 1971), 162, 182.

[14]Pierre Macherey, *A Theory of Literary Production,* trans. Geoffrey Wall (London: Routledge & Kegan Paul, 1978), 59.

Moreover, the Althusserian formulation would appear to take into account the effect of ideological contradiction routinely accompanying the mimetic contract. As Lewis notes, "The text disturbs ideology . . . by juxtaposing within itself alternative or competing ideological clusters (partial semantic fields) and articulating them within a common but conflictive semantic space so as to point out the artificial unity and false pretensions of individual ideological systems as such."[15] Fiction does not simply reproduce hegemony; it is empowered to air oppositional views.

If we examine the Althusserian theories of mimesis more closely, however, we see that their weakness in providing a description of the referent necessarily affects their formulations of the subject as well. For the Althusserians highlight, not an ideological contradiction within the author, but a contradiction between two hypostatized categories, Ideology and Literature. Mimesis thus emerges curiously free of the taint of ideology. As Macherey puts it, the fictional work "gives an implicit critique of its ideological content, if only because it resists being incorporated into the flux of ideology in order to give a *determinate representation* of it."[16] The price that mimesis pays for its subversive relation to ideology, however, is considerable. "Fiction, not to be confused with illusion, is the substitute for, if not the equivalent of, knowledge." Mimesis represents the procedures of representation, but, as metarepresentation, it is ontologically separated from the referent. The subject is eradicated; or more precisely, he or she is "inserted" into ideology, and authorial ideology is relegated to an insignificant position between "general ideology" on the one hand and the "ideology of the text" on the other.[17]

Despite their evident incompatibility on many points, the Lukácsian and the Althusserian approaches to fictional representation demonstrate a curious convergence. Both objectify forces beyond

---

[15]Thomas E. Lewis, "Notes toward a Theory of the Referent," *PMLA*, 94 (May 1979): 471.

[16]Macherey, 64.

[17]Eagleton, *Criticism and Ideology: A Study in Marxist Literary Theory* (1976; London: NLB, Verso, 1978), 59–60. Tony Bennett, in his critique of the Althusserians, suggests that the later work of Renée Balibar and Dominique Laporte corrects the idealist errors of the work of Macherey and Eagleton. I do not agree: the relation of literature to Science and Ideology is treated in more complexity in a study such as Balibar and Laporte's *Les Français fictifs* (Paris: Hachette, 1974), but there abides the notion that literature is somehow especially privileged to subvert the material "repressed" by ideology.

the subject (forces of production and of textuality) and both reduce the significance of authorial intervention in history. Lukács claims that the contradiction within the author is relatively unimportant—Balzac can be a Royalist, Scott a conservative—so long as the text replicates in nuce the contradictions of the historical moment. The dialectic of historical actuality writes the text, in other words: the novelist, preferably the realistic novelist, is its amanuensis. Despite its useful insistence that the text treats an independently existing object of representation, then, the Lukács/Goldmann formulation ultimately fetishizes the forces of production; the subject emerges as the object of historical forces. The Althusserians, on the other hand, marginalize the role of the subject because—despite occasional nods to "determination in the last instance" by economic forces—ideology becomes virtually omnipotent. Accordingly, the superstructure is fetishized, and the subject is enmeshed in a web of hegemonic ideological assumptions. Fiction heroically protests this hegemony, but its assertions are impotent, divested of status as knowledge, or Science. For the Althusserians, the act of fictional representation, rather than its substance, produces contradiction, which is objectified—in essentially formalistic terms—as a clash between epistemological categories.

The most useful definition of ideology remains that of Lenin, who asserted that the necessary incompleteness or distortion of an ideological posture does not preclude access to a reality existing beyond ideological appropriation. "In a society torn by class antagonisms there can never be a non-class or an above-class ideology,"[18] Lenin declared. But, "if truth is *only* an ideological form, then there can be no truth independent of the subject, of humanity."[19] One need not therefore endorse the positivistic doctrine that thought directly recapitulates the "real object," he argued, in order to propose a materialist theory of knowledge. "The existence of the thing reflected independent of the reflection (the independence of the external world from the mind), is the fundamental tenet of materialism." While all thought, including science, is ideological ("that science is non-partisan in the struggle of materialism against idealism and religion is a

---

[18]Lenin, *What Is to Be Done?* in *Collected Works,* trans. George H. Hanna, ed. Robert Daglish (Moscow: Progress, 1967), 5:384.

[19]Lenin, *Materialism and Empirio-Criticism,* in *Collected Works,* 14:123. The statements quoted below appear on pp. 123, 139, and 137.

favorite idea . . . of all modern bourgeois professors"), it does not follow that all ideological stances are equally limited in their appropriation of the "real object." On the contrary, dialectics "recognizes the relativity of all our knowledge, not in the sense of denying objective truth, but in the sense that the limits of approximation of our knowledge to this truth are historically conditioned." And, in this process of historical conditioning, political partisanship is the index to greater or lesser objectivity. Ideology is, finally, partisan discourse encoding partisan knowledge. Lenin thus declares unabashedly that "the task of the socialists" is to be the "ideological leaders of the proletariat";[20] "indeed, there is only one strictly proletarian ideology, and that is *Marxism.*"[21]

According to the Leninist formulation, the representations of discourse necessarily include distortions of some kind; even the "proletarian ideology" that would propose itself as the most advanced and objective form of knowledge must acknowledge its historical limitation. But this does not mean that ideology is foreclosed from a realm of truth accessible only to science, for science itself is constituted by procedures of ideological appropriation and construction. Ideology is not therefore placed in contradiction with science, as in the Althusserian formulation, but instead becomes an arena of contradiction: the class struggle takes place in the realm of conceptual abstraction as well as in the realm of social processes. The essence of historical understanding, remarked Lenin, is the "recognition of the contradictory, mutually exclusive, opposite tendencies in all the phenomena and processes of nature (including mind and society)."[22]

Mimesis and Ideological Contradiction

Of course, Lenin himself did not formulate a theory of mimesis, but his conception of consciousness as the battleground of ideology does, I believe, carry some significant implications for Marxist literary theory. I suggest, for example, that mimesis affords an abstraction of ideological contradictions within the author, contradictions that mediate in a unique way the broader contradictions shaping the soci-

[20]Lenin, "What the 'Friends of the People' Are," in *Collected Works,* 1:298.
[21]Lenin, "A New Revolutionary Workers' Association," in *Collected Works,* 8:505.
[22]Lenin, *Collected Works,* 38:357–58.

ety at large. Since any given social formation at a particular historical juncture is characterized by the contradictory interplay of many ideologies, any given individual is therefore likely to endorse not one but a constellation of ideological stances—separately univocal and unproblematic, perhaps, but by no means logically compatible when yoked together. For example, an ideology of Christian humanism can contradict, and yet coexist with, an ideology of racism; likewise an ideology of pacifism with an ideology of patriotism. We see such apparently illogical admixtures everyday; writers, I propose, are not more exempt from this condition than are other people. Indeed, I would argue that the highlighting of contradiction is central to the particular kind of cognition that mimesis projects. Philosophy, political theory, and other modes of discourse that codify ideology strive toward not merely the containment but the eradication of contradiction. These modes allow complexity, but not contradiction; a primarily analytical system of thought derives its effectiveness from the logical consistency of its assertions, as well as from the explanatory power of its central propositions. To the extent that the central presuppositions of a body of philosophical or political thought contain contradictions, they lessen its explanatory force. Although formulated by an individual or individuals, an analytical system of thought is therefore transindividual. One can be a Platonist or a Marxist (Plato and Marx have at least this much in common), but one cannot in the same sense be a Dickensian; an individual may be only a Dickens fan or a Dickens scholar, orientations that clearly lead one toward the particularity of the Dickensian mode of appropriating historical actuality.

I am not, it should be noted, reiterating in Marxist form a recycled version of the New Critical axiom that fiction conveys irony or paradox, but nothing like determinate explanatory propositions. Quite the contrary: I am arguing that *the knowledge that fiction conveys is the knowledge of the contradictory subjective appropriation of an objective social reality.*[23] As a result, aesthetic categories that are frequently thought

---

[23]Bakhtin also argues for the centrality of contradiction in mimesis. Compare his description of "heteroglossia" in language: "Every concrete utterance of a speaking subject serves as a point where centrifugal as well as centripetal forces are brought to bear. The processes of centralization and decentralization, of unification and disunification, intersect in the utterance; the utterance not only answers the requirements of an individualized embodiment of a speech act, but it answers the requirements of heteroglossia as well; it is in fact an active participant in such speech diversity. And this participation of every utterance in liv-

of as exclusively technical or structural should instead be viewed as rhetorical articulations of the text's attempt at synthesizing its informing contradictions. The feature that we often term "conflict," or "tension," could be fruitfully viewed as the structural embodiment of the main ideological contradiction in the text. Similarly, the evaluative criterion that we term "aesthetic coherence" could be seen as an assessment of how persuasive the author was in attributing primacy to one aspect of that main contradiction. Alternate possibilities—moral, political, psychological—are entertained, savored in their potentiality, but finally subordinated to a specific choice that makes a rhetorical claim upon the reader's allegiance. The aspect we term "complexity" is the full imaginative play given to alternate tendencies and possibilities. And the completeness we expect for successful closure is a recognition of the fact that the author has plausibly moved the text's represented contradiction toward a synthesis that takes into account the multiple minor contradictions that shape the main contradiction. Yet we are under no compulsion to produce a unified theory of the text that eliminates every contradiction under the guise of a broader principle of formal unity. If the text projects irreconcilable propositions, so be it. Such propositions are not necessarily assimilable to an ironic principle of synthesis; they simply testify to the author's inability to resolve all the contradictory ideological abstractions that the text has set forth for consideration.[24]

---

ing heteroglossia determines the linguistic profile and style of the utterance to no less a degree than its inclusion in any normative-centralizing system of a unitary language" (*The Dialogic Imagination: Four Essays,* ed. Michael Holquist, trans. Caryl Emerson and Holquist [Austin: University of Texas Press, 1983], 272). Clearly Bakhtin would take a strong stand against any literary version of the "dominant ideology thesis." Because Bakhtin insists upon locating contradiction within language, however, rather than within the subject who deploys language, he runs the risk of fetishizing the linguistic medium. The utterance, he declares, is a "contradiction-ridden, tension-filled unity of two embattled tendencies *in the life of the language*" (272, italics added).

[24]In *Language and Materialism: Developments in Semiology and the Theory of the Subject* (London: Routledge & Kegan Paul, 1977), Rosalind Coward and John Ellis quite correctly argue that the Althusserian theory of ideology reduces the subject to a contradiction-free unity incapable of purposive opposition to dominant ideology. Their argument is, however, largely vitiated by their Lacanian contention that the primary locus of contradiction within the subject is the conflict between the unconscious and the conscious rather than within the sphere of ideology itself. To be sure, ideological contradiction need not be fully conscious, and often contradiction within the subject can be located between conscious beliefs and unconscious proclivities. But to hypostatize the contradiction as one between the unconscious and the conscious and to posit that coherent subjectivity is itself an ideological illusion is, it seems to me, to divest internal contradiction of its full political significance.

In short, the critic, by treating the text as a projection of ideological contradiction internal to the author, can account for the characteristic admixture of conflicting evaluative attitudes in the mimetic text's representation of its referent. That is, the text's postulation of relationality in its referent—analogous configuration—mediates the ideological relationality within the subject at the same time that it offers an interpretation of actual relationships and processes in the social world. Textual contradictions and ambiguities do not therefore signal the freedom of art working against the determinism of ideology; rather, they represent the author's involvement with opposing possibilities existing right within the ideological class struggle. The author's conception of these possibilities is determined by the configuration of social forces in his or her time (by the prevalent form of the exchange relation, as I shall argue), which disturbs us only if we assume that consciousness is more autonomous than social. Indeed, when we grant that texts composed in class society ordinarily—though not always—synthesize their contradictions along the lines of dominant ideology, we simply reaffirm what we already know: the ruling class possesses hegemony. Nonetheless, an investigation into the process by which any given mimetic text produces ideological synthesis affords a view of the subjective arena of class struggle. By bringing to light the conflict that precedes synthesis, mimesis reveals the provisional character of ruling-class hegemony. So long as there is contradiction, secondary aspects may become primary; emergent, submerged, or adversarial tendencies may become dominant. The radical insight produced by Marxist criticism here is not the delineation of the determinism of productive forces nor the celebration of the oppositional relation of literature to ideology but the demonstration that ideology, as lived, is never a seamless whole, that where there is hegemony there is also contradiction. This knowledge, I believe, is useful.

Abstraction, Mimesis, and Mediation

Lenin's theory of ideology gives us the basis for resurrecting the authorial subject in Marxist criticism and for understanding the centrality of ideological contradiction in mimesis. It is still necessary, however, to describe the nature and function of ideological abstraction—that is, the procedure by which the concrete particulars of the referent are abstracted and then reconcretized in the particulars of the fictional text. It is especially important to develop such a description for a study of the documentary novel, for we shall be examining a series of mimetic contracts in which the author would have the reader think that the text replicates its referent (or at least certain features of its referent) in an unabstracted and unmediated way.

The key term on which I shall focus here is "abstraction," to which I attach the cluster of meanings developed by Alfred Sohn-Rethel in his *Intellectual and Manual Labor: A Critique of Epistemology*. Sohn-Rethel argues that the "socially necessary forms of thinking of an epoch are those in conformity with the socially synthetic functions of that epoch." In particular, the prevalent form of the "social synthesis"—which he defines as "the network of relations by which society forms a whole"—is determined by the "network of relations" that constitutes the dominant form of the exchange relation.[25] This exchange relation is, essentially, an abstraction, for it requires a dualism between concrete use-values and their abstract character as embodiments of equivalent labor. Thus, the "first nature" of commodities becomes subordinated to their "second nature"—that is, their function as use values becomes subordinated to their function as representatives of an entire system of abstract equivalences. By a curious paradox, then, the concrete and material existence of commodities becomes less real than the "real abstraction"—that is, the structural incorporation of the second nature of commodities into the configuration of society as a whole.

The specific form of this exchange relation varies, of course, from epoch to epoch. In societies in which exchange is facilitated by money (the universal equivalent) but does not penetrate the labor process itself, generality can be discerned in particularity, but it does not assume a fetish character divorcing it entirely from particularity. As Marx put it, "In the exchange of money for labour for service, with the aim of direct consumption, a real exchange always takes place; the fact that *amounts of labour* are exchanged on both sides is of merely *formal* interest for measuring the *particular* forms of the utility of labour by comparing them with each other. This concerns only the *form* of

---

[25]Sohn-Rethel, *Intellectual and Manual Labor: A Critique of Epistemology*, trans. Martin Sohn-Rethel (Atlantic Highlands, N.J.: Humanities, 1978), 6.

their exchange; but it does not form its *content*."[26] In societies characterized by capital formation in its various phases, by contrast, the real abstraction comes to pervade all spheres of existence, since the exchange relation comes now to penetrate the process of production itself, the very "interior of the commodity." The phenomena of commodity fetishism and reification, described by Marx and elaborated subsequently by many theorists, are the fruits of this development, describing both real conditions of existence and the conceptual abstractions to which these conditions give rise.

Abstraction is thus a paradoxical historical phenomenon. On the one hand, it provides the material basis for all advances in theoretical knowledge, since it establishes the actual immanence of general equivalences within particulars. On the other hand, it increasingly prohibits the move that Hegel termed the "return to the concrete," whereby abstraction can realize its progress by altering the concretion to which it is bound.[27] Moreover, abstraction is at once a reflection of existing social and economic realities and also a force that can produce new social and economic realities. It is constitutive of both the base and the superstructure, and it furnishes the principal means for mediation between the two. For, as Sohn-Rethel is careful to point out, the connection between the abstractions of intellectual production and those characterizing the exchange relation does not consist merely in their structural resemblance, and abstraction is not simply a heuristic device. "Not only analogy but true identity exists between the formal elements of the social synthesis and the formal constituents of cognition," Sohn-Rethel insists. "The conceptual basis of cognition is logically and historically conditioned by the basic formation of

[26]Marx, *Grundrisse: Foundations of the Critique of Political Economy*, trans. Martin Nicolaus (New York: Random House/Vintage, 1973), 469.

[27]For more on the relation between abstraction and objectification, see below, Chapter 6. "It is not the fact that the human being *objectifies himself inhumanly*, in opposition to himself, but the fact that he *objectifies himself* in *distinction* from and in *opposition* to abstract thinking," Marx remarked in his critique of Hegel, "that constitutes the posited essence of the estrangement and the thing to be superseded." For Hegel, the "return to the concrete" was rendered problematic not because the social organization of reality prevents such a move but because it is thought itself that produces alienation from the concrete in the first place. For Hegel, Marx observed, "The whole *history of the alienation process* and the whole *process of the retraction* of the alienation is therefore nothing but the history of the production of abstract (i.e., absolute) thought—of logical, speculative thought" (*Economic and Philosophic Manuscripts of 1844*, trans. Martin Milligan, ed. Dick J. Struik [New York: International, 1969], 175).

the social synthesis."[28] Thus, for example, the conceptual abstractions of bourgeois empiricism are, Sohn-Rethel declares, in their essence "non-empirical," for they take as their premise the fundamental separation of the activities of the abstracting intellect from the realm of the first nature. The Cartesian compulsion to view the world as an object awaiting the experimental activity of the *ego cogitans* mediates the emerging dominance of the second nature over the first nature in early capitalist society, producing a "knowledge of nature" in "commodity form." Similarly, the later hypostatization of a realm of transcendental subjectivity mediates the consolidated hegemony of the second nature abstraction: Kant's transcendental subject, Sohn-Rethel declares, is a "fetish conception of the capital function of money."

Sohn-Rethel develops his theory of abstraction in relation to his critique of bourgeois science, but it is also useful, I believe, for approaching the knotty problems of reference and ideology in mimesis. His description of abstraction as a feature both of the social synthesis and of the ideas people develop to understand the social synthesis has important bearing upon the procedures of abstraction involved in fictional creation. The mimetic text presents its people and events as concrete, but these elements, as we have seen, are in fact reconcretized representations of a referent that has undergone a process of abstraction in the author's consciousness. I hypothesize that, just as dominant conceptual abstractions in any era mediate the prevalent form of the exchange relation—whether as explicitly formulated social theories or, more likely, as common sense epistemological assumptions—so the mimetic text mediates these conceptual abstractions. It is, in other words, a mediation of a mediation, reproducing both real social relations and ideological constructions of those relations. And its distinctive feature, qua mimesis, is its articulation of both real and conceptual abstractions by means of a constructed concreteness; its assertive power resides in its production of illusion.

Sohn-Rethel's description of the dual nature of abstraction should

[28]Sohn-Rethel, 61. The statements quoted below appear on pp. 132 and 77. While Lukács, in *History and Class Consciousness,* holds that the abstraction of thought is engendered by capitalist reification, Sohn-Rethel argues—and I think he is right—that conceptual abstraction accompanies much less sophisticated social formations in which money comes to serve as the "universal equivalent." Marx stated, "Money may exist, and did exist historically, before capital existed." . . . "As a result, the path of abstract thought, rising from the simple to the combined" corresponds "to the real historical process" (*Grundrisse,* 102).

be helpful for the present study in a number of ways. First, it enables us to locate the problem of mimetic mediation squarely within the base-superstructure paradigm—a procedure that is, as I have indicated, necessary in any account of literary production that purports to be genuinely materialist. The equivalences that the text asserts between its representation and its referent are of course ideological equivalences, since they arise from a process of generalization and abstraction that articulates the author's attempt to make sense of the social world. At the same time, the conceptual abstractions that mimesis takes as it premise are not chimerical constructs unable to illuminate real states of affairs; on the contrary, they mediate actual social relations. Abstraction is, in short, a property of both the subject and the referent.

Furthermore, Sohn-Rethel's formulation of the relation between conceptual and real abstractions enables us to resolve some of the problems that, as we have seen, beset the Lukácsian and Althusserian theories of mimesis. We need not eradicate the subject if we wish to argue that the text renders cognition of its referent. Rather, we see that the subject's characteristic method of abstraction is itself a mediation of the referent and that conceptual abstraction is a force of production, as well as a reflection of existing realities. Novelists therefore are not simply passive reproducers of dominant ideologies but subjects who at times press inherited epistemological confines to their limits, preparing the way for revolutionary new types of abstraction, both conceptual and real. At the same time, we need not claim that ideological abstraction produces a screen that filters, distorts, or hides the referent. Rather, the mode of abstraction reproduced in the text can itself be seen as a social reality, articulating real practices of production, consumption, and exchange in the social world. For the referent to come to us through this procedure of mediation in no way negates its "reality." We are free to argue, in short, that the mimetic text, through its operations of dual mediation, replicates both the object and the subject—and that it also asserts this replication.

Finally, the view of fiction as the mediation of both conceptual and real abstractions is useful to this study of the documentary novel because it requires us to grasp the problem of mimetic representation as an intrinsically historical problem. If the text's abstracting procedures mediate contemporaneous modes of abstraction, then it makes no sense to give an account of representational strategies without examining the specific social situation from which the text arises. Hence we can pay more than lip service to Marx's admonition that

> in order to study the connection between intellectual and material pro-
> duction it is above all essential to conceive of the latter in its determined
> historical form and not as a general category. For example, there corre-
> sponds to the capitalist mode of production a type of intellectual pro-
> duction quite different from that which corresponded to the medieval
> mode of production. Unless material production itself is understood in
> its specified historical form, it is impossible to grasp the characteristics
> of the intellectual production which corresponds to it or the reciprocal
> action between the two.[29]

Sohn-Rethel's theory of abstraction provides a crucial bridge between the "determined historical form" of the exchange relation and the continually altering forms of "intellectual production" constituted by the mimetic contract. This model should prove especially helpful in our examination of the documentary novel, which, in its various phases, lays claim to different sorts of privileged access to the "real." We turn now to a consideration of the historical specificity of these various claims.

[29]Marx, *Theories of Surplus Value*, 1:276.

PART II

PRACTICE

5

The Pseudofactual Novel

I write nothing but what I have seen, or heard from persons of unquestionable credit: and therefore shall conclude with assuring you that you
have here not novel, or story, devised at pleasure; but an exact and most
true account of what I met with in my travels.
—Marie-Catherine d'Aulnoy

The major mode of the documentary novel in the eighteenth
century is the pseudofactual novel. By "pseudofactual novel" I mean a
genre of prose fiction that invokes an intrinsically ironic, even a parodic contract. According to such a contract, the reader is asked to accept the text's characters and situations as invented, which means seeing the text not as having no referent but as referring to relations
rather than to particulars allegedly existing apart from their representation in discourse. At the same time, however, the writer asks the
reader to approach the text as if it were a nonfictional text—a memoir, a confession, a group of letters. The generic contract of the
pseudofactual novel thus involves an agreement, in Mary Louise
Pratt's words, to "flout" the conventions of a familiar mode of nonfictional discourse.[1] This contract plays with the rabbit-duck Gestalt
I mentioned in Chapter 1, asking to be read as one kind of discourse
but mobilizing perceptual habits and responses routinely associated
with another kind of discourse. The pseudofactual novel is therefore
an invitation to irony. Indeed, I shall argue that the parodic imitation
of nonfictional discourse was the primary convention which first enabled prose fiction to usurp the terrain previously held by the ro-

[1]Mary Louise Pratt, *Toward a Speech-Act Theory of Literary Discourse* (Bloomington: Indiana University Press, 1977), 152–200.

mance: discursive irony was the defining characteristic of the novel in its early phases.

But to say that the pseudofactual novel invokes such a self-conscious contract is not to say that the imitation of nonfictional discourse is the defining quality of all fiction, as some theorists have urged. Barbara Herrnstein Smith, we will recall, argues that all "poetry" is "fiction": "The various genres of literary art—e.g., dramatic poems, tales, odes, lyrics—can to some extent be distinguished according to what types of discourse—e.g., dialogues, anecdotes of past events, public speeches, and private declarations—they characteristically represent."[2] For Smith, *all* mimetic texts signal their fictionality by simulating nonfictional writing—*War and Peace* as much as *Moll Flanders, Native Son* as much as *Pamela.* Moreover, Smith argues that mimetic texts relinquish their status as assertions when they model themselves on nonfictional discourse: they become pseudostatements. My contention is quite different. The pseudofactual novel's parodic invocation of nonfictional models constitutes a marker of fictional intentions that is historically specific: Tolstoy and Wright were not imitating chronicle and biography in anything like the way that Defoe and Richardson were imitating the rogue's confession or the set of letters. Moreover, the pseudofactual novelists' parodic relation to nonfictional discourse does not constitute an evasion of propositionality; on the contrary, this relation enables them to invest fiction with new and expanded powers of assertion.

Precursors of the Pseudofactual Novel

The pseudofactual novel attains a definitive generic identity in the work of Defoe, but it comes out of a long tradition of fictional writing purporting to tell a truth that is more than the projection of the poetic imagination. Apuleius avers that even the more improbable tales in his *Golden Ass* possess a certain plausibility. "In practice, things do occasionally happen to you and me, as to everybody else," he reminds his reader, "which are so outrageous that we can hardly believe in them ourselves, and which any ordinary person would cer-

[2] Barbara Herrnstein Smith, "Literature as Performance, Fiction, and Art," *Journal of Philosophy,* 67 (August 20, 1970): 557.

tainly reject as mere fiction."[3] Wolfram von Eschenbach holds that his telling of the grail legend in *Parzival* is based not on the fictional account of Chretien de Troyes but on a centuries-old "original" rescued from oblivion by the tireless efforts of one Kyot. Thomas Deloney asserts that his *Jack of Newbury* "raised out of the dust of forgetfulnesse a most famous and worthy man."[4] Thomas Lodge, in the fantastical *Robert Duke of Normandie,* attempts to retain his authority as historian. "Many things have happened in time past incredible in our age," he declares in his preface. "And in our age such things have falne out, as had our fathers knowne they had mervailed."[5]

The play with spurious pretensions to documentary verifiability that characterizes these fictional works also resonates through a good deal of classical, medieval, and Renaissance discourse that we would now term nonfictional. Ancient historians are notorious for including materials of highly questionable authenticity in their narratives. Herodotus depicts the gods as functioning causally in the world of human affairs, and he gives detailed transcriptions of dialogues that had no witnesses. Thucydides may assert that his narrative "rests partly on what I saw myself, partly on what others saw for me, the accuracy of the report being always tried by the most severe and detailed tests available";[6] he accepts as historical fact, however, such a dubious proposition as the existence of Deucalion. Seneca voices a common skepticism about the ancient historian's rights and responsibilities when he wryly remarks, "Who ever demanded affidavits from a historian?"[7] Medieval theological tracts and historical chronicles also make all sorts of specious claims to authenticity, even though, as Erich Auerbach points out, the necessity of establishing the historical existence of Christ gave a new seriousness to these claims.[8] Fabulous

---

[3]Apuleius Maurensis, *The Transformation of Lucius, Otherwise Known as "The Golden Ass,"* trans. Robert Graves (New York: Farrar, Straus & Young, 1951), 18.

[4]Francis Oscar Mann, ed., *The Complete Works of Thomas Deloney* (Oxford: Clarendon, 1912), 2.

[5]*The Complete Works of Thomas Lodge* (Glasgow: Anderson, 1883), 2:4.

[6]Thucydides, *The Peloponnesian War,* trans. John F. Finley, Jr. (New York: Modern Library, 1951), 14.

[7]Seneca, *Apocolocyntosis,* in *The Satire of Seneca,* trans. Allan P. Ball (New York: Columbia University Press, 1902), 132.

[8]Erich Auerbach, *Mimesis: The Representation of Reality in Western Literature,* trans. Willard Trask (1953; Garden City: Doubleday/Anchor, 1957), 1–20. For more on prenovelistic forms of prose fiction in Europe, see Arthur Heiserman, *The Novel before the Novel: Essays and Discussions about the Beginnings of Prose Fiction in the West* (Chicago: University of Chi-

saints' legends about talking beasts are routinely asserted to be true; Froissart and Geoffrey of Monmouth declare that their often fanciful and mythic tales are founded in unimpeachable sources.

It was only in the Renaissance that biography and historiography espoused new standards of rigor. Thomas Cooper's *Thesaurus* defined *historia* as "the declaration of true things in order set forth";[9] William Camden argued against the time-honored tradition of making up monologues and presenting them as fact: "Speeches and Orations, unless they be the very same *verbatim,* or else abbreviated, I have not medled withall, much less coined them of mine own Head."[10] Nonetheless, biographies and historical works of the time were unembarrassed about departing from the record. Polydore Vergil's life of Richard III, created to suit the needs of Tudor policy, promulgated the demonic myth of Richard III that persists to this day. Sir Walter Raleigh may have deprecated those cartographers who inserted imaginary "painters' wives" islands into their maps of recently discovered territories, but he approved of the historian's decision to fill comparable gaps in the historical record: "In filling up the Blanks of old Histories, we need not be so scrupulous," he noted. "For it is not to be feared that time should run backward, and by restoring the things themselves to knowledge, make our conjectures appear ridiculous."[11]

It is clear that modern empirical criteria for historical accuracy are not applicable to the fictions and histories I have just mentioned. It would be mistaken, however, to conclude that premodern historians, biographers, chroniclers, and writers of fiction lived in some sort of epistemological haze. Apuleius's intent in telling his diverting Milesian tales must clearly be differentiated from Herodotus's desire to "preserve the memory of the past by putting on record the astonish-

---

cago Press, 1977); Ben Edwin Perry, *The Ancient Romances* (Berkeley: University of California Press, 1967); Margaret Schlauch, *Antecedents of the English Novel, 1400–1600* (London: Oxford University Press, 1965); and Walter L. Reed, *An Exemplary History of the Novel: The Quixotic versus the Picaresque* (Chicago: University of Chicago Press, 1981).

[9]Quoted in William Nelson, *Fact or Fiction: The Dilemma of the Renaissance Storyteller* (Cambridge: Harvard University Press, 1973), 40.

[10]William Camden, *The History of the Most Renowned and Victorious Princess Elizabeth, Selected Chapters,* ed. W. T. MacCaffrey (Chicago: University of Chicago Press, 1970), 6.

[11]Sir Walter Raleigh, *The History of the World,* Early English Books, 1475–1640 (1617; Ann Arbor: University Microfilms, 1977), reel 1462, p. 1, bk. 2, chap. 23, sec. 4.

ing achievements both of our own and of the Asiatic peoples."[12] *Parzival* mobilizes expectations very different from those invoked in Froissart's *Chronicles*, even though both texts purport to be based on unimpeachable historical sources. Jacques Amyot's claim that history relates "la nue vérité"[13] is very different from Sir Philip Sidney's assertion that poetry's golden world delivers images of potentiality inaccessible in the brazen realm of quotidian reality. Ancient, medieval, and Renaissance writers exhibit no confusion about the difference between history and fiction; they simply require no empiricist credentials from the historian and take care to consign fictions to the realm of the abstract or the ideal. When writers of fiction invoke additional claims to veracity, then, they do so not because they pretend to be writing history or biography but because they wish to assure us that they tell the truth. This truth is not a "factual" truth, and they do not intend to fool us into thinking that it is.

Imposture and Invention: The Emergence of Pseudofactual Fiction

This relatively stable situation changes around the seventeenth century, when historians begin to take more seriously the empiricist credo set forth in the Renaissance and when a kind of pseudofactual discourse appears making more emphatic claims to veracity and verifiability. Bishop Pierre Daniel Huet, a theorist of the romance, signals his distaste for works of this emergent genre when he attacks them as "stories carefully shaped in whole and in part, but made up only to falsify truth."[14] These new stories differ from their forebears in that they lay claim to a distinct immediacy; since the nonfictional text that they simulate is generally a first-person account, rather than a chronicle or a biography, it is more difficult for readers to determine their authenticity. Indeed, for more than a century this mode of discourse would appear to have been conventionally ambiguous. The

---

[12]Herodotus, *The Histories*, trans. Aubrey de Selincourt (Baltimore: Penguin, 1954), 13.

[13]Jacques Amyot, "Aux lecteurs," in *Critical Prefaces of the French Renaissance*, ed. Bernard Weinberg (Evanston: Northwestern University Press, 1950), 167.

[14]Pierre Daniel Huet, *Traité sur l'origine des romans* (1669; Paris: Nizet, 1971), 49, my translation.

reader is asked to view the text's speaker as simultaneously part of the text's analogous configuration—and hence a fictional character—and as an autonomous voice commenting on the referent from a position external to fictionality. Since the text does not display ironic signals instructing the reader to view the speaker as part of the referent (to characterize the speaker, as it were), the generic contract requires an agreement to hold in suspension the question of verifiability. As Lennard J. Davis suggests, such works of fiction characteristically possess an "overt frame" proclaiming the text's veracity and a "covert frame" admitting to the text's fictionality. "Because the reader is never really certain . . . whether this covert frame indeed exists, a state of ambivalence is produced in the reader which extends throughout his or her experience of the novel."[15] These new pseudofactual works did not collapse the distinction between fictional and nonfictional discourse as such. When Huet angrily declared, "I say *falsified stories* to distinguish them from true stories,"[16] he was exhibiting a clear sense of the difference between reality and imagination. Nonetheless, these texts hovered around the borderline in such a way as to raise serious doubts about the accepted notion that prose fiction should be restricted to the subject matter of courtly love and heroic exploits.

These new pseudofactual fictions, while simulating such discursive forms as the chronicle, the traveler's report, or the set of letters, attached new force to their corroborative testimonials and emphatically denied the charge of mendacity.[17] Thomas Nashe, for example, in one of the earliest instances of the genre, announced in 1594 that his *The Unfortunate Traveller* would be "a reasonable conveyance of historie"[18] and presented his narrative as the first-person account of one Jack Wilton, the putative valet of the Earl of Surrey. Unlike Deloney's Jack of Newbury, who is asserted to be a historical figure but then readily assumes the fictional status of a jest-book character, Jack Wilton projects the ambience of a "real-life" person, one who

[15]Lennard J. Davis, *Factual Fictions: The Origins of the English Novel* (New York: Columbia University Press, 1983), 21.

[16]Huet, 46–47, my translation.

[17]For more on the authenticating procedures of early pseudofactual fiction, see Arthur Jerrold Tieje, "A Peculiar Phase of the Theory of Realism in Pre-Richardsonian Fiction," *PMLA*, 28 (1913): 213–52.

[18]Thomas Nashe, *The Unfortunate Traveller and Other Works*, ed. J. B. Steane (Harmondsworth: Penguin, 1972), 251. The passage quoted below is from p. 370.

frequently interrupts his own narration and apologizes for his forgetfulness. A curious quality thus attaches to his "conclusive epilogue":
"If herein I have pleased any, it shall animate me to more pains in this
kind. Otherwise I will swear upon an English Chronicle never to be
outlandish Chronicler more while I live." The admission of "outland-
ishness" obviously calls attention to the possible mendacity of Wilton's account. Interestingly, however, it is a genre of historical discourse that Wilton chooses to charge with distorting the truth. To the
extent that the reader distrusts chronicle as a reliable index to historical events (and surely the perceptive Elizabethan reader must have
done so), Nashe's own discourse retains its status as a "reasonable"
—or at least a plausible—"conveyance of historie," or teller of truth.

Aphra Behn, in her prefatory remarks to *Oroonoko; or, The History
of the Royal Slave,* maintained, "I do not pretend, in giving you the
history of this *Royal Slave,* to entertain my Reader with the adventures of a feigned hero, whose life and fortunes fancy may manage at
the poet's pleasure."[19] Behn herself was, she claims, "an eyewitness
to a greater part of what you will here find set down; and what I
could not be witness of, I received from the mouth of the chief actor
in this history, the hero himself." Behn frequently departs from the
terms of this pledge: Oroonoko's final dismemberment (through
which he calmly smokes his pipe) was certainly not "received from
the mouth of the chief actor," and Behn is astute enough to ascribe
her narration of this episode to another source. Nonetheless, the story
successfully simulates the format of the traveler's tale, which itself
frequently strained credibility; it remains an open question whether
the "chief actor" is feigned or real.

Mme d'Aulnoy prefaced her letter novel *The Lady ——— Travels
into Spain* with florid assurances of the text's veracity:

> I have not doubt there will be some who will accuse me of hyperboliz-
> ing, and composing romances; but such would do well to acquaint
> themselves first with the country, humour, and character of those I treat
> of. A fact must not be presently condemned as false because it is not
> public or may not hit every man's fancy. I cite no feigned names, no
> persons whose death may give me the liberty of attributing what I
> please to them.

[19]Aphra Behn, *Oronooko; or, The History of the Royal Slave,* in *The Novels of Mrs. Aphra
Behn* (London: Routledge & Sons, 1905), 88.

In a word: I write nothing but what I have seen, or heard from persons of unquestionable credit: and therefore shall conclude with assuring you that you have here not novel, or story, devised at pleasure; but an exact and most true account of what I met with in my travels.[20]

The text is in fact a fraud,[21] and such fervent overprotestations that it does not engage in the mendacious distortions of other epistolary discourse obviously tease the reader into considering this possibility. As in *The Unfortunate Traveller* and *Oroonoko*, however *The Lady ———— Travels* contains no explicit textual markers requiring the reader to posit the speaker as part of the referent. The reader may not necessarily take at face value the speaker's truth-telling assertions (the represented action poses too great a challenge to everyday canons of credibility). But neither does the reader automatically adopt the ironic attitude that the speaker's discourse primarily serves to characterize the speaker, thus subordinating him or her to the author's informing interpretive framework. Documentation goes on the offensive in these texts, securing a terrain for the propositional value of fiction by decrying the mendacity of other discursive modes charged with the responsibility of telling an unmediated truth.

While the early pseudofactual novelists routinely modeled their narratives on familiar types of nonfictional writing, their invocation of a conventionally ambiguous generic contract was made possible by the development of journalism in the seventeenth century. According to the *Oxford English Dictionary,* in the late sixteenth and early seventeenth centuries the term "novel" applied equally to both fictional tales and journalistic accounts and was often used coterminously with "news"; fiction and journalism were frequently conjoined in an undifferentiated discursive matrix that Davis calls the "news/novel discourse."[22] Invoking discursive conventions developed in the ballad-sheets of the late sixteenth century, fiction and journalism in-

---

[20]Marie-Catherine d'Aulnoy, *Madame D'Aulnoy Travels into Spain (The Ingenious and Diverting Letters of the Lady———— Travels into Spain)*, trans. and ed. R. Foulché-Delbosc (London: Routledge & Sons, 1930), 3.

[21]See Percy G. Adams, *Travelers and Travel Liars, 1660–1800* (Berkeley: University of California Press, 1962), 97–100. In "Madame d'Aulnoy in England" (*Comparative Literature,* 27 [Summer 1975]: 237–53), Melvin D. Palmer argues that the *Travels* enjoyed immense popularity in England and was a crucial text in the transition from the "true historie" to the novel.

[22]Davis, *Factual Fictions,* 42–70.

creasingly exploited a common fund of rhetorical—even typographical—devices. The creation of a "median past tense," the inclusion of the reader as an engaged spectator, the attribution of the status of "news" to any narrative rendition of the sensational in everyday life—all these activities became the constitutive features of a generic contract that enhanced experiential immediacy and de-emphasized the question of strict verifiability, even as it sometimes laid claim to that verifiability. Thus the testimonials accompanying the fictions of Nashe, Behn, and d'Aulnoy are hardly distinguishable from the sorts of guarantees that were attached to newspapers and journals of the time. Behn's and d'Aulnoy's proclamations that they possess privileged access to their materials find their rhetorical equivalent in the claim of *Mercurius Civicus* to be "London's Intelligencer or Truth impartially related from thence to the whole Kingdom to prevent disinformation."[23] Throughout most of the seventeenth century, a fictional writer was often as liable to legal suit as was a journalist: English licensing laws of the seventeenth century grouped together all material printed in a journalistic format. The Licensing Act of 1663, for example, covered "all narratives, advertisements, intelligencers, diurnals and other books of public intelligence."

The pseudofactual novel's early association with journalism is symptomatic of the way its practitioners were relinquishing the traditional subject matter of fiction and breaking new ground. The acknowledged model of prose fiction at this time was still the romance—a patently aristocratic genre that represented life at the highest level of abstraction and refrained from any representation of the rough grain of everyday life.[24] If writers wished to be taken seriously as interpreters of social reality, they were constrained to simulate familiar modes of nonfictional discourse. It is therefore no accident that Nashe wrote his *The Unfortunate Traveller* in the mode of a spurious chronicle; his text takes as its referent the key events of early sixteenth-century European history, from Henry VIII's 1513 siege of Terou-

---

[23]Davis, "A Social History of Fact and Fiction: Authorial Disavowal in the Early English Novel," in *Literature and Society: Selected Papers from the English Institute*, ed. Edward Said (Baltimore: Johns Hopkins University Press, 1980), 125.

[24]See Davis, *Factual Fictions*, chap. 2, "The Romance: Liminality and Influence," 25–41, and Ioan Williams, *The Idea of the Novel in Europe, 1600–1800* (London: Macmillan, 1979). While Davis's study is valuable for its many empirical findings about the relation of the novel to broadsheets and journalism, its methodology is flawed in some troubling ways. See my review of *Factual Fictions* in *Genre*, 17 (Winter 1984): 422–25.

anne to his 1520 encounter with Francois I, from Luther's 1519 doctrinal debates to the rising of the Anabaptists at Munster in 1534. Moreover, Nashe's Wilton delivers a witty lampoon on feudalistic decorum through his satirical depiction of Surrey—who hyperbolizes about his mistress's eyes and decks out his horse for the lists "in full proportion and shape of an estrich."[25] If Nashe wishes to tell the truth about aristocratic practices, he must do so through the discourse of the brazen world, not through that of the realm of gold.

Similarly, Mme d'Aulnoy's decision to tell her impressions of Spanish customs through a series of spurious letters signals her desire to expand the province of epistolary fiction beyond the realm of courtly intrigue. Her letter-novel contains its share of tales of passion and betrayal, to be sure, but these are always told to the intrepid traveler and thus incorporated into the text's investigatory ends. The presumed penchant of Spaniards for telling unbelievable stories ("'I never was in any place,' said I, smiling, 'where they relied so much on fabulous tales as they do in Spain'")[26] thus becomes a feature of the referent. *The Lady——— Travels* provides its readers with all the pleasures of romance but draws these into its reportorial design.

Even *Oroonoko*, which bears a closer resemblance to the romance than does *The Unfortunate Traveller* or *The Lady——— Travels*, uses its illusion of veracity to treat such urgent issues as the cruelties of slavery and the declining status of monarchy. As one critic has argued, in this work Behn was making a veiled plea for compassionate treatment of James II, in that there is a close resemblance between Behn's dethroned African ruler and the deposed Stuart king, for whom the writer retained a strong loyalty.[27] The social configuration which the text represents is thus a concretely historical pattern, rather than an abstracted realm where timeless passions play themselves out. When Behn declares that "there is enough of reality to support [the tale], and to render it diverting, without the addition of

---

[25]Nashe, 317. For more on the historicizing procedures and interests of Nashe and other Elizabethan writers of prose fiction, see Walter R. Davis, *Idea and Act in Elizabethan Fiction* (Princeton: Princeton University Press, 1969).

[26]D'Aulnoy, 348.

[27]See George Guffey, "Aphra Behn's *Oronooko*: Occasion and Accomplishment," in his *Two English Novelists: Aphra Behn and Anthony Tollope* (Los Angeles: William Andrews Clark Memorial Library, 1975), 1–41.

invention," she is arguing for the enfranchisement of fiction as a discourse to represent and interpret urgent contemporary realities.

While the conventionally ambiguous contract invoked in these early pseudofactual fictions permitted authors to explore issues and materials previously excluded from the realm of mimesis, the emergent genre also encountered certain difficulties that its eventual adoption of a greater degree of verisimilitude would resolve. The author's equivocal relation to the historical status of the text's characters and events effectively dehistoricized the very reality that the text meant to certify with the immediacy of an eyewitness report. Nashe's insistence upon the authenticity of his narrator threatens the integrity of the text's portraiture of historical events. In a tale presupposing the dubious veracity of its narrator, a juxtaposition of events in 1513 and 1534, and the subsequent termination of the narrative in 1520, would not create tremendous confusion. The modern reader, construing Wilton as a kind of ancestor to Huckleberry Finn, would simply dismiss the anachronism as a function of Wilton's desire to tell a "stretcher," and would see the speaker as a part of the story being told. Behn, too, undermines the credibility of her account when she expects us to take seriously the proposition that Oroonoko retained his majestic demeanor throughout his dismemberment. Had she simply asserted that Oroonoko exemplifies the cardinal virtues of monarchy, she could have offered a persuasive account of both the cruelties of slavery and the injustices presumably done to the Stuarts. As it is, however, Oroonoko's speech and demeanor—as well as his remarkably Caucasian features[28]—render him virtually indistinguishable from a typical Restoration nobleman and therefore negate his plausibility as an African analogue to James II. The early pseudofactual novel's postulation of veracity conflicted with its pretensions to verisimilitude: the "sense of the real" and "realism" experienced a truly uneasy coexistence.[29] The text's conventional participation in the "news/novel discourse" enabled fiction to experiment with a fas-

---

[28]That is, "The most famous statuary could not form the figure of a man more admirably turned from head to foot. His face was not of that brown nasty black which most of that nation are, but a perfect ebony, or polished jet. His eyes were the most awful that could be seen, and very piercing; the white of them being like snow, as were his teeth. His nose was rising and Roman, instead of African and flat: his mouth the finest shaped that could be seen; far from those great turned lips, which are so natural to the rest of the Negroes" (8).

[29]I owe this handy opposition of terms to Robert Gorham Davis, "The Sense of the Real in English Fiction," *Comparative Literature*, 3 (Summer 1961): 200–217.

cinating new subject matter, but the requirements of analogous configuration and reportage drew the text in opposite directions.

Between the Sense of the Real and Realism

The merging of parody with representation, argues M. M. Bakhtin, was the central linguistic development that produced the modern novel: "Languages cease to be merely the object of a purely polemical or autotelic parodying: without losing their parodic coloration completely, they begin to assume the function of artistic representation, of a representation with a value in its own right. . . . The hero's discourse about himself and about his world fuses organically, from the outside, with the author's discourse about him and his world."[30] The crucial phrase here is "from the outside": the conventions of novelistic mimesis required a contractual agreement that author and character are ontologically distinct, with the former empowered to incorporate the latter's discourse into an interpretive scheme that clearly emanates from an ethical position external to the discourse itself. The parodic play with nonfictional materials thus became increasingly identified as a marker of fictional intent. Hesitantly in the works of Defoe, then more boldly in subsequent novels of the eighteenth century, the pseudofactual imposture of veracious discourse signaled the invocation of a mimetic contract. Rather than simulating a putative nonfictional model, the text now openly imitated such a text, thereby flouting its own claim to nonfictional status. Irony is thus a crucial marker of the novelistic contract: the text parades its status as a mode of generalizing—and generalized—cognition by denying (or at least calling into question) its own capacity to offer authenticating statements about particular persons and events. Fictional assertion requires that verisimilitude supersede veracity.

Indeed, it would seem that, as the eighteenth century progressed, readers increasingly tired of tongue-in-cheek authorial disavowals of mimetic intent. Mary Davys remarked as early as 1729 that "probable

[30]M. M. Bakhtin, *The Dialogic Imagination: Four Essays*, ed. Michael Holquist, trans. Caryl Emerson and Holquist (Austin: University of Texas Press, 1983), 409.

feigned stories" had been "for some time . . . out of use and fashion."[31] As a predictor of immediate novelistic trends, Davys was
clearly mistaken, since pseudofactual imposture survived to the end
of the century and beyond. Nonetheless, the rise of the mode that we
term "realism" clearly involved an initial dependence upon, but an ultimate replacement of, the "sense of the real." The imposture that had
been dominant in the early phases of documentary fiction eventually
became a residual device, while realistic verisimilitude, previously a
by-product of the claim to veracity, became the central determinant
of mimetic conventions. As we examine the development of the
pseudofactual novel in the eighteenth century, the wonder is not that
the novel abandoned the pretense of factual truth-telling but that it
took so long to do so.

Defoe experimented with a complex and contradictory admixture
of veracity and verisimilitude; most of the critical debates about
Defoe's status as a watershed figure in the history of the novel rest
implicitly or explicitly upon the determination of which strategy
of representation more accurately characterizes the majority of his
works. Was he, as Ian Watt argues, the first practitioner of novelistic
realism? Or was he, as Ralph Rader suggests, a figure "whom studies
have shown to have ancestors but no posterity, . . . the last and most
perfect artist in a tradition of works designed to exploit the interest
naturally attaching to true stories"?[32] I believe that Defoe's works exemplify both qualities; some represent the final flowering of the tradition of the "false true story," while others experiment with analogous
configuration as the primary strategy of fictional assertion.

Defoe's *A Journal of the Plague Year*, a fictional reconstruction of the
Great Plague of 1688, is essentially a lie. Although it creates the great
majority of its particulars, it is intended to be read as—and succeeds
best when read as—a historical document. Defoe's goal here is to create a gripping portrait of London under biological and moral siege.

---

[31]W. H. McBurney, ed., *Four before Richardson: Selected English Novels, 1720–27* (Lincoln: University of Nebraska Press, 1963), 235.

[32]See Ian Watt, *The Rise of the Novel: Studies in Defoe, Richardson, and Fielding* (Berkeley:
University of California Press, 1967); Ralph W. Rader, "Defoe, Richardson, Joyce, and the
Concept of Form in the Novel," in *Autobiography, Biography, and the Novel*, ed. William
Matthews and Rader (Los Angeles: William Andrews Clark Memorial Library, 1973), 47.

H.F., the narrator, may see symbolic religious ramifications in his situation, but Defoe's primary purpose is to represent the engraving of experience on consciousness, rather than to propose a determinate judgment upon the ideological content of that consciousness. As in *The Unfortunate Traveller*, the putative historical status of the narrator primarily gives the text its effect of direct reference to reality. The detailed death rolls invest the text with a compelling authenticity, but the text convinces the reader that it is telling the truth mainly through its narrative stance. H.F. repeatedly interrupts his narrative to deal with the "shutting up of houses" and the behavior of the watchmen, themes for which he has a morbid fascination. He therefore takes shape not as a created character whose foibles and proclivities Defoe invites us to judge—whether ironically, sympathetically, or harshly—but as a real person to whom we react in a manner controlled only by our enforced acknowledgment of the enormity of his experience. As a result, the ideological conceptions that guide H.F.'s behavior and thought—Providence intends for him to survive the plague, the administrators of London maintain social control without unduly suppressing personal freedoms—stand in a peculiar relation to the mimetic text. Since Defoe does not proffer a novelistic contract, we may agree or disagree with H.F.'s views, admire or disrespect his responses; but we stand, in a sense, on equal discursive ground. The text contains few of the rhetorical overdeterminations (e.g., implicit assertions of typicality and synecdoche) that, in realism, compel—or at least demand—the reader's assent to the author's ideological stance. Definitive opinions on social relations are, it seems, the possession of the speaker, but not—at least not necessarily—of the author. Defoe thus manages to make his views on predestination and the prerogatives of the state a felt presence in the text without requiring that the reader imaginatively endorse these views in order to participate vicariously in the experience Defoe describes. Documentary validation serves not to corroborate a view of reality assumed to be true, but to enhance the authenticity of a voice that holds its own construction of truth to be self-evident.

The *Journal* does contain occasional signs of its fictional nature. For example, the lengthy interpolated story of Thomas and John—two Londoners who, it appears, escaped from the horrors of the city and sequestered themselves in the countryside—is told in a third-person narrative that would never be expected in a memoir such as the *Jour-*

nal purports to be.[33] H.F. attempts to cover his tracks, of course. "Their story has a moral in every part of it, and their whole conduct is a pattern for all poor men to follow, or women either, if ever such a times come again," declares H.F. "If there is no other end in recording it, I think this a very just one, whether my account be exactly according to fact or no."[34] But the fact remains that H.F. did not accompany Thomas and John, so he could not have witnessed the dialogue and events he relates. Defoe's eagerness to explore as many facets of the plague experience as possible threatens to override his pseudomemoiristic frame; clearly he wishes to construct an analogous portrait that aspires toward generalization. The episode is framed and contained within the rambling structure of the memoir, however, for it creates few of the thematic resonances that accompany digressive episodes in novelistic discourse. (Compare, for example, the Man of the Hill episode in *Tom Jones*.) Just as "factual" elements must be subordinated to the mimetic frame of *War and Peace*, this "fictional" element must be subordinated to the factual frame of the *Journal*. H.F. stands forth as a historical subject, one whom we encounter on the nonironic turf of a shared historical actuality. H.F.'s quirkiness is not a peculiarity that we must take into account in weighing the truth of his account but a voyeuristic means to cognition. The truth that he tells about the plague is a historical truth, even if it is a lie.

Robinson Crusoe shows Defoe moving toward undisguised mimetic representation and openly exploring the limits of pseudofactual imposture. The text is, to be sure, rife with testimonial materials and even contains several pages of the diary purportedly undertaken by Crusoe on his island. (Fortunately, this tedious document is terminated early in the narrative, through Defoe's well-planned exhaustion of his hero's ink supply.) Furthermore, *Robinson Crusoe* gains historical credibility by its close resemblance to the well-known tale of

[33]For the alternate view that "the *Journal*'s focus on its central character puts it in the category of fiction," see Everett Zimmerman, *Defoe and the Novel* (Berkeley: University of California Press, 1975), 107–25. The quoted sentence appears on p. 108. Maximilian E. Novak, in *Realism, Myth, and History in Defoe's Fiction* (Lincoln: University of Nebraska Press, 1983), argues that "narrative does not function in *A Journal of the Plague Year* as a mode of 'historical exploration'; to the contrary, it is history that functions as a subsidiary organizational device for various fictions in the narrative" (67).

[34]Daniel Defoe, *A Journal of the Plague Year*, Everyman's Library (London: J.M. Dent, 1966), 138.

Alexander Selkirk and to other extant and validated journals of voyages to the West Indies, which dissociate it from the apocryphal traveler's tales popular in Defoe's time. Indeed, Defoe absorbed factual and putative accounts so thoroughly that McKillop has characterized his method as a "compilation and reconstruction rather than a fabrication."[35]

Nonetheless, the conventional prefatory testimony to authenticity contains a telling overprotestation: "The Editor believes the thing to be a just History of fact; neither is there any Appearance of Fiction in it."[36] What is more, the hero—designated, we note, as "Crusoe," not "Selkirk"—stands forth as a generalized type of the resilient and self-reliant entrepreneur. His interactions with Friday signal a superiority that is rooted not in any distinct particularity but in his assured status as a "natural" (that is, European, male, bourgeois) leader. In its adherence to the narrative probabilites of memoiristic form, *Robinson Crusoe* makes its claim to pseudofactuality; in its signification of a Lockean *Homo economicus* exercising his natural right to property and dominance, the narrative proposes cognition by means of analogous configuration. Defoe's fortunate situation of his solitary hero on a desert island prevents a practical conflict between these divergent representational claims: veracity is not submitted to any binding test for verification and hence coexists with a compelling verisimilitude. Defoe thus manages to suggest that his Crusoe constitutes a contemporaneous type without committing himself to a full-fledged fiction taking the bourgeois hero as its theme.

In *Moll Flanders* we see Defoe returning to more commonplace terrain and staking out a more confident claim to mimetic representation as a way of making assertions about everyday reality. The author creates a convincing pseudofactual narrative based on the premise that reality can be stranger than fiction; we can accept Moll's outrageous pronouncements readily enough if we read them as the statements of

[35]Alan Dugald McKillop, *The Early Masters of English Fiction* (Lawrence: University of Kansas Press, 1956), 9. For more on Defoe's use of factual materials, see Arthur Wellesley Secord, *Studies in the Narrative Method of Defoe* (Urbana: University of Illinois Press, 1926).

[36]Daniel Defoe, *Robinson Crusoe* (New York: Norton, 1975), 3. In *The Farther Adventures of Robinson Crusoe* (1719), Defoe made a more open admission of fictionality. He declared, "The just Application of every Incident, the religious and useful Inferences drawn from every Part, are so many Testimonies to the good Reign of making it publick and must legitimate all the Part that may be call'd Invention, or Parable in the Story" (Oxford: Blackwell, n.d.).

a real person, similar to one we might encounter in a waiting room or on a bus. Moll's narration of her accidentally incestuous marriage, for example, assumes a bizarre moral neutrality—a quality only enhanced by her cheerful relegation of the experience to the past, never to be dwelled upon again. If Moll is not bothered by this circumstance, neither are we—as neither, apparently, is Defoe. Moll's personality is a wondrous phenomenon, remaining remarkably impervious to those environmental forces, that would, in full-fledged realism, become part of her social being. As Sheldon Sacks has argued, Defoe organizes *Moll Flanders* around few of the structuring devices ordinarily associated with the novel. There are no meaningful changes in her character after the opening chapters; the developmental pattern of the plot is additive rather than complicative; the main pleasure afforded by most of the episodes derives from the simple fact that Moll is present in them.[37] Accordingly, Sacks concludes, Moll's actions do not provoke the kinds of judgments that accompany the actions of, say, a David Copperfield or a Bigger Thomas.

Nonetheless, the generic contract governing *Moll* is subtly but crucially different from that invoked in the *Journal*. For the very outrageousness of Moll's presumably truthful discourse requires the reader to consider criteria of plausibility and verisimilitude: *could* all these things have happened to one person? Single episodes such as the incestuous marriage may be assimilated into a memoiristic Gestalt, but the text contains so many incredible episodes that their quantitative accumulation produces a qualitative change in the text's organizing frame. The perception of an actual historical subject chatting with us is transformed into the ironic appreciation of a character unwittingly shaped by her own discourse. As David Goldknopf has observed, Moll's talk contains a "confessional increment" that requires the reader to acknowledge the "mimetic membrane" separating the world of the novel from the world of the reader.[38] In her contradictory complexity, Moll relinquishes the self-censorship that routinely accompanies even the most candid spiritual autobiography or rogue's

---

[37]Sheldon Sacks, *Fiction and the Shape of Belief: A Study of Henry Fielding, with Glances at Swift, Johnson, and Richardson* (Berkeley: University of California Press, 1967), 267–70.

[38]In first-person narratives that we are intended to perceive as fictional, Goldknopf argues, "Everything that an I-narrator tells us has a certain characterizing significance over and above its data value, by virtue of the fact that he is telling it to us" (*The Life of the Novel* [Chicago: University of Chicago Press, 1972], 32–33).

confession; she constantly characterizes herself for the reader, and her statements therefore serve to draw attention to the author's implied ethical judgments. Unlike H.F., or even Robinson Crusoe, Moll is incapable of projecting convincing ideological abstractions of her own. The only coherent values represented in *Moll Flanders* are those of Defoe, located in the apparently unconscious disclosures of Moll's discourse.

The tone of Defoe's preface reveals the distance between this novel and his earlier pseudofactual discourses—and the gulf that separates his strategy from that of a Mme d'Aulnoy. "It is true that the original of this story is put into new words," the "editor" remarks, "and that the style of the famous lady we here speak of is a little altered; particularly she is made to tell her own tale in modester words than she told it at first, the copy which came first to hand having been written in language more like one still in Newgate than one grown penitent and humble, as she afterward pretends to be."[39] The author's posture as editor here entails an ironic objectifying of his narrator; it would appear that Moll, while chastened, is not above relishing the memory of her past sins nor, for that matter, above exaggerating her account here and there for effect. In *Moll Flanders*, then, Defoe relegates the pseudofactual imposture to his manner of representation and treats it as a device in the portrayal of personality. Moll is an agent of perception—we are required to see the world through her eyes, and hers alone—but she is also an object of perception: the story constructed around her, of which she is a part, becomes the primary means of offering generalized propositions about both her and her world.

Defoe's works mark a critical stage in the development of the documentary novel. In his novels the pseudofactual apparatus receded to subordinate status, and mimetic narrative achieved currency as a means of conveying determinate interpretations and evaluations of everyday reality. Textual claims to veracity were first decisively subordinated to the direct adoption of analogous configuration in Richardson's novels, however, and what Rader calls the "wish-fulfillment" devolving from participation in the mimetic contract took precedence over any presumed propositional value that could be gained from the designation of fictive characters as "real."[40] Thus

[39]Daniel Defoe, *The Fortunes and Misfortunes of the Famous Moll Flanders* (New York: Random House, Modern Library, 1950), xix.

[40]Rader, "Defoe, Richardson, Joyce," 31–72.

Richardson's prefatory assertion that *Pamela; or, Virtue Rewarded* is founded upon "Truth and Nature" announced his intent that the reader would be attracted by the moral lesson presumably encoded in the heroine's career: the narrative, he says, is related "in so probable, so natural, so *lively* a manner, as shall engage the Passions of every sensible Reader, and strongly interest them in the edifying Story."[41]

It is not surprising that Richardson moderated his claims to Pamela's historicity, for the complex structure of expectation and vicarious involvement erected upon Pamela's letters reveals that he was no longer simulating a form of nonfictional discourse, albeit for mimetic ends, but instead was using the epistolary form as a device to lend immediacy to his portraiture of semi-conscious social ambition and physical desire. The letters themselves become part of the plot of the novel: Pamela's concealment of the letters on her body and Mr. B.'s attempts to snatch them from her reveal the extent to which the protagonist's discourse about herself has become inseparable from the author's representation of that discourse. Richardson thus uses his residually pseudofactual manner of representation in order to air contradictory ideological positions. The heroine's social ambitions and her covert willingness to bargain her chastity in order to further those ambitions become part of the text's referent; as analogous configuration, *Pamela* proposes that the marriage of servant and master is socially acceptable. At the same time, the very immediacy of Pamela's presence and the almost palpable reality of the letters make it difficult for the reader to inhabit an empyrean position outside the text from which to evaluate Pamela's actions. We partially inhabit the consciousness that is Pamela, experiencing the same sensations and formulating the same shifting conjectures about the true nature of her antagonists. The reader sympathizes with Pamela's behavior, without quite knowing that he or she is doing so, since at any single moment Pamela evades judgment and interpretation. Richardson thus divests himself of full accountability for the somewhat subversive views encoded in his tale. The residual pseudofactual presence is not therefore merely a stylistic feature of the text; it is an ideological strategem enabling the author simultaneously to make an assertion and to deny responsibility for it. After all, he is just editing the letters, not composing them.

[41]Samuel Richardson, *Pamela: or, Virtue Rewarded* (Oxford: Blackwell, n.d.), ii.

While it must have been apparent to Richardson that he had discovered a powerful mode of fictional representation (wedding bells were rung all over England to celebrate the nuptials of Pamela and Mr. B.), he apparently felt unable to dispense altogether with the imposture of veracity in his "new species of writing." In *Clarissa* he insistently retained his hold upon pseudofactual devices and refused to attach an additional commentary by Bishop Warburton that acknowledged the tale to be fictional. "I could wish that the *Air* of Genuiness [*sic*] had been kept up, tho' not the Letters to be *Thought* genuine; only so far kept up, I mean, as that they should not prefatically be owned *not* to be genuine."[42] Such stubborn adherence to the posture of factuality involved risks of the most practical kind, however. When literary competitors eager to reap some of the returns of the lucrative *Pamela* market claimed that they too had access to the original *Pamela* documents, Richardson was caught in a bind: he could uphold his right to legitimate and exclusive *Pamela* royalties only by admitting that his editorial posture was a fraud.[43]

Not all eighteenth-century writers made such extensive use of authenticating documentation, of course: the sense of the real was also at this time gravitating toward the realism that would eventually supersede it. This alternate tendency was most notably exemplified by Fielding, who claimed to have founded a "new province of writing," wherein, he pronounced, "I am at liberty to make what laws I please."[44] In this statment, Fielding openly proclaimed his independence from the pseudofactual tradition and asserted the superiority of a fictional approach that would strive to portray generalized examples "copied from the book of nature."[45] In proposing that the novel could constitute an Aristotelian species of mimesis, the "comic Epic-Poem in Prose," Fielding was taking a radical step toward generic independence, for he was wresting from the romance the exclusive rights to representation in prose fiction.

Fielding's open endorsement of fictionality as the differentia of the novel would be given explicit theoretical formulation in Clara Reeve's later description of the novel as

---

[42]Samuel Richardson, quoted in McKillop, 42.

[43]For more on Richardson's legal dilemma, see Davis, *Factual Fictions*, 180–82.

[44]Henry Fielding, *The History of Tom Jones, A Foundling* (1749), ed. Fredson Bowers (Middletown: Wesleyan University Press, 1975), 1:77.

[45]Henry Fielding, *The History of the Adventures of Joseph Andrews* (1742), ed. Martin Battestin (Middletown: Wesleyan University Press, 1967), 10. The passage quoted below appears on p. 4.

a picture of real life and manners, and of the times in which it is written. . . . The Novel gives a familiar relation of such things, as pass every day before our eyes, such as may happen to our friend, or to ourselves; and the perfection of it, is to represent every scene, in so easy and natural a manner, and to make them appear so probable, as to deceive us into a persuasion (at least while we are reading) that all is real, until we are affected by the joys or distresses of the persons in the story, as if they were our own.[46]

Reeve's awareness of the novel as the successor to the romance is illustrated by her prefatory description of her own Gothic narrative in *The Old English Baron*, which, she claimed, grafted together "the most attractive and interesting circumstances of the ancient Romance and Modern Novel, at the same time that it assumes a character and manner of its own, that differs from both."[47]

It is important to note that the definitions offered by both Fielding and Reeve hinge in large part upon their rejection of pseudofactual imposture as a constitutive feature of the novelistic contract; the representation of generalized human experience in specific imaginary instances takes precedence over the illusion of actual historicity. It is also important to note that Fielding and Reeve are the first writers to outline a theory of the novel (which is also a theory of realism, even though the term "realism" would not attain currency until the middle of the next century). Pseudofactual novelists, by contrast, could not devise theories of their own discursive practice, for to do so would involve a contradiction in terms: it was only when the text's *analogized* referent was differentiated from its putative *veracious* referent that novelists could openly discuss the principles of their mimetic craft.

Yet we must realize that Reeve insisted that mimesis can "deceive

---

[46]Clara Reeve, *The Progress of Romance* (Colchester: W. Keymer, 1785), I: iii. The terms "novel" and "romance" have a complicated history in the seventeenth and eighteenth centuries. Clara Reeve articulated the common meanings these terms had gained by the late eighteenth century when she wrote, "The Romance is an heroic fable which treats of fabulous persons and things. The Novel is a picture of real life and manners, and of the time in which it was written" (111). James Beattie, however, proclaimed, in his *On Fable and Romance* (1783) that Defoe, Richardson, and Smollett—whom he described as "Novel-writers"—all wrote species of "Romance" (quoted in Ioan Williams, ed., *Novel and Romance, 1700–1800: A Documentary Record* [London: Routledge & Kegan Paul, 1970], 309–27).

[47]Clara Reeve, *The Old English Baron* (London: Nimmo & Bain, 1883), 11.

us into a persuasion (at least while we are reading) that all is real," and that Fielding, despite his openness in admitting the imaginary status of his characters, retained for the title page of *Tom Jones* the word "history." Fielding attempted to deflect the criticism leveled by the foes of imagined discourse: "Hence we are to derive that universal contempt which the world, who always denominate the majority, have cast on all historical writers, who do not draw their materials from the records. And it is the apprehension of this contempt, that hath made us so cautiously avoid the term romance. . . . Though indeed we have good authority for our characters, no less indeed than Doomsday Book, or the vast book of nature, . . . our labours have sufficient title to the name of history."[48] The distance between these prefactory remarks and those of a Mme d'Aulnoy is, of course, immense; where Mme d'Aulnoy denied writing not only "romance" but also any "novel, . . . or story, devised at pleasure," Fielding and Reeve openly admit to the fictionality of their practice. Nonetheless, it is significant that even the novel's boldest defenders were still compelled to urge that their representation carried the authority of a nonfictional discourse.

As the pseudofactual novel attained currency as a fictional mode in the eighteenth century, it gained more secure status as a mode of cognition. In novels as diverse as Henry Mackenzie's *The Man of Feeling*, Tobias Smollett's *Humphrey Clinker*, Denis Diderot's *La religieuse*, and Choderlos de Laclos's *Les liaisons dangereuses*, the implication of pretended veracious discourse served to enhance the text's claims to generality rather than to suggest its possible authenticity. Thus Mackenzie's claims that the manuscript of his tale was discovered being used as wadding for the local curate's fowling piece and that the text's fragmented plot is attributable to hiatuses in the manuscript are belied by the story's patently didactic intent. "It is no more a history than it is a sermon," declares the curate.[49] Smollett pretends that the letters constituting *Humphrey Clinker* were gathered by one Jonathan Dustwich, who, in the first of a prefatory pair of letters, assures his bookseller, Henry Davis, that the letters do not "contain any matter

---

[48]Henry Fielding, *Selected Essays*, ed. Gordon Hall Gerould (Boston: Ginn, 1905), 30.

[49]Henry Mackenzie, *The Man of Feeling* (1771; New York: Norton, 1958), xiv. The novel, Mackenzie wrote in the *Lounger*, should "aid the cause of virtue, and . . . hold out patterns of the most exalted benevolence" (June 18, 1785; reprinted in Ioan Williams, *Novel and Romance*, 329).

which will be held actionable in the eye of the law."[50] The tongue-in-cheek nature of this ruse is made explicit in Davis's reply; "There have been so many letters upon travels lately published—what between Smollett's, Sharp's, . . . The public seems to be cloyed with that kind of entertainment. . . . Nevertheless, I will . . . run the risque of printing and publishing." Diderot's guarantees about the truth of his tale of cloistral incarceration pale beside the text's more powerful thematic assertions. The banning of a movie version of *La religieuse* in France just twenty years ago suggests that the novel's satirical thrust resides more in its generalized critique of clerical corruption than in its exposure of certain individuals engaged in nefarious acts.[51] Laclos's "editor's" pronouncement that he simply selected and compiled the letters that make up *Les liaisons dangereuses* is subverted by his "publisher's" remark that "we do not guarantee the authenticity of this narrative, and have even strong reasons for believing that it is but a romance."[52]

In these and many other instances, ironizing coventions of fictionality enable the novelist to move beyond those constraints that, in the earlier forms of pseudofactual fiction, restricted the range of the text's interpretive commentary to the perceptual vantage point of its speaking voice (or voices). The later novelists are clearly offering generalized statements about ethical principles and social realities, and irony is directed toward the referent as much as toward the manner of representation. As Laclos's "publisher" notes, "Several of the personages whom [the editor] brings on his stage have minds so sorry that it were impossible to believe that they lived in our century, in this century of philosophy, where the light shed on all sides has rendered, as everyone knows, all men so honourable, all women so modest and reserved." But the eighteenth-century novelist's adherence to the

[50]Tobias Smollett, *The Expedition of Humphrey Clinker* (1771), ed. Lewis Knapp (London: Oxford University Press, 1966), 1. The passage quoted below is from pp. 2–3.

[51]As Jean-Luc Godard commented regarding André Malraux's suppression of the movie, "It's really sinister to see a Gaullist minister in 1966 afraid of an Encyclopedist of 1789" (quoted in Denis Diderot, *The Nun*, trans. Eileen B. Hennessey [Los Angeles: Holloway, 1968], 1).

[52]Choderlos de Laclos, *Dangerous Acquaintances*, trans. Ernest Dowson (London: Nonesuch, 1940), xiii. The passage quoted below appears on the same page. In pointing up a general similarity between the uses of pseudofactual imposture in English and French novels of the eighteenth century, I am not asserting that novelistic developments in these two countries were parallel in many other respects. For more on the differences between the evolution of prose fiction in England and France, see Williams, *The Idea of the Novel*.

pseudofactual mode of narration also enforces a separation between the speaking voice and the informing ideological abstraction projected by the author: in many pseudofactual novels, from *Moll Flanders* to *Les liaisons dangereuses*, it is difficult to determine exactly what the author thinks. The author has not yet achieved the transcendental subjectivity afforded by full-fledged realism, which would posit an Archimedean position outside the text, from which a plurality of ideological stances could be counterposed, reconciled, and assimilated to a governing perspective.

The business of interpreting and judging social reality therefore remains the province of fictional characters who have not yet been assimilated to a fictional representation that appears to emanate from a position beyond ideology. Each text projects characters with different conceptions of that reality, of course, and each signals a uniquely contradictory way of appropriating it. *Les liaisons dangereuses* suggests a contradiction between Laclos's aversion to and fascination with his decadent wordmongers, while *La religieuse* suggests a contradiction between Diderot's radical polemic against the church and his uneasy identification with the social system that sustains that institution. My main point, however, is that these documentary novels of the eighteenth century tend to play out their ideological contradictions by projecting some sort of disparity between the text's divergent claims to cognition. As analogous configuration, the text makes certain generalizing propositions about its referent; as a putative true document, the text implies that its pretensions to reference are confined to the opinions and speculations of memoirists and letter-writers. Pseudofactual novels of the eighteenth century routinely project a certain hesitancy, not about whether to make fictional assertions, but about how to make them in a convincing way. This hesitancy, I suggest, reflects the contradictory epistemological stance of the contemporaneous bourgeois subject, who is in the process of achieving hegemony but has not yet consolidated for itself a position from which the relation of perception to cognition can be taken as self-evident and unproblematic.

The Pseudofactual Novel and Empiricism

The primary conceptual abstraction shaping the representational strategy of the pseudofactual novel in its various phases is the epistemology of nascent empiricism. The somewhat cavalier attitude toward factuality characterizing ancient, medieval, and, to a lesser extent, Renaissance discourse, both fictional and historical, suggests that the verifiability of particular assertions was not necessarily taken as the most important criterion of their value. If a text purported to be telling the truth, that truth generally was moral or religious not empirical. In the seventeenth and eighteenth centuries, however, the view emerges that facts are meaningful in their own right and function as reliable indices to truth—an empiricist credo that visibly sets in motion the mechanics of a corroborative apparatus that distinguishes the conventions of the pseudofactual novel from those of the romance. For the pseudofactual novel routinely features in its protagonist a consciousness engaged in the activity of perceiving and understanding its world. In Jack Wilton's conclusion that Surrey's helmet resembles a garden waterpot, in H.F.'s voyeuristic speculations about the experiences of Thomas and John, in Pamela's subconscious manipulation of Mr. B., we see a series of Lockean selves busy in the procedure of codifying perception into cognition. Experience, they proclaim, is that from which, as Locke said, "our knowledge . . . derives itself": "Our observation, employed either about external sensible objects, perceived and reflected on by ourselves, or about the internal operations of our minds, perceived and reflected on by ourselves, is that which supplies our understanding with all the materials of thinking. These two are the fountains of knowledge, from whence all the ideas we have, or can naturally have, spring."[53] The fictional characters' ambition to know the lineaments of their worlds also articulates the insurgent epistemological program of Descartes, who aspired to liberate philosophy from the "infirm foundation" of scholastic speculation and to formulate a "knowledge highly useful in life," by means of which, "knowing the force and the actions of fire, water, air, the stars, the heavens, and the other bodies that surround us . . . as distinctly as we know the various crafts of our artisans, we might also apply them in the same way to all the uses to which they are adopted, and thus render ourselves lords and possessors of nature."[54]

[53]John Locke, *An Essay concerning Human Understanding* (1690), in *The English Philosophers from Bacon to Mill*, ed. Edwin A. Burtt (New York: Modern Library, 1939), 248.

[54]René Descartes, *A Discourse on Method and Selected Writings*, trans. John Veitch, Everyman's Library (New York: Dutton, 1951), 53–54. For the view that Descartes's *Discourse* constitutes "an ur-novel in which we can trace the coming to be of the space the novel will be assigned," see J. M. Bernstein, *The Philosophy of the Novel: Lukács, Marxism, and the Dialectics of Form* (Brighton: Harvester, 1984), 165, 166–84.

Portraying an ego cogitans who takes the res extensa of the social world as his or her object of inquiry, the pseudofactual novel represents an exploratory consciousness attempting to be "lord and possessor" of its environment.[55]

Just as empiricism mounted a challenge to the old idealism of medieval science, the narrative strategy of the pseudofactual novel implied a criticism of the aprioristic abstractions of the romance. Indeed, any subversive impact of the pseudofactual novel derives primarily from its insurgent epistemology; in *The Unfortunate Traveller* and *Pamela*, in *Robinson Crusoe* and *La religieuse*, cognition is insistently scrutinized as the activity of determinate individuals confronting concrete social situations. Abstraction does not mean the invocation of eternal truths, but instead designates the procedure whereby, as Locke defines it, "ideas taken from particular beings become general representatives of all the same kind."[56] Conclusions are shown to be the result of the represented subject's inquiry into the res extensa, rather than as the *quod semper quod ubique ab omnium creditum est* implicit in the romance and codified in the normative universals of neoclassical aesthetic theory. Defoe's foregrounding of a highly individualized and exploratory voice in *Moll Flanders* thus runs completely counter to Shaftesbury's prescription that "the variety of Nature is such, as to distinguish every thing she forms by a *peculiar* character; which, if strictly observed, will make the subject appear unlike to anything extant in the world besides. But this effect the good poet and painter seek industriously to prevent. They hate *minuteness*, and are afraid of *singularity*."[57] Moll is preeminently singular, and the effect of Defoe's portrayal of her is to make the reader wonder whether she resembles "anything extant in the world besides." The pseudofactual

---

[55]I am not alone, of course, in claiming that the eighteenth-century novel is profoundly shaped by empiricism. Watt, for one (*The Rise of the Novel*, chap. 1), argues for a close correlation between empiricist epistemology and fictional form. But Watt takes more or less at face value the empiricist pretension to a neutral and precise replication of the objection of perception. I am clearly indebted to Watt, but I am more interested in empiricism as an ideological paradigm, one that is shaped primarily by changes in the forces of production. For the alternate view that the pseudofactual apparatus of the early novel is attributable principally to the Puritans' distrust of the imagination, see Sidney J. Black, "Eighteenth-Century 'Histories' as a Fictional Mode," *Boston University Studies in English*, 1 (1955): 33–44.

[56]Locke, *Human Understanding*, 281.

[57]Anthony, Third Earl of Shaftesbury, "Essay on the Freedom of Wit and Humour," in *Characteristics of Men, Manners, Opinions, Times, Etc.*, ed. John M. Robertson (London: Grant Richards, 1900), 1:95–96.

novelist's very hesitancy about incorporating the speaking voice fully into the text serves to highlight all the more the provisional nature of any discourse's claim to cognition. The documentary materials accompanying the text thus serve not to validate a posteriori the assertions of the text's narrative voice but to authenticate its sincerity. Even when, as in later pseudofactual fiction, these documentary materials ironize the speaker's discourse, they do not furnish determinate judgments, for to do so would involve a totalizing activity alien to the empiricist project. *"Judgment,"* Locke reminds us, *"is the presuming things to be so, without perceiving it."*[58]

The pseudofactual novel's empiricist epistemology constitutes its primary challenge to aristocratic hegemony. This is not to say, however, that it lacks an expressly political propositional content. On the contrary, the "singular" voices that we hear in the pseudofactual novel frequently pose clear challenges to received notions of decorum or social order. *Oroonoko*, it is true, may not in some respects occupy a particularly subversive relation to dominant ideology (despite its bold treatment of the slavery issue), but *The Unfortunate Traveller, Robinson Crusoe*, and *Pamela* provide a discursive terrain where distinctly bourgeois viewpoints and aspirations receive a hearing. Jack Wilton, after all, delivers a devastating satire on courtly tournaments and love rhetoric; Crusoe celebrates the bourgeois entrepreneur; Pamela the servant marries her master. The individualism embedded in the epistemology of the pseudofactual novel thus readily aligns itself with the premises of Lockean political economy, which posits a Homo economicus, unburdened by tradition, as the autonomous center of its contractual relations. In their very freedom from the constraint of performing an assigned function fully controlled from outside the text, the protagonists of pseudofactual fiction enact a version of Locke's definition of radical independence—that is, that "state of perfect freedom" where people may "order their actions and dispose of their perceptions and persons as they think fit, within the bounds of the law of nature, without asking leave, or depending upon the will of any other man."[59] Just as Locke's atomistic ego independently contracts his social relations in the state of nature, the memoirist or letter writer contracts to be understood on discursive

---

[58]Locke, *Human Understanding*, 377.

[59]Locke, *An Essay Concerning the True Original, Extent and End of Civil Government* (1690), in *The English Philosophers*, ed. Burtt, 404.

terms presumably uninfluenced by inherited conventions. As N. W. Visser points out, the pseudofactual novel's "marginal standing in the prevailing hierarchy of kinds" enabled it to be "a vehicle through which an emergent class could explore and codify its sense of itself and the world."[60]

While pseudofactual fictions of the seventeenth and eighteenth centuries express the revolutionary aspects of early bourgeois empiricism, however, they also reflect its limitations as an oppositional program. For in its confrontation with the res extensa, the ego cogitans denies the dialectical—and hence historical—relation between subject and object, taking as an ontological given its own empyrean position in relation to material reality. Locke, who described the mind as a "closet wholly shut from the light, with only some little openings left to let in external visible resemblances or ideas of things without,"[61] concluded that "the mind, in all its thoughts and reasonings, hath no other immediate object but its own ideas, which it alone does and can contemplate." Descartes decided that "except our thoughts, there is nothing absolutely in our power; so that, when we have done our best in respect of things external to us, all wherein we fail of success is to be held, as regards us, absolutely impossible."[62] While Descartes prided himself on his investigations in physics and anatomy and celebrated the value of experimentation, he also proclaimed the radical unreliability of sensory data and continually returned to the *cogito ergo sum* that constituted, for him, the "first principle of philosophy." The ego cogitans is therefore a peculiarly abstract identity, never altering through its participation in the world of things, and never contemplating, as Descartes remarked of himself, "anything higher than the reformation of my own opinions, and basing them on a foundation wholly my own." For the early empiricists, nature was to be known by contemplation but not by intervention; the exploratory consciousness that aspired to be "lord and possessor" of nature also took as an operative premise its own alienation from, and lack of determination by, its object of inquiry.

In the pseudofactual novel, this empiricist failure to discern the historical connection of subject and object manifests itself in the pecul-

[60]N. W. Visser, "The Novel as Liberal Narrative: The Possibilities of Radical Fiction," unpublished essay (Rhodes University, Cape Town, 1985), 6.
[61]Locke, *Human Understanding*, 282. The passage quoted below is from p. 317.
[62]Descartes, 21–22. The quotations below are from pp. 28 and 12.

iarly abstract relation of character to the represented social world. Jack Wilton's interaction with his historical world is beset with anachronisms. Oroonoko, with his courtly speech and Caucasian features, is not especially plausible as an African ruler of the early colonial period. Moll rolls through her environment with the freedom of a billiard ball in a Newtonian experiment: she may be hauled off to Newgate, but her character remains an emanation of her own nature. Even Pamela's psychology partakes of a mechanistic quality, for she responds to stimuli with unfailing consistency, forms a minimum of inductive generalizations, and readily abandons even these when the stimuli emanating from Mr. B. alter in their social content. Pamela's inability to bear a grudge is not simply a function of her unacknowledged ambitions; it is also intimately linked to her shallow contextualization in social relations, which take shape as background rather than as formative context. Where the realist Twain was to portray his character Chambers in *Pudd'nhead Wilson* as permanently and irrevocably stamped by his experience as a slave, Richardson makes his servant girl infinitely adaptable to her radically altered social status: speech and manners—the material expressions of class—are strangely irrelevant to Pamela's experience. The pseudofactual novelists' unwillingness to drop the imposture of veracity and to incorporate their characters fully into the stories they tell implies a static view of the text's social referent: historical actuality consists not in processes but in objects, and the perceiving subject discovers identity in opposition to, rather than in conjunction with, its environment.

The documentary strategy of the pseudofactual novel thus mediates the central ideological contradictions characterizing early empiricism. The text represents discourse as an activity of particular individuals. The act of perception leads to cognition, but cognition is not imposed—at least, not overdetermined—by the configuration of the text. The text's avoidance of interpretive totalization thus signals a critical relation to the apriorism of dominant aesthetic and social ideologies. "Historicity" is retained in a residual apparatus of documentary authentication to the extent that "history"—as the totalizing field of force informing that referent—is not recognized as the primary determinant of the activities of perception and cognition. If characters have not attained full credibility as *objects* of perception, they must inhabit a realm as *subjects* of perception that is (or at least claims to be) coterminous with that of the reader.

The Pseudofactual Novel and Merchant Capitalism

To posit that the pseudofactual novel mediates the contradictory conceptual abstractions of nascent empiricism does not tell the whole story, however. For empiricism itself constitutes a quintessential articulation of the new form of the exchange relation accompanying the emergent capitalist social formation. On one level, the connection between empiricism and capitalism is obvious and was in fact perceived and articulated by philosophers of the time. Bacon drew an explicit connection between the advancement of scientific knowledge and the voyages of discovery. Crossing the Atlantic had replaced the search for Atlantis, he declared, and "These times may justly bear in their motto . . . *plus ultra*—further yet—in precedence of the ancient *non ultra*—no further . . . in respect of our sea-voyages, by which the whole globe of earth has, after the manner of the heavenly bodies, been many times compassed and circumnavigated."[63] Similarly, Descartes's desire to make man the "lord and possessor of nature" expressed the ideological imperatives of a class that needed to abolish the mystifications of feudal apologetics in order to attain its political and economic ends. Descartes, we will recall, aimed to produce a "knowledge highly useful in life" that would enable man to apply the elements to "the uses to which they are adopted," thus bringing the knowledge of nature into the same sphere as the knowledge of "the various crafts of our artisans." The postulation of an ego cogitans taking the res extensa as its object was therefore linked to the commercial project of the bourgeoisie; Descartes's regulatory and proprietary language is hardly an accidental construct. As Engels rather grudgingly admitted, in the early phases of the bourgeois era

the bounds of the old *orbis terrarum* were pierced, only now for the first time was the world really discovered and the basis laid for subsequent world trade and the transition from handicraft to manufacture, which in its turn formed the starting-point for modern large-scale industry. The dictatorship of the Church over men's minds was shattered. . . .

[63]Francis Bacon, *Works* (London: 1857–74), 4:169. For more on the influence of the oceanic voyages on Elizabethan writing, see Robert Ralston Cawley, *Unpathed Waters: Studies in the Influence of the Voyagers on Elizabethan Literature* (Princeton: Princeton University Press, 1940).

It was the greatest progressive revolution that mankind had so far experienced.[64]

As part of this process of global exploration, the revolution in scientific method, with its necessary dismantling of older forms of speculative philosophy, was for Engels clearly founded in the economic imperatives of the rising bourgeoisie.

It has been pointed out, however, that the utility of the empiricist platform was ultimately more ideological than pragmatic and that the theory of the empiricists was in actuality greatly advanced beyond their practice. Christopher Caudwell, for example, proposes that early bourgeois natural philosophy tells us a good deal more about property relations than it does about methods that were used in scientific inquiry: "Man is the subject; Nature is the object. Therefore in bourgeois society, the object appears solely as 'things' over which man has rights, and whose laws or 'necessity' he discovers in order to satisfy his desires." According to Caudwell, empiricism, in spite of its pretensions to experimentalism, is an intrinsically noninterventionist philosophy. "Nature is always known as a passive object—as something not subject to man's activity nor the antagonist of his striving, but as something self-contained and shut in by its necessities. Hence Man's whole relation to Nature bears the stamp of the property relation, in which his right over it is the reward of his consciousness or cleverness—never of his activity."[65] The empyrean stance of the ego cogitans is therefore primarily an ideological posture, one that transposes a relation of ownership into an epistemological category.

Sohn-Rethel has further developed the connections between the epistemological and political premises of Cartesian dualism and the "real abstraction" of early capitalist relations of production and exchange. The gradually increased division of mental from manual labor, Sohn-Rethel argues, determines the cognitive procedures of bourgeois science, from the time of Galileo to the present. "It is . . . not science but ideology," he declares, "when, in the seventeenth century, philosophers like Descartes and Hobbes looked upon the

[64]Frederick Engels, *Dialectics of Nature* (Moscow: Progress, 1974), 21–22.
[65]Christopher Caudwell, "The Crisis in Physics," in *The Concept of Freedom* (London: Lawrence & Wishart, 1965), 205.

outer world as a whole and in all its parts, organic no less than inorganic, as self-operating mechanisms."[66] According to Sohn-Rethel, the empiricist compulsion to conceptualize the material world as object of inquiry expresses above all else the increasing need of capital to impose upon production the abstraction of a self-regulating mechanism: conceptual appropriation takes as its model the appropriation of an abstracted and transferable exchange value. The growing influence of empiricist paradigms is a crucial signal of the development of bourgeois hegemony, but the significance of this influence resides more in the realm of ideology than in that of technology.

The principal historical development that sustained—and was rationalized by—empiricist epistemology was therefore not the development of the applied sciences needed for expanding commerce and industry but the gradual subordination of the social relations and the forces of production to the automatism of capital. This process would attain its full development only in the nineteenth century, when workers relinquished their tools and became appendages to machines propelled by nonhuman sources of energy. From the late sixteenth through most of the eighteenth century, however, changes in the social formation were initiated that would render capitalist production virtually a self-regulating phenomenon. The primitive accumulation of the capital necessary for the developments Engels described consisted primarily in the accumulation of a fund of labor power. The early capitalists embarked upon their enterprises, not by amassing wealth from trade or even by discovering precious metals in the Americas, but primarily by separating laborers from their means of production—a process of social compulsion. In the era of handicraft industry, the social division of labor was moved from the society at large to the workshop, where wage laborers possessing specialized skills were brought together under one roof. In the era of manufacture, workers were trained to perform segmented tasks requiring less knowledge and expertise: manufacture was, in Marx's words, "a productive mechanism whose parts are human beings."[67] With the subjugation of workers to the discipline of wage labor, capital gradually brought the entire social formation under the hegemony of the exchange relation. Where in precapitalist modes of production social re-

---

[66] Alfred Sohn-Rethel, *Intellectual and Manual Labor: A Critique of Epistemology*, trans. Martin Sohn-Rethel (Atlantic Highlands, N.J.: Humanities, 1978), 123.

[67] Karl Marx, *Capital*, 1:338. The passage quoted below is from p. 737.

lations took the form of visible, personal dependencies, in the era of handicrafts, and especially of manufacturing, relations among persons increasingly became objective dependency relations, characterized by growing economic abstraction and by the apparent neutrality of the market. Marx caustically remarked,

> It is not enough that the conditions of labour are concentrated in a mass, in the shape of capital, at the one pole of society, while at the other are grouped masses of men, who have nothing to sell but their labour-power. Neither is it enough that they are compelled to sell it voluntarily. The advance of capitalist production develops a working-class, which by education, tradition, habit, looks upon the condition of that mode of production as self-evident laws of Nature.

But the era of merchant capital and manufacture was beset by contradictions, for capitalist hegemony was by no means consolidated or complete. For one thing, the capitalist class encountered continual opposition from the landed aristocracy, who, while assimilating a good deal of agricultural production to the capitalist model, still retained control of the state and the economy. Furthermore, the capitalist class itself was hardly the monolithic presence that it would be in the era of industrialism. As Elizabeth Fox-Genovese and Eugene Genovese have recently argued,

> Although [merchant capital] provided a powerful solvent to feudal and seigneurial relations and contributed mightily to the emergence of a world market, it could not create capitalist social relations or a new system of production. To the extent that it remained commercial and money-dealing capital—to the extent that it escaped becoming an agent of industrial capital—it eventually became an impediment to the emergence of the capitalist mode of production.[68]

Merchant capitalist enterprises often served as financial auxiliaries to the entrenched landed aristrocracy; even the "historic overseas expansion," Fox-Genovese and Genovese argue, was "a desperate if heroic effort to shore up a crisis-ridden feudal mode of production."

In addition, the owners of manufacturing enterprises experienced

---

[68]Elizabeth Fox-Genovese and Eugene Genovese, *Fruits of Merchant Capital: Slavery and Bourgeois Property in the Rise and Expansion of Capitalism* (New York: Oxford University Press, 1983), 6–7. The statement quoted below is from p. 10.

continual—if, to be sure, largely spontaneous—opposition from their workers, who maintained a modicum of control over the conditions and terms of production. "Since handicraft skill is the foundation of manufacture," remarked Marx, "and since the mechanism of manufacture as a whole possesses no framework, apart from the labourers themselves, capital is constantly compelled to wrestle with the insubordination of the workmen."[69] The early phases of the capitalist era thus witnessed a tremendous expansion in commodity exchange but they were not completely regulated by it; the principle of equivalence characterized emergent tendencies in the social synthesis but did not extend to the labor process itself. The "interior of the commodity," as Marx put it, was not yet dominated by the exchange relation. Marx defined the intermediary nature of merchant capital in this way:

> The quantitative ratio in which products are exchanged is at first quite arbitrary. They assume the form of commodities inasmuch as they are exchangeables, i.e., expressions of one and the same kind. Continued exchange and more regular reproduction for exchange reduces this arbitrariness more and more. But at first not for the producer and consumer, but for their go-between, the merchant, who compares money-prices and pockets the difference. It is through his own movements that he establishes equivalence. *Merchant's capital is originally merely the intervening movement between extremes which it does not control and between premises which it does not create.*[70]

The important idea here is that the principle of equivalence is situated between "uncontrolled" and "uncreated" processes of production and consumption. Merchant capital played a growing role in regulating the market, but it could not yet propose itself as a "self-evident law of nature."

The Cartesian hypostatization of the ego cogitans and the res extensa, I suggest, mediates this "intervening movement" between uncontrolled and uncreated extremes and premises. "Descartes," Marx wryly remarked, "saw with the eyes of the manufacturing period."[71] Disjunctions would necessarily exist between the theory and

---

[69]Marx, *Capital: A Critique of Political Economy*, ed. Frederick Engels, trans. Samuel Moore and Edward Aveling (New York: International Publishers, 1967), 1:367.

[70]Marx, *Capital*, 3:324.

[71]Marx, *Capital*, 1:390.

the practice of the sovereign bourgeois ego that aspires to take the material world as its object and to appropriate to itself the fruits of production. That object possesses, after all, a contradictory social nature: it is characterized by the universal equivalence accompanying a highly developed market economy, but it has not yet been subdued to the imperatives of those industrial capitalist forces of production that will extend the principle of abstract equivalence to the totality of the labor process. To the extent that the abstraction of the exchange relation has not fully penetrated the social relations of production, the epistemological paradigms articulating early capitalist development will be highlighted *as ideology*—conceptual abstractions necessary for appropriating the configuration of nature and society, perhaps, but hardly cognitive structures that can be said to emanate from the nature of the object itself. "Our knowledge," Locke observed, "comes not only short of the reality of things, but even of the extent of our own ideas. . . . It would be well with us if our knowledge were but as large as our ideas, and there were not many doubts and inquiries concerning the ideas we have, whereof we are not, nor I believe, ever shall be in this world, resolved."[72] As long as "abstraction" is seen as a generalizing activity of the perceiving subject, and not experienced as the pervading atmosphere of a reified daily life, such "doubts and inquiries" will continue to enforce a separation between perception and cognition.

The historical contradictions characterizing the development of bourgeois economic and political hegemony, I speculate, reproduce themselves in the fundamental contradictions informing the ironic strategy of documentary representation in the pseudofactual novel. History per se also enters the pseudofactual novel, of course. Moll tells us a good deal about the brutality of the primitive accumulation of capital in the early eighteenth century, and the Vicomte de Valmont reveals a good deal about the proclivities of the leisure class that lived off the surplus created by peasants before the French Revolution. But historical actuality enters the text through various levels of mediation and permeates not only its referent but its strategy of representation as well. The pseudofactual novel's insistent inclusion of an authenticating documentary apparatus reveals a hesitancy about engaging in a procedure of analogous configuration that will assert

---

[72]Locke, *Human Understanding*, 328.

the generality of the text's representation of life. It is, paradoxically, only when the reifying tendency of industrial capitalism effects the full severance of mental and manual labor that the sense of the real is decisively supplanted by realism and that the documentary novel undertakes a totalizing representation of the very historical process that produces the text's alienation from its referent.

6

The Historical Novel

Through the plot [of the historical novel], at whose centre stands [the typical hero], a neutral ground is sought and found upon which the extreme, opposing social forces can be brought into a human relation with one another.

— Georg Lukács

In the nineteenth century, the "sense of the real" has been superseded by "realism," and the dominant mode of the documentary novel becomes the historical novel. The term "historie" now disappears from the title pages of novels, since they no longer aspire to invoke what Richardson called "that kind of Historical Faith which Fiction itself is generally read with, tho' we know it to be Fiction."[1] Banished from the manner of representation, however, history resurfaces in the referent. Where pseudofactual novelists represented an abstract and undialectical relation between character and environment, and even the realist Fielding declared his lawyer in *Tom Jones* to have been alive for four thousand years, documentary novelists of the nineteenth century are historical novelists, for they view historical process as the crucible in which character and destiny are formed. Even those texts that recapitulate certain features of the pseudofactual novel's documentary strategy—such as Dickens's *David Copperfield* or Charles Reade's *The Autobiography of a Thief*—incorporate the speaking "I" into a novelistic frame that locates the character's identity in a historically specific fictional realm, rather than in a speciously authentic mode of discourse. Other modes of documentary fiction enjoy

---

[1]Samuel Richardson, *Selected Letters*, ed. John Carroll (Oxford: Clarendon, 1964), 85.

residual status in the nineteenth century, but the historical novel emerges as the paradigmatic mode of the genre.

The shift from pseudofactuality to realism marks a major transformation in the conceptions of history that guide the practice of nineteenth-century novelists. When the novel's referent comes to be seen as possessing a dynamis in its own right, historicity need no longer be invoked to guarantee the text's representation of that referent. By a curious paradox, mimesis is empowered to interpret and judge historical actuality when it finally acknowledges its own distinctness as a mode of discourse: the novel loses its hesitancy about its propositional status when it admits that its assertion is fictional. The historical novel's separation from nonfictional kinds of writing such as history and journalism thus signals its adoption of a new view of the historical process shaping the relation of character to event. As Raymond Williams points out, it is only in the nineteenth century that the term "history" comes to denote not merely a mode of discourse or a universal process of change, but a crucial context for understanding the present.[2] This altered notion of historical process, we shall see, profoundly influences historiography of the time as well. From the Romantic history of Bancroft and Michelet to the "scientific" history of Ranke and Taine, nineteenth-century historical narratives take as their premise a view of history as the formative context of the present that sharply differentiates them from histories written during the century before. The historical novel thus participates in a broader transformation of historical consciousness. Its emergence as an unabashedly fictional kind of writing signals not its abandonment of the claim to represent historical actuality but its reformulation of this claim in accordance with a changing conception of that actuality.[3]

The representational strategy of the historical novel differs in three respects from the practice of earlier documentary fiction. First, the text now proposes cognition through an undisguised adoption of analogous configuration. Characters make their claim to truthfulness

[2]Raymond Williams, *Keywords: A Vocabulary of Culture and Society* (New York: Oxford University Press, 1976), 119–20.

[3]For the view that the major transformation in modern historical consciousness occurred in the eighteenth century—and hence manifests itself in the eighteenth-century novel—see Leo Braudy, *Narrative Form in History and Fiction: Hume, Fielding, and Gibbon* (Princeton: Princeton University Press, 1970).

not through their imposture of veracity but through their function as representative types; hence they convey cognition of the referent through their relationality. Moll compels interest by her billiardlike movement through a static world, but Cooper's Harvey Birch, in *The Spy*, gains credibility only as he is embedded in the context of a revolutionary crisis. Second, the plot of the historical novel relinquishes the historical probabilities accompanying the pseudofactual novel and directs its narrative energy to the elaboration of a pattern of complication and resolution that interprets and evaluates the social world. The historical novel posits complication as an essential component of the historical dialectic; resolution becomes a teleological necessity, and totalization emerges as the principal strategy for reproducing the lineaments of historical actuality. Third, empirical data enter the historical novel not to validate the author's honesty but to reinforce the text's claim to offer a persuasive interpretation of its referent. Where details in the pseudofactual novel could be outrageous and anomalous so long as they purported to be true (we recall Mme d'Aulnoy's fantastic tales of intrigue), factual references in the historical novel must be plausible, yet they need make no pretension to a literal retelling of events. When a figure from world history enters the fictional world, he or she verifies the trajectory of the plot; when a corroborative preface or footnote is attached to the text, it authenticates the propositionality embedded in the analogous configuration. Telling the truth has become a matter of accurate generalization.

The representational strategy of the historical novel bespeaks, in short, a new epistemological program. In the closing section of this chapter, I shall argue that this epistemological program points to the qualititative alteration taking place in the relations of production characteristic of an emergent industrial capitalist society. Realism, I shall propose, articulates the triumph of reification; the historical novel's powerful synthesis of the dialectics of social change mediates the emergence of capital itself as the supreme social subject. Industrial capitalism is thus in one sense the hero of my tale here. Following the lead of Marx, who grudgingly admired the achievement of nineteenth-century capital in drawing the economy of the entire globe into a universal market, I acknowledge the higher level of mimetic abstraction made possible by the more fully developed abstraction of the exchange relation in the era of the mechanically powered machine. But the very abstraction that derives from the increased complexity in the realm of the concrete makes it increasingly difficult to return to the realm of the concrete; by rendering capital the supreme social subject, reification posits the equivalence of the different subjects who are subordinated to capital's hegemony. In most nineteenth-century historical novels, the vantage point of the authorial subject thus presents itself as interchangeable with that of the reader. The ideological coloration of the consciousness that shapes the text is no longer foregrounded for critical consideration, as it was in the pseudofactual novel. Instead, the text's goal of rendering empirically grounded representation readily lapses into positivism, and totalization threatens to become self-evidence. In its contradictory blend of disability and empowerment, the historical novel mediates the reification that both expands and limits the epistemological horizons of nineteenth-century discourse.

It should be apparent that the representational strategy of the historical novel creates new problems at the same time that it solves old ones. The historical novel indeed makes possible a comprehensive portraiture of past events that was unavailable to the pseudofactual novel. But where the empirical self-consciousness of the pseudofactual novel continually called attention to the epistemological relation between fact and generalization, the more confident empiricism of the historical novel tends to simplify this relation. The historical novel's "facts" appear to anchor the text's analogous configuration in historical actuality by proposing that particular corroborative data bear an unmediated reference to the public historical record. Actually, however, these data function to validate a posteriori the text's particular ideological construction of its referent. Documentation in the historical novel is intrinsically tautological; rather than confirming the text's assertions about social reality, it corroborates a reality assumed to be self-evident. This documentary practice was bound to recoil upon itself. In the course of the century, the historical novel's empiricist claims enter into a state of crisis, ultimately issuing in the profound epistemological skepticism characterizing modernist documentary fiction.[4]

---

[4]The debate over the meaning of the term "realism" is heated and never-ending. In recent years, of course, the notion that nineteenth-century realism aims at transparent "reflection" has been widely challenged. See, for example, Leo Bersani's *A Future for Astyanax: Character and Desire in Literature* (Boston: Little, Brown, 1976). Bersani argues, "The or-

The Classical Historical Novel

Lukács's writings on nineteenth-century realism remain the locus classicus of the theory of the historical novel, and any Marxist discussion of the genre should take them as the point of departure. The central critical category in Lukács's theory of realism is the "type," who, as fictional protagonist, provides

> a peculiar synthesis which organically binds together the general and the particular both in characters and situations. What makes a type a type is not its average quality, not its mere individual being, however profoundly conceived; what makes it a type is that in it all the humanly and socially essential determinants are present on their highest level of development, in the ultimate unfolding of the possibilities latent in them, in extreme presentation of their extremes, rendering concrete the peaks and limits of men and epochs.[5]

---

dered significances of realistic fiction are presented as immanent to society, whereas in fact they are the mythical denial of that society's fragmented nature. . . . The formal and psychological reticence of most realistic fiction makes for a secret complicity between the novelist and his society's illusions about its own order. Realistic fiction serves nineteenth-century society by providing it with strategies for containing (and repressing) its disorder within significantly structured stories about itself" (61, 62). There is much of value here; as I shall argue throughout this chapter, realism does entail ideological operations of containment and repression. But we should not lose sight of the empiricist goals—and achievements—of nineteenth-century realism, which did in fact manage to capture the totality of social relations with a new degree of precision. As Harry Levin observes, "Etymologically, realism is thing-ism. . . . Platonic idealists and scholastic 'realists'—and let us not be confused by the misnomer—had believed in the priority of universals, *universalia ante rem*. Specific objects were mere accidents, or at best symbolic correspondences with the actualities of a transcendent otherworld. That they should be valued for their own sake, that things should have meaning in themselves, marked the triumph of empiricism, materialism, and worldliness" (*The Gates of Horn: A Study of Five French Realists* [New York: Oxford University Press, 1963]). For the various formulations of "realism" that have been influential in writing this chapter, see George Levine, *The Realistic Imagination: English Fiction from Frankenstein to Lady Chatterley* (Chicago: University of Chicago Press, 1981); Taylor Stoehr, "Realism and Verisimilitude," *Texas Studies in Language and Literature*, 11 (1970): 1269–88; Ioan Williams, *The Realist Novel in England: A Study in Development* (London: Macmillan, 1974); Robert Alter, "Mimesis and the Motive for Fiction," *TriQuarterly*, 42 (Spring 1978): 224–49; Everett W. Knight, *The Novel as Structure and Praxis: From Cervantes to Malraux* (Atlantic Highlands, N.J.: Humanities, 1980); Mary Louise Pratt, *Toward a Speech-Act Theory of Literary Discourse* (Bloomington: Indiana University Press, 1977), 201–23; and of course Lukács's many writings on realism.

[5]George Lukács, *Studies in European Realism*, Universal Library (New York: Grosset & Dunlap, 1964), 6.

The fate of the typical hero thus embodies in microcosm the essential trajectory of the historical dialectic: "Through the plot, at whose centre stands the hero, a neutral ground is sought and found upon which the extreme, opposing social forces can be brought into a human relationship with one another."[6] Moreover, the complications and resolutions constituting the plot of the historical novel represent what the author sees as the essential dynamic of historical process. The world-historical hero here plays a necessarily subsidiary role. As Lukács says of Scott's novels, the great representatives of the age "can never be central figures of the action. . . . The important leading figure, who embodies an historical movement, necessarily does so at a certain level of abstraction. Scott, by first showing the complex and involved character of popular life itself, creates this being which the leading figure then has to generalize and concentrate in an historical deed." Articulating the lesson of the French Revolution—that history is the product of mass activity, rather than of the subjective intentions of kings and generals—the world-historical hero functions, in Hegelian fashion, as an index to the unconscious strivings of the masses of people. But the real "struggles and antagonisms of history" are best represented by "mediocre" heroes who, "in their psychology and destiny, always represent social trends and historical forces." In this context, "it matters little whether individual details, individual facts are historically correct or not. . . . Detail . . . is only a means of achieving historical faithfulness, for making concretely clear the historical necessity of a concrete situation."

In many ways Lukács offers an accurate and penetrating description of the ideological premises of the historical novel. Certainly Scott's novels, which Lukács repeatedly invokes as pure instances of the form, fulfill Lukács's criteria for realistic representation. In *Ivanhoe*, for example, fictional characters such as Cedric the Saxon and Front-de-Boeuf act out the historical contradiction between Saxons and Normans; historical personages such as Robin Hood and Richard the Lion-Hearted assume ancillary roles that emphasize the primary function of the anonymous populace in effecting historical change. In *Waverley; or, 'Tis Sixty Years Since*, the typical hero emerges as the dialectical embodiment of vast social forces. Thus Waverley's alternating attraction to Rose Bradwardine and Flora Mac-Ivor sets forth

---

[6]Lukács, *The Historical Novel*, trans. Hannah Mitchell and Stanley Mitchell (London: Merlin, 1962), 36. The statements quoted below appear on pp. 39, 34, and 59.

in microcosm the contrary appeals of Lowland concession and Highland rebellion; his initial rejection of, and ultimate reconciliation with, his own aristocratic status illustrate Scott's melioristic view of the path of historical change. When Bonnie Prince Charlie enters the tale, he furnishes a specific link with the historical record, but it is relatively unimportant whether or not the real Pretender followed the exact circumstantial course that Scott outlines for his fictional counterpart. What matters most is that Bonnie Prince Charlie's quixotic actions validate Waverley's eventual decision to repudiate the Stuart rebellion; the world-historical hero is a catalyst, not a cause.

Lukács pays little attention to the question of documentary corroboration, but we can expand upon his analysis by noting the ways in which Scott's testimonial materials are intended to reinforce the propositional claims of his novels. In the various prefaces and the postscript to *Waverly*, for example, Scott announces his departure from Gothic antiquarianism and his ambition to represent the historical forces that have projected Scotland into modern times. His goal is, indeed, to use fiction to delineate the trajectory of history: "The change, though steadily and rapidly progressive, has, nevertheless, been gradual; and, like those who drift down the stream of a deep and smooth river, we are not aware of the progress we have made until we fix our eye on the now distant point from which we have been drifted."[7] While Scott is careful to point out that his novel is based on historical research and the testimony of participants in the Highland Rebellion, he openly admits that his narrative is a "romance" and that he has "embodied in imaginary scenes, and ascribed to fictitious characters, a part of the incidents which I then received from those who were actors in them." The difference between this statement and Behn's claim to be relating neither "novel" or "story" is striking, and it bespeaks a qualitative shift in the cognitive capacities attributed to mimesis. Romance, imagination, and fiction are now means, rather than barriers, to assertion.

Moreover, *Waverley's* apparatus of footnotes testifies to the novel's presumption to be a reliable guide to the characteristic features of eighteenth-century Scottish history and culture. Thus one note tells us that "the sanguine Jacobites, during the eventful years 1745–46,

[7]Sir Walter Scott, *Waverley; or, 'Tis Sixty Years Since* (1814; London: Nelson, n.d.), 553. The passages quoted below appear on pp. 554, 234, and 154.

kept up the spirits of their party by the rumour of descent from France on behalf of the Chevalier St. George." Another, referring to Fergus Mac-Ivor's regaining the estate that had been forfeited after his father's participation in the insurrection of 1715, remarks that "it was not till after the total destruction of the clan influence, after 1745, that purchasers could be found, who offered a fair price for the estates forfeited in 1715, which were then brought to sale by the creditors of the York Buildings Co., who had purchased the whole or greater part from the government at a very small price." Unlike the documentary materials in the pseudofactual novel, which testify to the text's authenticity but not necessarily to its truth, these documentary materials establish the verifiability of the text's generalized portraiture of customs and historical movements. The text must present a valid analogy to history, these notes imply, if the author has taken such pains to research his subject. (Indeed, one might note, even the typographical presence of the notes serves to anchor the text in an authenticated reality. The very act of leaving the story and moving one's eyes to the small print at the bottom of the page has the effect of invoking an extratextual source of information.)

Cooper's novels, which Lukács also praises as exemplars of classical historical fiction, adopt a comparable strategy in their project of narrating and explaining the early years of the Republic. In *The Spy: A Tale of the Neutral Ground*, for example, the battle over war-torn Westchester County projects in microcosm the collision of opposed historical forces. Even the rather insipid lovers, Dunwoodie and Frances, take on the status of historical actors, in that the barriers to their romantic fulfillment are thrown up by the contention of rebels and loyalists. And the omnipresent figure of the double agent, Harvey Birch, points to the shifting nature of political allegiances: his interactions with both camps give full play to the attractiveness of the British cause (Cooper is something of an Anglophile) at the same time that they mobilize the reader's sympathies on the side of the rebels. In this context, the text's documentary apparatus serves an important validating function. Cooper's preface, which informs us that the novel is based on a story he was told about the experiences of an actual double agent during the Revolutionary War, parades the narrative's fictionality and openly asserts the generalization encoded in the text: "[My] theme," he declares, "is patriotism," and "the hero of the anecdote just related is the best illustration of this subject."[8] Moreover, the mysterious figure who turns out to be George Washington corroborates the nationalistic theme. "That Providence destines this country for some great and glorious fate I must believe," beams Washington, "while I witness the patriotism that pervades the bosoms of her lowest citizens." The novel ends, indeed, with a "document" that directly links the world-historical hero to the fate of Harvey Birch, who, having died fighting for his country once again in the War of 1812, is found clutching to his bosom a paper that reads: "Circumstances of political importance, which involve the lives and fortunes of many, have hitherto kept secret what this paper now reveals. Harvey Birch has for years been a faithful and unrequited servant of his country. Though man does not, may God reward him for his conduct!"

The Spy most clearly shows Cooper as a self-consciously historical novelist.[9] It bears noting, however, that even the Leatherstocking novels, which do not portray world-historical heroes, introduce documentary materials in strategically similar ways. In the largely autobiographical *The Pioneers*, for example, Cooper includes a set of corroborative statements that reverse the role assigned to documentation in the pseudofactual novel. The preface, informing us that the novel replicates many personalities from the Cooperstown of Cooper's youth, makes the peculiar claim that generalization is superior to precise historicity. In response to inquires about "how much of [the novel's] contents is literal fact, and how much is intended to represent a general picture, . . . the author is very sensible that, had he confined himself to the latter, *always the most effective, as it is the most valuable mode of conveying knowledge of this sort*, he would have made a far better book" (italics added). He later adds, "The incidents of this tale are purely a fiction."[10] The role of the corroborative preface, it now seems, is to reclaim the authorial role that was previously disavowed;

---

[8]James Fenimore Cooper, *The Spy: A Tale of the Neutral Ground* (1821; New York: Putnam's, n.d.), vi. The passages quoted below appear on pp. 421 and 429–30.

[9]For a thorough discussion of Cooper's strategy as a historical novelist, see "Cooper: The Range of the American Historical Novel," in Harry B. Henderson III, *Versions of the Past: The Historical Imagination in American Fiction* (New York: Oxford University Press, 1974), 50–90.

[10]Cooper, *The Pioneers; or, The Sources of the Susquehanna: A Descriptive Tale* (1823; New York: Putnam's, n.d.), ii.

we have come a long way from Mme d'Aulnoy's denial that she composes "novel . . . or story." All the same, the text contains a number of footnotes that verify the fiction's grounding in personal experience. Thus, describing the bass-seining episode, Cooper remarks, "Of all the fish the writer has ever tasted, he thinks the one in question the best"; recounting Judge Temple's munificence to the pioneering poor (presumably a fictive rendition of the activities of Cooper's own father, William Cooper), the author assures us that "all this was literally true." The unmediated assertion of something "literally true" nestles in the bosom of a narrative that is "purely a fiction," providing personal corroboration that a text that does "represent a general picture" does indeed tell the truth.

In some ways, then, the above analysis of the uses of documentation in Scott and Cooper confirms and even extends Lukács's discussion of the representational strategy of the realistic historical novel. But my analysis also challenges Lukács's contention that, by virtue of its objectivist epistemology, the realistic historical novel is therefore privileged to portray from a neutral standpoint "all the humanly and socially essential determinants . . . present on their highest level of development." According to Lukács, writers like Scott and Cooper could transcend the limitations of their class perspectives and present objectively valid portrayals of historical process because of their strategic location in that process. In the wake of the French Revolution, but before the proletarian upheavals of 1848, the bourgeoisie were still a residually progressive class, engaged in the process of consolidating their victory over feudalism. Their interest was not yet inalterably opposed to that of the masses with whom they had marched under the banner of liberty, equality, and fraternity; they could, therefore, pose themselves as exemplars of universal humanity. As a result of the presumably nonantagonistic contradiction shaping the historical dialectic, writers of this period could view the emergence of national destiny from a nonpartisan position: for Lukács, realism is the fruit of the privileged ideological stance made possible by the political configuration of pre-1848 Europe. The early nineteenth-century historical novel is therefore beyond ideology. Lukács stipulated, we will recall, that the plot of the historical novel constitutes a *"neutral ground . . .* upon which the extreme opposing social forces can be brought into a human relationship with each other" (italics added). The echo of Cooper's subtitle to *The Spy* is not entirely accidental: both writer and critic see historical process as affording a position of political—and epistemological—objectivism.

But a close scrutiny of both literary and political modes of representation in this era produces, I believe, quite a different conclusion: the works of Scott and Cooper are saturated with ideology, at no time more so than when they seem to be engaging in an unmediated transposition of historical realities into fiction. The choice of an Edward Waverley or a Harvey Birch as typical hero, to begin with, hardly affords the author an empyrean view of political conflict. Waverley functions as a prescriptive rather than a neutral norm; Scott proffers a generic contract that requires the endorsement of a number of ideological assumptions, foremost among which is the notion that an Englishman, by virtue of his accession to the "steadily and rapidly progressive . . . change" through which the Highlanders were defeated, is a better index to historical process than is a member of the race that "has now almost entirely vanished from the land." Were Fergus Mac-Ivor presented as the typical hero, and the plot's resolution centered around his tragic fate, *Waverley* would bear a very different relation to the raw materials constituting its referent.[11] Similarly, Cooper's delegation of typical status to Harvey Birch carries a number of implications. Birch's position as a figure marginal to the very society he is trying to liberate suggests that the revolutionary process that relies upon the participation of such outsiders need not incorporate them into its postrevolutionary resolution. Birch remains, fortunately, celibate, requiring no marital denouement to his personal destiny; he therefore is freed from any permanent association with lower-class characters speaking crude English, yet also kept from too close a contact with the Whartons and Dunwoodies who inherit the reins of power. Birch's glad acceptance of Washington's fa-

[11]In arguing that Scott commits himself to a certain view of progress by positing Waverley as the typical hero, I am not claiming that Scott's portrayal of the supersession of the Highlanders is free of ambivalence. As Avrom Fleishman has noted, Scott absorbed from Scottish speculative history—particularly Adam Ferguson's *Essay on the History of Civil Society* (1767) and the teachings of Dugald Stuart—a highly contradictory view of the relation of tradition to progress in historical development. Fleishman declares, "One of the reasons . . . the historical novel begins with Scott is that the tension between tradition and modernity first achieved its definitive form in Scotland." The Scottish speculative historians were, Fleishman maintains, "scientific Whigs" who viewed the course of Scottish history as a combination of tragedy, melodrama, and above all historical necessity (*The English Historical Novel: Walter Scott to Virginia Woolf* [Baltimore: Johns Hopkins University Press, 1971], 38, 46).

vor, moreover, obscures the fact that he does not belong to the class that will (if Washington has anything to say about it) be enfranchised after the war is over.

In short, the heroes of *Waverley* and *The Spy* project anything but a neutral typicality signaling essential historical truths. Rather, typicality becomes coterminous with synecdoche: the bourgeois protagonist "stands for" the dynamic totality of society in a way that sloughs over very real historical contradictions among very real social groups. Enclosing social conflicts within the apparently benign framework of a representative fictional microcosm, the classical historical novel articulates the rationale of representative government, which masks the reality of class conflict and social inequality by positing a pluralistic social order in which all antagonisms are presumably voiced, considered, and then reconciled.

The politically synecdochic status of the classical historical novel's protagonist is reinforced by the ways in which the text characteristically marshals its documentary apparatus. The world-historical hero, pace Lukács, does not simply "grow out of the being of the age"; rather, he corroborates a myth of nationalistic progress that is quintessentially class-bound. Scott's Pretender illustrates the folly of monarchical rebellion that would turn back the clock of history; he prepares the reader for the text's endorsement of Waverly's accession to English hegemony, even as he allows full play to the attractiveness of the Highland cause. Cooper's Washington acknowledges the energy and integrity of the anonymous Harvey Birches who guarantee the success of the Revolution, even as he lays the basis for their later marginalization. The historical novel gives play to the historical dialectic, to be sure, but this historical dialectic is mediated by the ideological contradictions internal to each writer, and it is synthesized in accordance with the dominant aspect of that ideological contradiction. The world-historical hero characteristically enters the plot in its final phases, but this does not therefore imply (or exclusively imply) the author's fascination with the purposive agency of the rank and file makers of history. The maneuver also glosses over the covert nature of bourgeois rule, which equates class interest with popular nationalism. Moreover, the use of prefaces and footnotes in classical historical novels can be seen as further evidence of the text's embeddedness in various political premises. When Scott tells us that it was only after 1745 that "fair" prices could be obtained for the chieftans' forfeited lands by the creditors of the York Building Co., he is endorsing a distinctly partisan view of equity. When Cooper reassures us that the account of Judge Temple's kindness to his tenants is "literally true," he espouses a landholder's view on class relations in the United States at the end of the eighteenth century: these were, after all, also the years of Shay's Rebellion.[12]

Lukács's theory of realism thus offers only a partial account of the referential activities of the classical historical novel. Lukács quite correctly points to the historical circumstances that gave historical novelists the confidence to position themselves above and outside the historical process they described, but he gives far too much credence to their posture of neutrality.[13] The classical historical novelist's implicit claim to stand above ideology is itself an ideological position, one positing the equivalence of essence and phenomenon, cognition and perception. The text's representation of its referent is, quite simply, offered as equivalent to the referent itself; its configuration proposes itself as not only analogous but in fact homologous with that of historical actuality, and the empirical corroboration it provides is tautological.[14] In the shift from pseudofactual to historical modes of documentary mimesis, ideological abstraction has been transferred from the represented subject to the representing author. Where the pseudofactual novel reinforced a disjunction between the asserting

[12]Shari Benstock, in an analysis of the rhetorical function of footnotes in fiction, argues that "the notational system implies an extrareferentiality that does not exist in fiction (where all is fiction, even the notes), so that the notes can only extend the authority of the text by seeming to enlarge the context in which the fiction takes place" ("At the Margin of Discourse: Footnotes in the Fictional Text," *PMLA*, 98 [March 1983]: 219–20). Benstock's remark may well be applicable to such writers as Fielding, Joyce, and Sterne, but it offers an inaccurate account of works residing squarely in the realistic tradition—which, when they use footnotes, insistently refer beyond the text to corroborate the explanatory paradigm of the text.

[13]In a chapter of my "The Politics of Criticism: Historical Contexts of Marxist Literary Theory" (forthcoming), I explore the connection between Lukács's theory of realism, his advocacy of nationalism, and the politics of the United Front against Fascism endorsed by the Third International in 1935.

[14]By the distinction between "analogy" and "homology" in relation to the problem of fictional reference, I mean that the former implies a correspondence in function, while the latter implies a correspondence in structure, origin, and development as well as function. Homology involves a contractual agreement that the world of the novel replicates its referent in a totalizing way: every particular is drawn into a configuration that purports to replicate reality diachronically as well as synchronically. For more on the distinction between analogy and homology, see Raymond Williams, *Marxism and Literature* (Oxford: Oxford University Press, 1977), 104–6.

speaker and the disavowing author, the historical novel proposes a transcendental standpoint outside the text from which the text's competing ideological voices can be juxtaposed and then reconciled. As Heidegger commented of the epistemological transition from Descartes to Kant, "'I think' becomes 'I bind together.'"[15] To read a classical historical novel is to be invited to participate in a generic contract with an authorial presence that "binds together" the text, empyrean in its pretensions to autonomy but in fact implicated in every shade of characterization and turn of plot.

From Typicality to Anachronism: The Historical Novel as Genre

Scott's influence on mimetic practice was enormous, and by mid-century the historical novel was established as a genre in its own right. Leslie Stephen voiced a prevalent nineteenth-century fascination with historicism when he praised Scott for his ability to "describe no character without assigning to it its place in the social organism which has been growing up since the earliest dawn of history."[16] Stephen's echo of Darwin's phrase "the earliest dawn of history" (from the conclusion to *On the Origin of Species*) is by no means accidental, even if it was perhaps unintentional. Where the model of mechanistic atomism provides a metaphor for the informing epistemological assumptions of the pseudofactual novel, the model of biological organism articulates those of the historical novel.

But Scott's legacy, as we have seen, was contradictory—capable of a totalizing, dialectical synthesis of the particular and the universal, but prone to an empiricist overdetermination that simply renders self-evident the relation between fact and generalization, text and referent. Both tendencies are visible in the novels of Scott's descendants. In some novels, the interest in the historical genesis of the "social organism" involved the reader in a sophisticated and self-critical mi-

---

[15]Quoted in J. M. Bernstein, *The Philosophy of the Novel: Lukács, Marxism, and the Dialectics of Form* (Brighton: Harvester, 1984), 181.

[16]Leslie Stephen, "Sir Walter Scott," in *Hours in a Library* (1871; London, 1907), 1:221. The point that Stephen echoed Darwin was first made by John Henry Raleigh, "What Scott Meant to the Victorians," in *Time, Place, and Idea: Essays on the Novel* (Carbondale: Southern Illinois University Press, 1968), 119.

metic contract. The documentary apparatus accompanying such works as *Henry Esmond* and *War and Peace*, for example, expresses a complex awareness of history as both process and discourse; the tautological footnote is abandoned, world-historical figures are treated with a skeptical irony, and the authorial preface calls attention to the ideological perspective that shapes the text's totalizing portraiture of past events. Even in the early decades of the nineteenth century, however, Scott's model had prompted some novelists (for example, W. H. Ainsworth and G. P. R. James) in the direction of a florid costumery that left out the material premises of Scott's representation of past events. Increasingly, then, historical novels substituted psychological anachronism or superfluous detail for historically concrete specificity, and the Hegelian "identical subject-object of history" became either the transcendental subject of the antiquarian historical novel or the nonpurposive object of the naturalistic novel. The use of documentary materials reflects this shift in consciousness: data that would presumably anchor the text in an extratextual reality becomes absorbed into the fictional representation, with the result that the analogous configuration, while more densely concretized than ever, loses the possibility of formulating a critical relation to its referent.

Much of the self-critical historicism of *Henry Esmond* and *War and Peace* derives from the conjunction of authorial commentary with the mimetic representation of historical events. Where Scott and Cooper tend to offer their plots as self-propelling mechanisms and to present the authorial preface as a discourse external to the plot, Thackeray and Tolstoy, as conscious authorial presences, explicitly theorize the views of historical process that their narratives imply. Thus the very marginality of the world-historical hero becomes a thematic proposition. In *War and Peace*, for example, Kutuzov and Napoleon continue to fulfill the ancillary function described by Lukács; clearly it is the Rostovs and Betzukovs who embody the dynamis of historical process. But, in his two epilogues to *War and Peace*, Tolstoy explicitly discusses the theory of history that shapes his portraiture of the two generals. Confronting the "specialist historians," the "universal historians," and the "historians of culture," Tolstoy declares the inadequacy of any philosophy of history that locates the springs of historical causality in the subjective wills of "heroes and rulers": "So long as histories are written of separate individuals, whether Caesars, Alexanders, Luthers, or Voltaires, and not the histories of all, absolutely *all* those who take part in an event, it is quite impossible to describe the movement of humanity without the conception of a force compelling men to direct their activity toward a certain end."[17] In depicting the divergent fates of Napoleon and Kutuzov, Tolstoy refutes the fervid nationalism that envisions the leader as a repository of the "collective will of the people": Kutuzov succeeds where Napoleon fails precisely because he understands his own subsidiary role in the historical process. Authorial commentary thus asserts the accuracy of its mimetic representation (*"wherever in my novel historical persons speak or act, I have invented nothing, but have used historical material of which I have accumulated a whole library during my work"*), at the same time that it acknowledges the text itself to be the product of a theory of history that takes issue with other theories of history. Documentation validates not by effacing the relation between evidence and generalization but by arguing for the text's particular construction of that relation.

Henry Esmond, while less expressive of a formulated theory of historical process than *War and Peace*, also comments explicitly on its lampoon of the Great Man theory of history. "Why shall History go on kneeling to the end of time?" Thackeray wonders in the opening chapter. "I am for having her rise up off her knees, and take a natural posture: not to be for ever performing cringes and congees like a court chamberlain, and shuffling backwards out of doors in the presence of a sovereign. In a word, I would have History familiar rather than heroic."[18] Marlborough, Addison, and Swift are thus memorable in *Henry Esmond* mainly for their pettiness, while the Pretender is enshrined in historical absurdity for his lustful "dangling after Trix"—a propensity that, in Thackeray's version of historical affairs, loses him the throne. Indeed, Thackeray is, of all the nineteenth-century historical novelists, perhaps the most audacious in his tampering with the historical record; he enacts a daring extension of Herbert Butterfield's suggestion that "sometimes a wrench has to be given to history in order to subdue it to the demands of the novel."[19] Scott's Pretender is at least plausibly a participant in the rebellion that

---

[17]Leo Tolstoy, *War and Peace* (1865–69), trans. Louise Mande and Aylmer Mande (New York: Simon & Schuster, 1947), 1321. The passage quoted below appears on pp. 1358–59.

[18]William Makepeace Thackeray, *The History of Henry Esmond, Esq.* (1852; New York: Holt, Rinehart & Winston, 1962), 2. The statement quoted below is from p. 487.

[19]Herbert Butterfield, *The Historical Novel: An Essay* (Cambridge: Cambridge University Press, 1924), 32.

Waverly joins; Thackeray's entirely flouts the canons of historical probability. The text's pseudomemoiristic form, moreover, compounds its satire upon the authority of received historical discourse. Presenting itself as the memoir of Henry Esmond, "written by himself," the novel is introduced by a preface supposedly composed by Esmond's daughter Rachel in 1778; as Thackeray admits in the dedication preceding this preface, the text "copies the manners and language of Queen Anne's time."[20] While *Henry Esmond* operates squarely within the conventions of realism—it is written in the third person and possesses little of the sense of the real characterizing fictions in "Queen Anne's time"—the effect of this documentary overdetermination is to direct attention to the question of narrative authority. The text offers a generalized interpretation of a past epoch without posing that interpretation as a neutral replication of that epoch; the author's privileged epistemological stance proposes totality, but not tautology.

Tolstoy's and Thackeray's awareness of history as both a series of past events and a mode of inquiry proved the exception rather than the rule, however; most nineteenth-century historical novels adopted a relatively unproblematic and naturalized formulation of the relation between text and referent. In *Barnaby Rudge*, for example, Dickens proposed an analogy between his microcosmic fictional world and that in which the actual Gordon riots occurred. Thus Gabriel Varden exemplifies the stable and nonalienated craftsman; Sim Tappertit, the borderline lumpenproletarian; the older Chester, the decadent gentility; the idiot Barnaby, all the nameless victims of aristocratic brutality and social disorder. The George Gordon who enters the book is a thoroughly despicable creature. Employing a bolder satiric pen than Scott or Cooper, Dickens stresses the tragic social consequences of the pride and greed of the declining aristocracy. But, even in its partiality toward the popular forces typified by Varden, *Barnaby Rudge* effects an ideological resolution fully assimilable to bourgeois liberalism. The enormity of Gordon's historical crimes is muted by Dickens's attribution of the novel's key historical acts to Gordon's fictitious accomplice George Gashford, who is depicted as manipulating the anti-Papist riots—and Gordon himself—in order to satisfy his own hunger for power. The marginalization of the ac-

---

[20]Thackeray, xxxv.

tual historical figure thus lessens the burden of historical blame: documentation mutes the force of historical assertion at the same time that it anchors the text in a known public actuality. Dickens thus successfully encompasses social contradictions within the framework of a petty bourgeois meliorism. Joe Willett marries Dolly Varden, receives from the king a silver snuff box as a reward for his role in containing the riots, and assumes proprietorship of the Maypole Inn, which, nodding in its sleep at the end as at the start of the narrative, symbolizes the accommodation of England's most venerable institutions to the incursions of struggle and change.

In one historical novel after another, this paradigm repeats itself. Characters constitute a microcosmic portrayal of representative social types; they experience complications and conflicts that embody important tendencies in historical development; one or more world-historical figures enters the fictive world, lending an aura of extra-textual validation to the text's generalizations and judgments; the conclusion reaffirms the legitimacy of a norm that transforms social and political conflict into moral debate. When the novel addresses domestic crises, as in *Barnaby Rudge*, the depiction of warring historical forces takes on real urgency, for the author must acknowledge the full dimension of the conflict that precedes resolution and synthesis. Heightened ideological contradiction mediates an intensification of social contradiction in the referent. In *The Pioneers* and *Waverley*, the authorial conscience reluctantly accedes—but accedes nonetheless —to the defeat of the Highlanders or the extermination of the Indians; in *Barnaby Rudge*, it can less readily come to terms with the subordination of a proletarian class that can hardly be seen as a vanishing race. Nonetheless, in all these novels the informing ideological perspective is that of an emergent and then consolidated liberalism, which claims to encapsule universal human aspirations and needs in the synecdochic figure of the bourgeois hero. The text's documentary apparatus, presumably providing from extratextual sources an empirical validation for the generalizations the fiction implies, lapses into a positivist invocation of factuality that legitimates the text's informing assumptions.

The tendency toward this sort of empiricist rubber-stamping became especially pronounced in the later part of the century, when the historical novel came to assume stature as a quasi-official genre in its own right. An early instance of this development is contained in

George Eliot's *Romola*, which serves as a kind of bridge between fictions deriving from the tradition of Scott and later antiquarian fictions abandoning the classical historical novelist's aspiration to portray historical processes as what Lukács called "the concrete precondition of the present."[21] In *Romola*, Eliot grapples with the critical shifts in consciousness that accompany a transitional historial moment; the decaying marriage of Romola and Tito illustrates the deeply divisive nature of the debate over the religious and secular basis of ethics, a debate articulating the contradictory tendencies toward medieval asceticism and Renaissance individualism in fifteenth-century Florence. Eliot's morbid Savonarola effectively shapes the terms of this debate, for his initial appeal to Romola's moral nature is superseded by her—and the reader's—realization of the social cost that his fanaticism entails.

Despite its careful reconstruction of fifteenth-century backdrops and debates, however, *Romola's* historicity is in many ways superficial. As Eliot comments in the introductory "Proem," the "eternal marriage of love and duty" is her principal theme; "We still resemble the men of the past more than we differ from them,"[22] she declares. As more than one critic has noted, there is something anachronistic about Eliot's protagonist: despite her situation in a carefully etched environment, her consciousness is peculiarly modern, more akin to that of Browning's Victorianized Renaissance people than to a plausible fifteenth-century psychology.[23] It is therefore significant that, in formulating her protagonist's final endorsement of a Comtian "religion of humanity," Eliot finds it necessary to leave behind the historical world of Florence, transporting Romola to a village suffering from the plague, where the problems of humanity appear sub specie aeternitatis and Savoronola is suddenly strangely irrelevant. Noting that these closing episodes were "by deliberate forecast adopted as romantic and symbolical elements," Eliot was apparently aware that the analogous configuration constructed around Romola's Florentine ca-

---

[21]Lukács, *The Historical Novel*, 21.

[22]George Eliot, *Romola* (1863; London: Oxford University Press, 1971), 2, 9.

[23]See, for example, Fleishman, 124, and Andrew Sanders, *The Victorian Historical Novel, 1840–1880* (London: Macmillan, 1968), 168–96. Sanders declares, "[Eliot] is not concerned to show how the past has moulded the present, but that history can be alive to us, through our awakened awareness of the 'internal conditions' of the men of the past." She plants "a nineteenth-century seed in a fifteenth-century soul" (174, 176–177). The statement by Eliot that I quote below appears in Sanders, 191.

reer could not bear the weight of the text's moral resolution; hence the critical determination of her fate apart from historical process. The transcendental subjectivity that, in the classical historical novel, is restricted to the author's vantage point, now becomes a property of the protagonist. Despite her dense contextualization, Romola is an essentially private being, and her discovery of moral order constitutes a peculiarly modern "separate peace."

The departure from historical imagination implied in the conclusion to *Romola* becomes a headlong retreat from the historical process in most later nineteenth-century historical fiction. In the last decades of the century, the historical novel dons a flamboyant costumery. While it appears still committed to the concrete representation of a past actuality, its conception of historical development has become increasingly abstract. In Lew. Wallace's *Ben Hur: A Tale of the Christ* and Gustave Flaubert's *Salammbô*, for example, there is little attempt to present character and event as issuing from the contradictions of the historical dialectic; history is no longer the "concrete precondition of the present," but a remote and exotic ground for the incarnation of religious truths and timeless human passions. The text's referential relation to historical actuality is thus undergirded by what might be termed a "pseudoempiricism": the corroborative "facts" make no pretense to verifiable factuality. *Ben Hur* bristles with photographs of the modern Holy Land, but these only enhance the reader's sense of the text's separation from the referent. A nineteenth-century Bedouin standing by a camel in front of a ruined Crusader castle provides a curious sort of corroboration for the text's propositional claim that Jesus Christ actually walked the earth and performed miracles. In *Salammbô*, Flaubert undertakes a similarly "archaeological" (the phrase is Sainte-Beuve's)[24] representation of the past. Flaubert repudiates the one ancient source detailing the Punic war upon which the novel is based: "Hanno's *Periplus* is hateful to me," he declared; it is "a subject for [dissertation] theses." Flaubert thus engages in a reconstruction of past events that is patently invented from beginning to end. Replying to Sainte-Beuve's complaint that *Salammbô* was too "fantastical," Flaubert remarked that his "empirical" reconstruction

[24]Quoted in Gustave Flaubert, *Salammbô* (1862), trans. J. S. Chartres (London: J. M. Dent, 1931), 305. Flaubert's responses appear on pp. 311–19. The quotation from Flaubert appears on p. 312.

of physical details was as accurate as possible. Hanno's account was, however, too close to the events it described to provide an objective basis for historical reconstruction. Apparently the novelist's transcendental presence is best able to tell the truth about the Punic wars if it frees itself entirely from the trammels of documentary testimony.

Flaubert's mode of historical reconstruction mystifies the past and closes it off from the present. Usually such antiquarianism does not imply a particular political agenda. The plantation novels of Thomas Nelson Page and Thomas Dixon, however, exemplify one kind of particularly distasteful polemic that could be veiled in historical costumery. Portraying the defeat of Reconstruction as the triumph of those who, Page tells us in his preface, "reconquered their section and preserved the civilization of the Anglo-Saxon,"[25] Page sets his *Red Rock* in a peculiarly mythic environment, "somewhere in that vague region partly in one of the old Southern States and partly in the yet vaguer land of Memory"—a realm where "sincerity dwells and the heart still rules—the realm of old-time courtesy and high breeding." In *Red Rock*, nostalgia constitutes an apology for slavery. The documentary preface makes no pretension to anchor the text in a continuing historical dialectic but instead asserts the superiority of a vanished past. In the preface to *The Clansman*, which makes a more decisive claim to historicity (the abolitionist father of the pure white heroine is a veiled representation of Thaddeus Stevens), Dixon testifies to the veracity of his tale: "The men who enact the drama of fierce revenge into which I have woven a double love-story are historical figures," he declares. "I have merely changed their names without taking a liberty with any essential historic fact."[26] He follows this empiricist claim with a peculiar sort of corroborative argument:

> In the darkest hour of the life of the South, when her wounded people lay helpless amid rags and ashes under the beak and talon of the vulture, suddenly from the mist of the mountains appeared a white cloud the size of a man's hand. It grew until its mantle of mystery unfolded the stricken earth and sky. An "Invisible Empire" had risen from the field of Death and challenged the Visible to mortal combat.

[25]Thomas Nelson Page, *Red Rock: A Chronicle of Reconstruction*, in *The Works of Thomas Nelson Page* (New York: Scribner's, 1908), 4:vii, ix, xi.

[26]Thomas Dixon, *The Clansman: An Historical Romance of the Ku Klux Klan* (New York: Doubleday, Page, 1905), v–vi.

When references to rags and ashes, beaks and talons, and white clouds from the realm of the Invisible authenticate a text's claim to historicity, we clearly have come some distance from the mode of the classical historical novel. Where Scott used corroborative detail to reinforce the explanatory claims of his text, Page and Dixon repudiate even the pretense of empiricism. Where Scott at least attempted to delineate the contradictory social and political forces informing his referent, Page and Dixon confine their representations of the South to selected sets of characters whose claims to typicality rest on a patently spurious racial stereotypicality.[27] *Waverley* signals the discursive concerns of a progressive liberalism that envisions in pluralism a genuine resolution to contradiction. *Red Rock* and *The Clansman*, by contrast, treat historical dialectic as coterminous with racial destiny. The "Invisible Empire" of the "vanished race" becomes the locus of all value, and the "visible" realm of an emergent historical race is assaulted with all the weapons that pseudoempiricism can muster.

If some novelists in the late nineteenth century directed their attention to a mythical past, others—ordinarily of a much more progressive political inclination—postponed the assignation of historical significance to a distant future. The late nineteenth century witnessed a revival of utopian novels, in which authors came to terms with the harsh realities of their time by constructing ideal worlds in which these difficulties had been overcome. For example, Edward Bellamy, in *Looking Backward: 2000–1887*, reacted to the strikes and financial panics of his day not by exploring their roots in the configuration of past class struggle but by positing a world in which such occurrences would be no longer conceivable. Indeed, in one sense Bellamy achieved an apotheosis of the liberal conception of progress, since his utopia is attained without the loss of a drop of blood, through the exercise of reason and parliamentary democracy. Yet the labor process—the battleground of the old society—is hidden from view in the new society, and commodities magically pop out of tubes from central warehouses. Moreover, the exemplary citizens of the future, the Leete family, are distinctly anachronistic projections, since their undisturbed, middle-class gentility negates the transformation of human personality that would accompany any genuine transformation

---

[27]For more on the relation of racism to typicality and stereotypicality, see below, Chapter 8.

of the social relations of production. For all its socialist proclivities, *Looking Backward* projects a fundamental fear of the actual nature of historical change; its exhaustive descriptions of industrial armies and communal kitchens lack grounding in a commensurate grasp of the dynamics of class conflict. Indeed, Bellamy closely resembles the "Socialistic bourgeois" whom Marx and Engels ridiculed in *The Communist Manifesto*—that is, those reformers who "want all the advantages of modern social conditions without the struggles and dangers necessarily resulting therefrom. They desire the existing state of society minus its revolutionary and disintegrating elements. They wish for a bourgeoisie without a proletariat."[28]

Posing itself as an exemplary fiction written for the enlightenment of citizens of the twenty-first century, *Looking Backward* occupies a peculiar relation to the tradition of the documentary novel. Knowing that his readers cannot possess an experience to which the text can correspond by analogy, Bellamy somewhat playfully posits this readership in the future. Presenting his text as Julian West's autobiographical reminiscence, Bellamy remarks in an "author's" preface:

> Living as we do in the closing year of the twentieth century, enjoying the blessings of a social order at once so simple and logical that it seems but the triumph of common sense, it is no doubt difficult for those whose studies have not been largely historical to realize that the present organization of society is, in its completeness, less than a century old. The object of this volume is to assist persons who, while desiring to gain a more definitive idea of the social contrasts between the nineteenth and twentieth centuries, are daunted by the formal aspect of the histories which treat the subject.[29]

This strategem circumvents but cannot finally avoid the question of historical reference. Bellamy carefully avoids reference to events in the class struggle of the 1880s that would locate his utopia in a continuing historical dialectic; the novel's reconcretization of its referent eschews any documentary invocation of extratextual actualities of Bellamy's own time.[30]

[28]Marx and Engels, "Manifesto of the Communist Party," in *The Marx-Engels Reader*, 2d ed., ed. Robert C. Tucker (New York: Norton, 1978), 496.

[29]Edward Bellamy, *Looking Backward, 2000–1887* (1888; New York: New American Library, 1960), xxi.

[30]I do not mean to imply that all the time-traveling novels of the 1880s and 1890s—utopian or otherwise—were as fetishistic and idealist as *Looking Backward*. Mark Twain's *A*

The Naturalistic Novel

There is a peculiar paucity of documentary references to actual historical persons and events in the historical novel of the late nineteenth century. Curiously enough, this sort of nonspecific referentiality is also a distinctive feature of the exhaustive reportage of the naturalistic novel. At first, this may seem an anomalous claim, since the naturalistic novel, with its passion for encyclopedic portraiture, would seem to exemplify the documentary novel in its purest form. If, however, we take "documentary" as denoting a specified invocation of data known to exist in an extratextual reality, we see that the naturalistic novel in fact participates in the same reluctance to anchor fiction in a known actuality that characterizes contemporaneous works of historical fiction.

Edmond de Goncourt made a revealing statement of purpose in his preface to *Les frères Zemganno.* "The novel," he advocated, should be "made with documents narrated or selected from nature, just as history is based on written documents."[31] Working-class people, he continued, "can be captured only through an immense storing up of observation, by innumerable notes taken through a lorgnette, by the amassment of a collection of *human documents,* like those heaps of pocket sketches which, assembled at a painter's death, represent his life-time of work." There is a curious logic here. First, the writer asserts that fiction must possess a "documentary" base; he is supremely conscious of his sociological mission. But Goncourt does not specify exactly what the naturalistic novelist's "documents" actually are, nor how these are to be differentiated from the "written documents" on which the historian relies. And yet these "human documents" consist of "an immense storing up of observations, by innumerable *notes*" (italics added). How can these "documents" be both unwritten and written? The answer is, of course, that his "documents" are written

---

Connecticut Yankee in King Arthur's Court (1889) undertakes a fairly earthy and concrete examination of the theme of historical progress, and William Morris's *News from Nowhere* (1891) does not shy away from representing the role of class struggle in producing "visionary" change. Nonetheless, even these novels evade a direct confrontation with the historicity of the present and the recent past: historical process is, significantly, displaced to distant centuries.

[31]Edmond de Goncourt, Preface to *Les frères Zemganno* (1879), reprinted in George Becker, ed., *Documents in Modern Literary Realism* (Princeton: Princeton University Press, 1963), 245–46.

by the author; they arc not borrowed from the public fund from which historians draw their data. This invocation of an absent authority points to the peculiar nature of the naturalistic novel's empiricist claims. The naturalistic novel purports to replicate and expose social conditions with scientific objectivity, yet it offers no documentary guarantee that the text's mediation between referent and analogous configuration is validated by extratextual realities. The dialectic between evidence and generalization informing the epistemology of the classical historical novel—however tautological this relation may be—has been superseded by a positivist epistemology positing the unmediated *equivalence* of document and fact, extratextual reality and intratextual representation. Despite its frequently radical commitment to demystifying and exposing existing social and economic relations (in the preface to *Germinie Lacerteux*, the Goncourt brothers "ask . . . whether what one calls 'the lower classes' have no right to the novel"),[32] the naturalistic novel is guided by a distinctly conservative epistemology.

Naturalistic novelists thus generally repudiated any kind of testimonial apparatus and offered their texts as authoritative representations. There are no prefaces, postscripts, or footnotes accompanying texts such as *The Pit, Germinal, The Red Badge of Courage, Sister Carrie,* and *The Financier,* even though these texts are grounded in personal experience or careful research and could very easily be anchored in extratextual reality. These texts are intended to represent their referents by analogous configuration, and analogous configuration alone; even within the totalizing framework of fictionality, indeed, they characteristically avoid reference to specific historical events. In *The Red Badge of Courage,* for example, Crane omits all mention of the actual Battle of Chancellorsville, on which his narration is based. His intent is to reveal the biological roots of human behavior, and Henry Fleming's heroic aspirations have no historical specificity. They reenact, indeed, the futile attempt of human consciousness to escape from the trap of biological instinct (poor Henry Fleming is, all within one page, a "jaded horse," a "rabbit," and a "proverbial chicken")[33] from the time of the ancient "Greek-like

[32]Edmond de Goncourt and Julius de Goncourt, quoted in Alan Swingewood, *The Novel and Revolution* (London: Macmillan, 1975), 59.
[33]Stephen Crane, *The Red Badge of Courage,* in *Great Short Works of Stephen Crane* (1895; New York: Harper & Row, 1965), 39–40.

struggle" to the present. In *Germinal*, Zola even goes so far as to distort nineteenth-century political developments in order to enhance his representation of the emergence of the revolutionary proletariat as a Darwinian necessity. Projecting back into class struggles of the 1860s a political battle between anarchism, evolutionary socialism, and Marxist revolutionism that acquired significance only in the 1880s, Zola attained sociological exactitude only at the expense of historical anachronism.[34] For all its apocalyptic force, then, there is a strangely timeless quality in Zola's closing prophecy: "Men were springing forth, a black avenging army, germinating slowly in the furrows, growing towards the harvests of the next century, and this generation would soon overturn the earth."[35] Class struggle is, it seems, a natural force, having little to do with the political course that the proletariat will choose to follow. In *The Financier*, Dreiser omits all reference to the actual Charles Yerkes, on whose career Dreiser based his saga of Frank Cowperwood. Even though, as with the Gillette case in *An American Tragedy*, whole pages of the Yerkes trial transcript have been incorporated into the narration, these materials are presented as part of the analogous configuration; the text provides the reader with no signal that its reconcretized materials replicate the particulars of the referent.[36]

The generic contract accompanying the naturalistic novel thus requires the reader to focus on the configuration of the events portrayed, even when the reader may sense that many details of the text also possess an independent referential power of their own. The novel insists upon the pervasiveness of the conditions it represents, and the reader is not permitted to dismiss the story as a retelling of events that may be bizarre or atypical, with no broader social signification. At times, the naturalistic novel's denial of its grounding in particular lives powerfully reinforces its generalized assertions. The protagonist of *Sister Carrie*, for example, is not simply a fictional replication of Dreiser's sister but a wholly plausible character whose fate necessi-

[34]See Richard H. Zakarian, *Zola's "Germinal": A Critical Study of Its Primary Sources* (Geneva: Droz, 1972), 143–44.

[35]Emile Zola, *Germinal* (1885), trans. Havelock Ellis (New York: Knopf, 1925), 472.

[36]For more on Dreiser's incorporation of documentary materials into his novels, see Haskell Block, *Naturalistic Triptych: The Fictive and the Real in Zola, Mann, and Dreiser* (New York: Random House, 1970), 54–77. Even though Dreiser placed about thirty pages of trial testimony and letters in the final portion of *An American Tragedy*, Block argues, "the poignant and arresting portrayal of character in moments of crisis forcefully asserts the dominance of the fictive over the real in Dreiser's art" (67).

tates a trenchant judgment on the economics of sexual morality. The commodity fetishism pervading Carrie's world would reduce her, like the other shop girls, to the status of a thing; Dreiser's totalizing portraiture of her fate and his insistence upon her typicality constitute a compelling critique of capitalist dehumanization. At the same time that it emphasizes the broad application of the truth it tells, however, the naturalistic novel runs the risk of presenting social conflicts as natural phenomena and therefore of denying the historical specificity of its referent. If the Battle of Chancellorsville is all wars, if the struggle between miners and capitalists exemplifies the germination and harvest of a natural necessity that will "overturn the earth," if Cowperwood's career enacts the struggle of the fittest to survive, then what is the possible role of conscious agency in the historical process? Is there a particularity to the configuration of natural necessity at any given historical juncture? The lack of any documentary apparatus presuming to ground the naturalistic novel's assertions in an extratextual reality provides a telling index to the mechanistic determinism guiding the process of mimetic abstraction and reconcretization, for the inclusion of references to public figures and events is a constant reminder to the reader that history is the product of human acts. Even if it simplifies and distorts these acts by positing the embodiment of national destiny in the typical hero, the historical novel treats the intersection of individual praxis with forces beyond individual agency. By contrast, the naturalistic novel's omission of historically specific documentation—particularly in novels representing actual public events and personages, such as *The Red Badge of Courage* and *The Financier*—produces a curiously static effect. The view of history as nature, which departs through the front door of the historical novel in the early decades of the nineteenth century, reenters through the back. In short, the many sociological particulars in the naturalistic novel do not produce historically specific cognition. Rather, they reproduce re-cognition of a reality that, in its underlying laws and epiphenomenal features, is assumed already to be known.

Empiricism and Positivism in Nineteenth-Century Historiography

As it moves through the various phases I have described here, the documentary novel of the nineteenth century mediates the conceptual abstractions of a now-confident empiricism. Speaking of the assumptions guiding the practice of nineteenth-century realism, George Levine remarks, "In requiring the validation of imagination in the visible world, . . . realism posits a tension between imagination . . . and reality. Values are reversed in that the realistic method proceeds to what is not visible—the principles of order and meaning—through the visible; the *a priori* now requires validation."[37] Where the pseudofactual novel only partially signals "principles of order and meaning" through the documentary "validation" of the "visible," the historical novel invokes a contract presupposing the reader's endorsement of an empiricist epistemology. As even the best historical novels move toward costumery in the last decades of the century, however, and the task of documenting quotidian realities passes to the naturalistic novel, the "tension between imagination . . . and reality" collapses. The hypostatization of subject and object mediates the transition of empiricism into positivism: fact becomes coterminous with law, and the transcendental observer is absorbed into the object of perception.

Empiricist assumptions permeated many areas of nineteenth-century intellectual activity, but perhaps few as fully as historiography. If we seek to understand the conceptual abstractions shaping the representational strategy of the historical novel, it is useful to analyze the paradigms guiding contemporaneous historical writing, particularly since historians and novelists of the time were quite explicit about their mutual influences. Macaulay, for instance, acknowledging his indebtedness to Scott, stated that

> the perfect historian is he in whose work the character and spirit of an age is [*sic*] exhibited in miniature. . . . By judicious selection, rejection, and arrangement, he gives to truth those attractions which have been usurped by fiction. Sir Walter Scott, in the same manner, has used those fragments of truth which historians have scornfully thrown behind them in a manner which may well excite their envy. . . . But a truly great historian would reclaim those materials which the novelist has appropriated.[38]

Thackeray modeled *Henry Esmond* on Macaulay's historical narratives and enviously exclaimed, "It takes as much trouble as Macaulays [*sic*]

---

[37]Levine, *The Realistic Imagination*, 18.
[38]Thomas Babington Macaulay, "History," in *Critical and Historical Essays* (Boston: Houghton Mifflin, 1900), 1:236.

History almost and he has the vast advantage of remembering everything he has read, whilst everything but impressions I mean facts dates & so forth slip out of his head."[39] Parkman constructed his frontiersman after the model of Natty Bumppo, who, he remarked, seems "so palpable and real" that "the reader might in some moods of mind . . . easily confound" Cooper's hero with "memories of his own experiences."[40] Carlyle's depiction of the French Revolution as a fiery moral drama was clearly a central subtext for *A Tale of Two Cities*; his writings on the role of "representative men" exercised a widespread influence upon Victorian novelists treating historical themes. Yet Carlyle, in turn, drew much of his inspiration from Scott: "Bygone ages of the world were actually filled by living men, not by protocols, state-papers, controversies, and abstractions of men." Carlyle wrote:

> Not abstractions were they, not diagrams or theorems; but men, in buff or other coats and breeches, with colour in their cheeks, with passions in their stomach, and the idioms, features, and vitalities of very men. [History's] faint hearsays of "teaching by experience" will have to exchange themselves everywhere for direct inspection and embodiment; this, and this only, will be counted experience. . . . It is a great service, . . . this that Scott has done; a great truth laid open by him.[41]

Interestingly, writers in each genre seem to value in their counterparts in the other the ability to clarify the experiential relation between fact and generalization. Macaulay lauds Scott for his seizing upon abandoned "fragments and truth" and calls upon historians to

---

[39]William Makepeace Thackeray, *The Letters and Private Papers of William Makepeace Thackeray*, ed. Gordon N. Ray, 4 vols. (Cambridge: Harvard University Press, 1945–46), 3:38.

[40]Francis Parkman, "James Fenimore Cooper," in *Essays from the North American Review*, ed. Allan Thorndike Rice (New York, 1879), 358–62.

[41]Thomas Carlyle, "Sir Walter Scott," in *Critical and Miscellaneous Essays* (London, 1888), 3:214–15. Carlyle was, however, very much biased toward historical forms of discourse. As he exclaimed in his "Biography," "Consider but the whole class of Fictitious Narrative; from the highest category of epic or dramatic Poetry, in Shakespeare and Homer, down to the lowest of froth Prose, in the Fashionable Novel. What are these but so many mimic Biographies? . . . Let anyone bethink him how impressive the smallest historical *fact* may become, as contrasted with the grandest *fictitious event*; what an invaluable force lies for us in this consideration: The Thing which I here hold imaged in my mind did actually occur; was, in very Truth, an element in the system of the All, whereof I too form a part; had therefore, and has, through all time, an authentic being; is not a dream, but a reality!" (100, 106).

use "selection, rejection, and arrangement" of their materials so as similarly to exhibit "in miniature" the "spirit of an age." Parkman praises Natty Bumppo for seeming "so palpable and real." Carlyle praises Scott for his "direct inspection and embodiment" of experience. Thackeray chides himself for losing track of the "facts dates and so forth" that render Macaulay's "impressions" so valuable. It would seem that novelists and historians are engaged in comparable empiricist enterprises; interestingly, when the novel has staked out its claim as a distinctive mode of cognition, it then can grant its indebtedness to—rather than simply simulate—other kinds of writing.

If Scott is most frequently mentioned as an influence by novelists and historians, Hegel's writings most clearly set forth the assumptions guiding both fictional and historical depictions of historical process in the nineteenth century. Rejecting the dominant eighteenth-century notion that history is governed by either universal "unchanging laws" or "providence," Hegel argued that "World-history . . . represents the rationally necessary course of the World Spirit, the Spirit whose nature is indeed always one and the same, but whose one nature unfolds in the course of the world."[42] The universal thus manifests itself in the succession of distinct particulars: "Every age has conditions of its own and is an individual situation; decisions can and must be made only within, and in accordance with, the age itself." History's actors exercise a freedom generated by the contradictions internal to the historical moment, but they work within the limits of a necessity external to subjective will. The "manifestations of vitality on the part of individuals and peoples in which they seek and satisfy their own purposes are, at the same time, the means and tools of a higher and broader purpose of which they know nothing, which they realize unconsciously." In Hegel's philosophy of history, people are at once the subjects and the objects of historical process. Where the Cartesian ego cogitans contemplated the world from a detached and ahistorical vantage point, the Hegelian subject is dialectically involved with a changing object of contemplation. The Spirit hovers over historical actuality, then, but its "manifestations of vitality" are necessarily concretized in agents who follow its dictates of their own volition.

Hegel's conception of the dialectical emergence of Reason had both

[42]Georg Wilhelm Friedrich Hegel, *Reason in History: A General Introduction to the Philosophy of History* (1822), trans. Robert Hartman (New York: Liberal Arts, 1953), 12. The passages quoted below appear on pp. 8, 31, 39, and 54.

revolutionary and conservative implications. On the one hand, the "inner development of the Idea" generates "momentous collisions between existing, acknowledged duties, laws, and rights and those possibilities which are adverse to this [established] system, violate it, and even destroy its foundations and existence." The state of nature posited by eighteenth-century philosophers was, he declared, "one of those nebulous images which theory produces . . . . Freedom . . . does not *exist* as original and natural. It must first be acquired and won." Attacking the atomistic and static presuppositions of early bourgeois political theory, Hegel posited the necessity of struggle and change. On the other hand, Hegel's conception of the Idea was readily assimilable to the hegemony of the bourgeois world order. Proposing that the stages in the development of Spirit are embodied in "world-historical national Spirits," he argued that national spirit was in turn embodied in the state, which he designated as "the externally existing, genuinely moral life." The recognition that the Spirit must be concretized in order to be Real meant, in practical terms, a very premature concretion in the self-evident—that is, the Prussian state. The motion within essence is, for Hegel, "the moment of becoming and of transition which remains within itself." Describing the tension of the historical dialectic as a feature of pure Spirit, Hegel thus subdued the potentially revolutionary aspects of his dialectic to the political imperatives of bourgeois nationalism. Calling upon philosophers to grant the contradictoriness of natural and social processes, Hegel himself projected a contradiction that locates him squarely within the ideological nexus of emergent capitalism.

Hegel's dialectical conception of history profoundly influenced the narratives of Romantic and Victorian historians. First, they recognized the centrality of conflict to historical process and celebrated the role of the masses. Thus Michelet declared that the history of humankind was the history of "interminable struggle" and stressed the subordinate role of "brilliant, powerful speakers" in the "drama" of history. Probing into the archives of the Commune, he concluded, "The chief actor is the people. In order to find and restore the latter to its proper position, I have been obliged to reduce to their proportions those ambitious puppets whom they have set in motion and in whom till now, people have fancied they saw . . . the secret transactions of history."[43] Carlyle warned that "hunger, nakedness and righteous

[43]Jules Michelet, *History of the French Revolution* (1847–53), trans. Charles Cocks, ed. Gordon Wright (Chicago: University of Chicago Press, 1967), 1:12.

oppression lying heavy on 25 million hearts; this, not the wounded vanities or contradicted philosophies of philosophical advocates, rich shopkeepers, rural noblesse, was the prime mover in the French revolution; as the like will be in all such revolutions, in all countries."[44] Bancroft, in his *History of the United States*, treated Daniel Boone as a prototype of the whole class of woodsmen, rather than as an isolated heroic agent. Motley declared of William of Orange that "the whole nation thought with his thoughts, and spoke with his words."[45]

Second, nineteenth-century historiography often crossed the fine line between the argument that historical process creates its heroes and the proposition that history's powerful are the chosen arbiters of national destiny. Just as Hegel's Idea found its concrete apotheosis in the nationalist design of the Prussian state, Macaulay complacently envisioned the reign of Victoria as the culmination of England's development toward liberty, an interpretation that merely codified the Whig interpretation of history. "The history of our country during the last hundred and sixty years is eminently the history of physical, of moral, and of intellectual improvement," he declared. "No man who is correctly informed as to the past will be disposed to take a morose or desponding view of the present."[46] Motley believed in the "inexorable law of Freedom and Progress";[47] Prescott and Bancroft characterized as politically—even biologically—retrograde all those nations and peoples that presumably retarded the fulfillment of the Teutonic or Anglo-Saxon historical mission. Thus, in *The Conquest of Mexico*, Prescott saw an irresistible march of destiny in Cortez's defeat of the decadent civilization of Montezuma, while Bancroft stated that it was the "strong tendency to individuality and freedom" that allowed the "Teutonic race" to "become the master from the Gulf of Mexico to the poles."[48] Even Carlyle, despite his sympathetic de-

[44]Thomas Carlyle, *The French Revolution: A History* (1837; London: Chapman & Hall, 1888), 3:140.

[45]John Lothrop Motley, *The Rise of the Dutch Republic* (1855), quoted in David Levin, *History as Romantic Art: Bancroft, Prescott, Motley, and Parkman* (New York: Harcourt, Brace & World, 1959), 50.

[46]Macaulay, *The Life and Works of Lord Macaulay* (London: Longmans, Green, 1898), 1:2.

[47]Motley, "Historic Progress as American Democracy," in *John Lothrop Motley: Representative Selections*, ed. C. P. Higby and B. T. Schantz (New York: American Book, 1939), 105.

[48]George Bancroft, *History of the United States from the Discovery of the American Continent* (Boston: Little, Brown, 1862–75), 4:456.

scription of the class oppression that erupted in the French Revolution, eventually favored the side of bourgeois right. As Engels remarked of Carlyle in disgust,

> All real class conflicts, for all their variety in various periods, are finally resolved into the one great, eternal conflict, between those who have fathomed the eternal law of nature and act in keeping with it, the wise and noble, and those who misunderstand it, distort it, and act against it, the fools and the rogues. . . .
>
> The trump card in all [Carlyle's] attacks on bourgeois relations and ideas is the apotheosis of the bourgeois individual.[49]

It should be evident that historical novelists and historians of the nineteenth century founded their narratives on certain common ideological presuppositions. The novel was constructed around the typical hero, whereas the history focused upon the activities of "great men"; yet both held that "representative men" could successfully embody the contradictions of their historical moments. Scott's depiction of Waverley's hesitation between Rose and Flora thus has its analogue in Bancroft's assertion that "the trials of Washington are the dark, solemn ground on which the beautiful work of his country's salvation was embroidered."[50] Moreover, the novelist's treatment of the formal problems of resolution and closure bore a marked resemblance to the historian's narrative rendition of the theme of progress: Scott's marriage of Waverley to Rose has its counterpart in Motley's celebration of the defeat of Spanish decadence by Dutch resourcefulness. The novelist generalized upon the private, whereas the historian personalized the public, but the effect is the same: character emerges as a Hegelian concrete universal, but it also takes on inevitably class-bound qualities. Antagonistic historical forces were not so opposed, it seemed, that they could not be incarnated in the career of a single synecdochic individual, and the unfolding of national destiny superseded the conflict of opposed classes. As David Levin shrewdly remarks of the American Romantic historians, "Whatever value facts had for their own sake, it was the story, and the kind of story, that counted."[51] The "story" was the triumph of liberal nationalism, and

[49]Marx and Engels, *On Literature and Art* (Moscow: Progress, 1976), 333, 336.
[50]Bancroft, 9:218.
[51]Levin, 22.

the "facts" chosen to validate it a posteriori were carefully subordinated to its informing teleology.

The so-called scientific historians of the later nineteenth century castigated their forebears for what Homer Hockett called the "appetite for literary effects."[52] "The substance of all science," wrote Taine, consists in "little facts that are well chosen, important, and significant."[53] Taine's little significant fact became almost as notorious as Ranke's dictum that the historian's task is to recount "what really happened" (*wie es eigentlich gewesen*). George Burton Adams echoed Ranke when he urged his colleagues to "ascertain as nearly as possible and to record exactly what happened."[54] Frederic Harrison envisioned the accurate collocation of data as the supreme accomplishment of the historian: "If there is one thing which, more than another, is the mark of Oxford today, it is the belief in contemporary documents, exact testimony of authorities, scrupulous verification of citations, minute attention to chronology, geography, paleography, and inscriptions. When all these are right, you cannot go wrong."[55] This description contrasts sharply with Parkman's declaration that "the task of exploring archives and collecting documents" was "repulsive at best."[56]

The positivist orientation of the scientific historians is unmistakable: facts speak for themselves, laws emerge from the dispassionate survey of facts, and the historian's task is to be a neutral facilitator of the connection between the two. It seems obvious to us now that this project was doomed in advance. It was, of course, impossible for historians to eliminate their own perspectives. Taine may have declared that "the movements of the spiritual automaton which is our being are governed by laws to the same extent as those of the material world in which it is contained,"[57] but this proclamation of neutrality did not prevent him from branding the leaders of the French Revolu-

---

[52]Homer Hockett, "The Literary Motive in the Writing of History," *Mississippi Valley Historial Review*, 12 (1926): 476.

[53]Hippolyte Taine, *De l'intelligence*, 16th ed. (Paris: Hachette, n.d.), 1:2, my translation.

[54]George Burton Adams, quoted in Richard Hofstadter, *The Progressive Historians: Turner, Beard, Parrington* (New York: Random House, 1968), 38.

[55]Frederick Harrison, *The Meaning of History* (1893; London, 1902), 118–38.

[56]Francis Parkman, quoted in Charles H. Farnham, *Life of Francis Parkman* (Boston: Little, Brown, 1900), 331n.

[57]Taine, quoted in Edmund Wilson, *To the Finland Station: A Study in the Writing and Acting of History* (1940; New York: Farrar, Straus & Giroux, 1972), 63, 59.

tion as a "race of crocodiles." In fact, the scientific historians' posture of objectivity routinely masked a complacent conservatism. Michelet freely admitted that his *Introduction to Universal History* had been composed "on the burning pavements" of Paris.[58] Comte, by contrast, suppressed the personal voice in his disourse but proclaimed that "the positive spirit tends to consolidate order, by a rational development of a wise resignation to incurable political evils. A true resignation . . . can proceed from a deep sense of the connection of all kinds of natural phenomena with invariable natural laws."[59] As Charles Beard noted of Ranke, "Written history that was cold, factual and apparently undisturbed by the passions of the time served best the cause of those who did not want to be disturbed."[60]

The positivist epistemology upon which the scientific historians relied did not simply mask political conservatism in a specious objectivity; it also ultimately mystified the very historical processes that it set out to describe with scientific rigor. Comte conceded that there was an epistemological limitation to the enterprise of the scientific investigator, who "recognizes the impossibility of reaching an absolute understanding, and abandons the search for the destination of the universe and the inmost causes of phenomena."[61] Where Marx saw in the greasy sausages distributed by Louis Napoleon both the actual evidence of bribery and the ironic symbolic embodiment of the bourgeois bid for imperial grandeur, Taine consigned to metaphysics "research into first causes." Phenomena have only an apparent reality, concluded Taine. "Basically, there exist only abstractions, universal principles of general cases that appear to us as particulars."[62] Renan argued that his scientific approach to the history of religion would simply replace religious faith with a "faith which believes in the ideal without the need of belief in the supernatural, and which . . . sees the divinity better in the immutable order of things than in derogations from the eternal order."[63] John Stuart Mill posited that the "phae-

[58]Quoted in ibid., 8.

[59]Auguste Comte, quoted in Swingewood, 9n.

[60]Charles Beard, "Written History as an Act of Faith," in *The Philosophy of History in Our Time*, ed. Hans Meyerhoff (Garden City: Doubleday/Anchor, 1959), 142.

[61]Comte, *Cours de la philosophie positive* (Paris: J. Baillière, 1864), 1:9 , my translation.

[62]Taine, *Hippolyte Taine: Sa vie et sa correspondance, 1902–07*, quoted in D. G. Charlton, *Positivist Thought in France during the Second Empire, 1852–70* (Oxford: Clarendon, 1959), 148, my translation.

[63]Ernest Renan, *Studies of Religious History* (London: Heinemann, 1893), xxvi.

nomena" that furnish the object of scientific inquiry are opaque and static, precluding any access to determinate knowledge:

> We have no knowledge of anything but Phaenomena; and our knowledge of phaenomena is relative, not absolute. We know not the essence, nor the real mode of production, of any fact, but only its relations to other facts in the way of succession or of similitude. These relations are constant; that is, always the same in the same circumstances. The constant resemblances which link phaenomena together, and the constant sequences which unite them as antecedent and consequent, are termed their laws. The laws of phaenomena are all we know respecting them. Their essential nature, and their ultimate causes, either efficient or final, are unknown and inscrutable to us.[64]

For all its aspiration to render a materialist description of phenomena, the positivist program led to a new metaphysics of essence.

The positivist epistemology that shapes the practice of the scientific historians is the same one that shapes the picture of social reality in documentary novels of the late nineteenth century. Like the scientific historians, the antiquarian historical novelists and the naturalists fetishized the "little significant fact." The detailed description of Florentine life in *Romola* and the dizzying succession of battle sequences in *The Red Badge of Courage* furnish fictive counterparts to Renan's compendious research in *The Origins of Christianity*: presumably the reader can never learn, and the writer never tell, too much about the subject at hand, which is in fact defined as the sum of its component data. Totality is imagined to be an additive entity, so that the writer's job is to pile up enough data until the working of a law becomes apparent. In both scientific histories and documentary fictions, however, the laws that the data are supposed to supply bear a highly problematic relation to their empirical base. In *Romola*, for example, the presence of Savonarola suggests a specific link between the dilemma facing the typical hero and larger world-historical forces. In the plot, however, his relation to Romola's moral development remains ambiguous; her endorsement of a Comtian pragmatic humanism provides an anachronistic ideological resolution, one distinctly at odds with her represented historical experience. But if essence consists, as Renan and Mill proposed, in immutable laws, then the imposition of

---

[64]John Stuart Mill, *Auguste Comte and Positivism*, 2d ed. (London: Routledge, 1866), 6–8.

moral categories in vogue some four hundred years later is of little account: ultimate realities are, after all, timeless. Similarly, Crane's reliance upon an elaborate sequence of zoological metaphors to describe Henry Fleming suggest that the laws regulating Henry's behavior stem from an intrinsic biological mechanism. The particulars of the plot, in order words, assert Taine's "abstractions, universal principles of general cases." Phenomenon recapitulates law, and law springs forth from the dispassionate observation of phenomenon. The concrete is only concrete in appearance: its essence is abstract. The empiricism that would probe the meaning of the thing (the *res*) has become the positivism that affirms the structure to which the thing belongs (reification).

Automatism and Alienation: The Historical Novel and Industrial Capitalism

The empiricism and positivism shaping the altering representational strategy of the documentary novel in the nineteenth century are themselves conceptual mediations of changes in the nature and degree of abstraction characterizing the social world at large. The principal development here is the emergence of industrial capitalism, which signaled the complete subordination of the production process to the automatism of capital. In the era of manufacture, we will recall, laborers still retained a residual control over the process of production, for the instruments of production, while owned by the capitalists, required deployment at the initiative of the laborer. According to Sohn-Rethel,

> As long as [the artisan producer's] means of production had not actually been taken from him, no matter how heavily they were pledged to the capitalist, we still move in the era of the production relations of artisanry. . . . The manner of production and of its physical conditions were still conceived in terms of artisanry and these were basically the terms of the unity of head and hand of the artisan in person.[65]

With the institution of steam-powered machinery, however, the tool no longer serves to link laborers with the raw materials upon which they work. Marx observed,

[65]Sohn-Rethel, *Intellectual and Manual Labor*, 68.

Labour no longer appears so much to be included within the production process; rather, the human being comes to relate more as watchman and regulator to the production process itself. (What holds for machinery holds likewise for the combination of human activities and the development of human intercourse.) No longer does the worker insert a modified natural thing as middle link between the object and himself; rather, he inserts the process of nature, transformed into an industrial process, as a means between himself and inorganic nature, mastering it. He steps to the side of the production process instead of being its chief actor.[66]

Accordingly, the machine enforces the complete hegemony of capital.

> Every kind of capitalist production, in so far as it is not only a labour-process, but also a process of creating surplus-value, has this in common, that it is not the workman that employs the instruments of labour, but the instruments of labour that employ the workman. But it is only in the factory system that this inversion for the first time acquires technical and palpable reality. By means of its conversion into an automation, the instrument of labour confronts the labourer, during the labour-process, in the shape of capital, of dead labour, that dominates, and pumps dry, living labour-power. *The separation of the intellectual powers of production from the manual labour, and the conversion of those powers into the might of capital over labour, is . . . finally completed by modern industry erected on the foundation of machinery.* [Italics added]

This " 'postulate of automatism' presents itself as a feature of technology," Sohn-Rethel observes, yet "it does not spring from technology, but arises from the capitalist production relations and is inherent in the capital control over production. It is, as it were, the condition controlling this control."[67] Thus, the machine removes the last barrier between the abstractness of the exchange relation and the labor process. When workers themselves have become interchangeable parts in a production process controlled by machines and when their labor power itself has become a commodity that facilitates their insertion in this production process, then the abstract second nature of the commodity form has clearly achieved a new position of dominance.

[66]Marx, *Capital: A Critique on Political Economy*, ed. Frederick Engels, trans. Samuel Moore and Edward Aveling (New York: International, 1967), 1:422. The statement quoted below is from p. 423.
[67]Sohn-Rethel, 121.

Indeed, it is a dominance so complete as to obscure the fact of its dominance. Since all exchanges—including the exchange of labor power for a wage—are now equivalents in quality as well as quantity, the process of exploitation itself, based upon the nonequivalence of wages and labor, is shrouded in the abstractness of the exchange relation.

The concepts generated by the development of this self-regulating automatism in the "real abstraction" assume, accordingly, an added degree of abstraction. Marx's parenthetical aside ("What holds for machinery holds likewise for the combination of human activities and the development of human intercourse") has direct epistemological implication. Marx's own anatomy of capital, indeed, could be seen as the fullest exemplification of the connection between material and intellectual abstractions: it was only when capital itself had achieved the automatism of its industrial phase that it could genereate a theory of itself possessing corresponding abstraction. Such a hypothesis need not, of course, negate the political and historical importance of Marx's theory of class struggle. The automatism of capital would create a rebellious proletariat and a recalcitrant bourgeoisie at the same time that it subordinated the labor process to its structural imperatives. Nor does this hypothesis need to relativize the validity of Marx's own discourse, which, as an abstraction, might be seen as intrinsically a prioristic and bound by ideology. As Sohn-Rethel has noted, *Capital* is not only a description of actual relations of production and circulation but also a critique of prevailing views of these relations; as such, it provides a critique of prevailing abstractions. Its partisan position in the class struggle need not therefore imply a diminished explanatory power. As Marx repeatedly argued, abstraction is a necessary consequence of the development of the forces and social relations of production, but it does not in itself necessarily imply alienation and fetishism. Indeed, abstraction of social relations is a precondition to the development of explanatory abstraction:

As a rule, the most general abstractions arise only in the midst of the richest possible concrete development, where one thing appears as common to many, to all. Then it ceases to be thinkable in a particular form alone. On the other side, this abstraction of labour as such is not merely the mental product of a concrete totality of labours. Indifference toward specific labours corresponds to a form of society in which individuals can with ease transfer from one labour to another, and where the specific kind is a matter of chance for them, hence of indifference.[68]

It is only to the bourgeois economists, Marx noted, that "the *objectification* of the powers of social labour appears . . . as inseparable from the necessity of their *alienation vis-à-vis* living labour." The very process of consolidating production and exchange into an increasingly complex social division of labor also created the class that, constituted by abstraction alone (at least from the point of view of capital), would abolish the conditions of alienation (and of its own existence as a class) altogether.

Marx's theory of capital confronts and criticizes the nature of capitalist abstraction directly, in the realm of political economy. The representational strategy of the nineteenth-century documentary novel, I propose, more indirectly expresses the increasing complication and opacity characterizing the realm of production. Despite its circumstantial concreteness, the documentary novel at this time achieves a new level of abstraction. Again, to quote Marx: "The concrete is concrete because it is the concentration of many determinations, hence unity of the diverse. It appears in the process of thinking, therefore, as a process of concentration, as a result, not as a point of departure, even though it is the point of departure in reality and hence also the point of departure for observation and conception." The apparent autonomy of the fictive realm, its liberation from the cumbersome apparatus of pseudofactuality, its implicit claim that the text's reconcretized particulars replicate the concrete features of the referent—all these constitutive aspects of the generic contract of the historical novel mediate the "unity of the diverse" in nineteenth-century society. In one sense, then, the totalizing strategy of the historical novel—particularly in its classical phase—can be seen as an attempt to outline the vanishing lineaments of a world being rendered increasingly opaque by the hegemony of capital. The text's immersion in the dynamics of historical process and its insistent depiction of the workings of a society in its entirety involve an implicit rejection of reification and fragmentation. The totalizing strategy of the historical novel thus signals the epistemological achievement of a transcendental sub-

---

[68]Marx, *Grundrisse: Foundation of the Critique of Political Economy*, trans. Martin Nicolaus (New York: Random House/Vintage, 1973), 104. The passages quoted are from pp. 832 and 101.

jectivity which (like the transcendental subjectivity that "steps to the side" of the labor process) comprehends and describes the workings of the mechanism from which it is alienated. As Lukács noted in *The Theory of the Novel*, the nineteenth-century novel "is the epic of an age in which the extensive totality of life is no longer directly given, in which the immanence of meaning in life has become a problem, yet which still thinks in terms of totality."[69]

Even as the automatism of capital generates abstractions that possess increased explanatory power, it at the same time threatens to sever altogether the historical connection between subject and process, analogous configuration and referent. Alienation and commodity fetishism blur the configuration of the social formation and further distance the "second nature" of the exchange abstraction from the "first nature" of use values. Alienation—or, estrangement, as Marx termed it in the *Economic and Philosophic Manuscripts of 1844*—means the separation of wage laborers from the products of their labor, from their life activity as productive beings, from their fellow laborers, and from themselves.[70] In alienating laborers from the totality of the labor process, the abstraction of the wage relation thus creates material, social, and conceptual fragmentation. Commodity fetishism thus displaces alienation onto the products of labor. Marx concluded in *Capital*, "A commodity is therefore a mysterious thing, simply because in it the social character of men's labour appears to them as an objective character stamped upon the product of that labour; because the relation of the producers to the sum total of their own labour is presented to them as a social relation, existing not between themselves, but between the products of their labour."[71] When alienation and commodity fetishism exert dominant influence upon the epistemological

[69]Georg Lukács, *The Theory of the Novel*, trans. Anna Bostock (Cambridge: MIT Press, 1971), 56. The view of totality as a rejection of reification provides the epistemological basis for Lucian Goldmann's theory of realism. "The [realistic] novel of the problematic hero" arose, Goldmann declares, "from precisely the traits analyzed by the theories of reification dealing with commercial and nineteenth-century liberal capitalism. The novel form was founded precisely on the opacity of social life, and the individual's difficulty in orienting himself and giving his life meaning" (*Cultural Creation in Modern Society*, trans. Bart Grahl [Oxford: Blackwell, 1976], 43). Goldmann sees the realistic novel as intrinsically critical and adversarial; as is clear from the preceding discussion, I see the realistic novel as primarily incorporating dissent and reproducing dominant ideology.

[70]Marx, *Economic and Philosophic Manuscripts of 1844*, trans. Martin Milligan, ed. Dirk J. Struik (New York: International, 1969), 106–19.

[71]Marx, *Capital*, 1:72.

matrix within which consciousness confronts material reality, phenomena that are the products of purposive human activity appear natural and ahistorical; stasis takes the place of process; the self becomes privatized, hypostasized as an essence apart from, and antagonistic to, its actual embeddedness in the social world.

At the same time that the automatism of capital enables the formulation of increasingly comprehensive explanatory models (fictive, historical, or economic) for social processes, it also fosters a disjunction between these conceptual abstractions and their referents in historical actuality. Just as the exchange relation fetishizes the products of human labor, rendering equivalent those expenditures of labor power that in fact create widely varying use values, the nineteenth-century documentary novel—particularly in its later phases—fetishizes the very procedure of analogous configuration, suggesting an uncritical and unmediated equivalence between the represented social world and the contradictory complex of social processes for which the text purports to offer an explanatory account. The implicitly adversarial epistemological stance of the pseudofactual novel—its querying of the relation between perception and cognition, its foregrounding of the problem of ideological perspective—has been superseded by a mimetic strategy that presents as inevitable the epistemological and political hegemony of the industrial capitalist class. Authenticating documentation functions primarily to promote the illusion that the generalizations projected in the mimetic text possess an unproblematic legitimacy; authority replaces testimony. The very capacity for synthesizing totalization that constitutes the strength of the nineteenth-century historical novel also signals its crucial fragility. As the automatism of capital presses to its limits the principle of equivalence in the monopolist era, it is inevitable that the representational procedures of classical liberalism will also be pressed to their limits, ultimately producing qualitatively new kinds of documentary mimesis. Empiricist documentation is no longer a means to cognition, but a barrier that must be overcome if the text is to assert its appropriation of reality.

7

The Modernist
Documentary Novel

Pure essential truths do not make the slightest assertion concerning the facts.

—Edmund Husserl

In the early decades of the twentieth century, the empiricist and positivist epistemologies that sustained historical and naturalistic fiction of the nineteenth century enter into a state of crisis. The modernist documentary novel makes few of the pretensions to totalizing representation that accompany fictions of the previous century. Rather, in its use of documentary materials it parades its status as interpretation but calls into question the very necessity of offering determinate judgments of a concretely historical referent. As Michael Zéraffa has noted, "The historical development of the novel comprises two opposite tendencies: the novel was born and established itself as a genre on account of, and to account for, historical and social phenomena; it attained the status of art when it set itself over against them."[1] This does not mean that documentary fiction of the early twentieth century had less assertive power than before. As we shall see, the assertion of indeterminacy in the referent or of impotence in the authorial subject carries as much propositional force as does the assertion that the text transparently replicates its referent. The documentary procedures used in modernist fiction, however, bespeak a profound skepticism about the capacity of analogous configuration to effect a valid reconcretization of the text's referent. Ideological abstraction presents itself as not merely involved in, but constitutive of,

---

[1] Michael Zéraffa, *Fictions: The Novel and Social Reality*, trans. Catherine Burns and Tom Burns (Harmondsworth: Penguin, 1976), 11.

the representational process; the generic contract requires that the reader participate in a *de*concretization of the text's historical referent. The modernist documentary novel is as preoccupied with telling the truth as were its forebears, but it questions whether this truth has much to do with "the facts."

In the modernist era, the documentary novel splits into two strands.[2] First, the historical novel continues as a distinct fictional subgenre, but it becomes the *meta*historical novel. The linear progression and univocal causality of nineteenth-century realism are supplanted by the postulation of cyclicality and indeterminacy in the referent. Documentation serves either to highlight the epistemological problem of historical inquiry or to affirm a truth transcending the realm of the concrete altogether; it no longer reinforces the self-evidence of the text's representation of a particular moment in the historical dialectic. Second, the pseudofactual novel reappears in the modernist era, this time in the new guise of the fictional autobiography. Invoking a generic contract that requires the reader to see the text's characters and actions as replications of real persons and events, the fictional autobiography emphasizes, paradoxically, that it is nevertheless a fiction and cannot be other than a fiction, rendering cognition of its referent by means of analogous configuration. The sense of

---

[2] In the discussion that follows, I shall focus upon texts produced after the First World War and shall implicitly extend the definition of modernism into the 1940s: Warren's *All the King's Men* appeared in 1946, and Toynbee's *A Study of History* spanned the mid-1930s to the mid-1950s. I am aware that this procedure shifts the definition of modernism into a somewhat later temporal framework than is customary. Bradbury and McFarlane, for instance, call the years 1890–1930 the modernist epoch, arguing that the reaction against positivism predates the turn of the century and that the return to more explicitly political and historical concerns in the literature of the 1930s excludes the Depression era from the rubric of modernism. I do not quarrel with their stipulation that the modernist era begins in the 1890s—I simply find the most interesting instances of modernist documentary fiction appearing in later decades—but I would disagree with their argument that some literature of the 1930s, and even some of that of the 1940s, is not, properly speaking, "modernist." The representational strategies adopted in many fictions of the 1930s manifest some quintessentially modernist features, and as we shall see, the uses of modernist technique in the work of Brecht and Dos Passos signal one crucial aspect of modernist literary production—that is, its harnessing to an explicitly radical propositional content. For more on the definitive features of modernism, see *Modernism, 1890–1930*, ed. Malcolm Bradbury and James McFarlane (Atlantic Highlands, N.J.: Humanities, 1978), esp. the editors' introductory essay, "The Name and Nature of Modernism," 19–56. See also Renato Poggioli, *The Theory of the Avant-Garde*, trans. Gerald Fitzgerald (New York: Harper & Row, 1971); and Eugene Lunn, *Marxism and Modernism: An Historical Study of Lukács, Brecht, Benjamin, and Adorno* (Berkeley: University of California Press, 1982).

the real accompanying the modernist fictional autobiography is therefore very different from that characterizing its pseudofactual forebear. Where the eighteenth-century pseudofactual novel featured a clear disjunction between the perceptual stances of author and character, the fictional autobiography poses a differentiated but essentially nonironic relation between the two discourses. The protagonist is objectified without being judged; his or her subjectivity is regarded as the only possible lens through which to perceive historical actuality, rather than featured as one among many possible perceptual vantage points.

Though the metahistorical novel and the fictional autobiography use very different representational strategies, they share some common ideological premises. Central among these is an emphatic critique of the notions of subject and object that sustain empiricism, positivism and novelistic realism. Novelistic mimesis can no longer be presumed to convey authoritative generalizations, nor can the author presume to validate his or her private vision by invoking authenticating references to an extratextual reality. This skepticism about the cognitive range of the perceiving subject is routinely accompanied by the notion that historical process, the object, is in any case beyond the reach of individual agency or comprehension. The private self may inhabit a domain more real than that of public affairs, but this reality is largely a function of its refusal to try to make sense of these affairs. Epistemological indeterminacy thus frequently cohabits with a pronounced historiographical determinism. For Santayana, life consists of "two concomitant, yet strangely different streams"—one, "the vast cosmic flood of cyclic movements and sudden precipitations, in which man has his part, like the other animals"; the other, "the private little rivulet of images, emotions and words babbling as we move, and often hidden in sleep or forgetfulness."[3]

The modernist documentary novel—like much philosophy and historiography of the early twentieth century, as we shall later see —takes as its point of departure a critique of the reification that would render unproblematic the relation between datum and law, particularity and generality. But it often reproduces the very reification that it attacks. If history is a flux beyond purposive agency or de-

[3]George Santayana, quoted in John Henry Raleigh, *Time, Place, and Idea: Essays on the Novel* (Carbondale: Southern Illinois University Press, 1968), 43.

terminate interpretation and if the transcendental subject can represent a reality beyond itself only through a procedure of patently
subjective aesthetic intervention, then the modernist text replicates
—indeed, reinforces—the very separation of consciousnss from context that its antipositivist epistemology seeks to overturn. Though
some writers manage to make use of modernist defamiliarization as a
powerful tool in the critique of reification, most accede to the thor-
oughgoing fetishization of social relations that characterizes what
Lukács called the "problem of commodities" in the early twentieth
century.

The Fictional Autobiography

In the fictional autobiography, the validation of personal testimony
attaches to one of the central concerns of modernist fiction, namely,
the artist-hero's odyssey to self-knowledge. Focusing upon the protagonist's efforts to formulate a coherent representation of an evasive
historical actuality, the fictional autobiography gives a specifically
referential urgency to its depiction of the protagonist's discovery of
the redemptive powers of art. For the fictional autobiography proposes that its reader apprehend its central characters and incidents as
real entities rather than as mimetic constructs—filtered through the
consciousness of the protagonist and thereby endowed with shape
and significance, but real nonetheless. The fictional autobiography is
therefore founded on a paradox: a discursive activity that privileges
the transcendence of historical actuality is insistently anchored in a
felt historicity.

Joyce's *A Portrait of the Artist as a Young Man* can be taken as a paradigmatic illustration of this paradox. The plot of *Portrait* is peculiarly
indeterminate. Its resolution depicts the hero's adoption of a matur-
ing aesthetic—and thus completes the bildungsroman pattern of the
plot—but also suggests the open-endedness of "real-life" experience.
The novel's shift into a first-person, diaristic form in its final pages
signals its abandonment of those patterns of decisive closure that had
characterized most novels written in the preceding century. Where
the bildungsroman objectifies its hero as part of its analogous configuration, *Portrait* limits its explanatory claims to the perception of the
hero, whose vantage point becomes the only position from which to

view and judge social reality. Stephen is both a fictional character and, in his own words, an image of "life purified and reprojected from the human imagination."[4] The other characters are both components of a fictional construct and possessors of what Rader calls a "mysterious outwardness . . . independent of perceiving Stephen and . . . independent of Joyce also."[5] The Stephen who addresses the reader as "I" in the novel's closing pages is thus in a peculiar way exempt from controlling authorial judgment: the powerful valorization attached to his status as artist derives not so much from any heroic action or moral stance as from his position as the center of consciousness who "author-izes" the existence of the narrative itself.

Thus the heated debate that surrounds Joyce's depiction of Stephen's aesthetic (does the author intend this manifesto as a serious statement of his own artistic principles or as a sophomoric credo that the reader is to view ironically?) can be seen to derive largely from the ambiguity of the protagonist's ontological status. If Stephen is to be seen as a wholly fictive construct, then we may expect that Joyce would provide a framework of authorial judgment inviting us to evaluate Stephen's beliefs in a certain light. If, however, Stephen is a reprojection of Joyce, then we may anticipate that we, not Joyce, provide the final court of judgment upon Stephen's stated artistic goals. The author communicates the immaturity of his hero's theory of art and yet withholds signals of irony that would decisively imply the inadequacy of this theory. Accordingly, a crucial disjunction exists between Stephen's aesthetic and the actuality for which it presumably offers a symbolic account—a rupture that signals both Joyce's privileging of the transcendent vision available in art and his skepticism regarding its ultimate explanatory power.

Variants upon Joyce's documentary strategy in *Portrait* are discernible in other fictional autobiographies that focus upon the prophetic figure of the modernist artist-hero. In *The Autobiography of Alice B. Toklas*, for example, the text's invocation of a sense of the real enables Stein to project her own "monumental egotism" by presenting

---

[4]James Joyce, *A Portrait of the Artist as a Young Man*, ed. Chester A. Anderson (New York: Viking, 1964), 215.

[5]Ralph W. Rader, "Defoe, Richardson, Joyce, and the Concept of Form in the Novel," in *Autobiography, Biography, and the Novel*, ed. William Matthews and Rader (Los Angeles: William Andrews Clark Memorial Library, 1973), 51. I am indebted to Rader for my central argument about Stephen's aesthetic.

herself as a "character" in Alice B. Toklas's presumed memoir.[6] Thus Toklas, the putative author, repeatedly refers to her friend as a "genius"; the arrogance of the real author is transmuted into an objective feature of the character about whom Toklas naively writes. Yet Stein also retains for herself the final rights of authorship. As she remarks in the final chapter, still speaking through the voice of Toklas, "About six weeks ago Gertrude Stein said, it does not look to me as if you were ever going to write that autobiography. You know what I am going to do. I am going to write it for you. I am going to write it as simply as Defoe did the autobiography of Robinson Crusoe. And she has and this is it."[7] The reference to Defoe is revealing: abandoning her original plan to close the book in the style of Huck Finn ("Sincerely, Alice B. Toklas"), Stein disrupts both realism and the sense of the real by openly admitting her own identity as the transcendental subjectivity that has framed a novel about itself.

In playing with the Gestalts of antecedent modes of mimesis, however, Stein does not impede her novel's projection of fictionality. Defoe did not, after all, admit to having composed his pseudomemoir; *The Autobiography of Alice B. Toklas* is, by contrast, undisguisedly by Gertrude Stein. Stein thus avoids the generalizing claims implicit in realism—her text makes no pretensions to typicality or to totalization in its projection of Toklas's patently subjective perspective—at the same time that it retains its status as a fictional representation. Through Stein's collapse of the object into the agent of perception, the voices of Alice B. Toklas and Stein are merged rather than differentiated; indeed, the two women become, in the reading experience, virtually interchangeable identities. The text's ironic tone thus serves not to query the ideological stance endorsed by the pervasive Stein/Toklas voice but to assert the unquestioned superiority of that voice, which permits the reader access to the community of privileged sensibilities constituting the modernist movement.

Henry Miller, by contrast, presents himself in propria persona throughout *Tropic of Cancer*; there is no ambiguity about the identity

[6]Michael Hoffman, *Gertrude Stein* (Boston: Twayne, 1976), 116. For more on Stein's changes in the manuscript, as well as on the factual discrepancies contained in the *Autobiography*, see Richard Bridgman, *Gertrude Stein in Pieces* (New York: Oxford University Press, 1970). Apparently Matisse, Tzara, and Braque attacked the *Autobiography* for what they felt were serious errors in factual representation.

[7]Gertrude Stein, *The Autobiography of Alice B. Toklas* (New York: Harcourt, Brace, 1933), 310.

of the text's narrative voice. He bares his soul so readily, however, that the reader is invited to view his "confession" as the projection of an invented personality who should be objectified within the evaluative conventions of a mimetic contract. Like Moll Flanders, "Henry Miller" conveys a "confessional increment" that makes it possible for the reader to ironize his discourse. But where Defoe, in his preface to *Moll Flanders*, indirectly invites the reader to engage in such a judgment, Anais Nin, in the testimonial preface included in the first and all subsequent editions of the book, openly celebrates the regenerative power of Miller's candor and vouches for the prophetic insight of the narrative voice:

> Here is an artist who re-establishes the potency of illusion by gaping at the open wounds, by courting the stern psychological reality which man seeks to avoid through recourse to the oblique symoblism of art.
>
> . . .
>
> The gross caricatures are perhaps more vital, more "true to life" than the full portraits of the conventional novel for the reason that the individual today has no centrality and produces not the slightest illusion of wholeness. The characters are integral to the false cultural void in which we are drowning; thus is produced the illusion of chaos, to face which requires the ultimate courage.[8]

The text engages in the fictional representation of historical actuality—it "re-establishes the potency of illusion"—but it rejects the strategy of a realism embodied in "the conventional novel" that would posit a false typicality and resolution.

Miller's often outrageous flaunting of his ego is therefore to be construed as an artistic strategy necessary for countering the perceived fragmentation of mass society. As in *The Autobiography of Alice B. Toklas* and *Portrait*, the text's valorization of an artistic ego courageously facing the "illusion of chaos" involves a foregrounding of the sense of the real. But the novel lays bare the ideological preconceptions of its narrative voice only to reaffirm that voice's privileged epistemological stance; irony is directed more toward inherited conceptions of the explanatory role of mimesis than toward the particular discursive assertions of the artist-hero. What Nin's testimonial pref-

---

[8]Anais Nin, preface, in Henry Miller, *Tropic of Cancer* (1934; New York: Grove Press, 1961), xxxii.

ace authenticates, we note, is not the text's veracity but its fidelity to its self-appointed mission.

Christopher Isherwood and Thomas Wolfe examine the figure of the artist-hero in a more concretely specified historical context; their tendency to transcendentalize the ego cogitans enters into contradiction with their acute awareness of the historical situation within which the subject produces its discourse. Isherwood, in *Goodbye to Berlin*, frames his mimetic rendition of pre–World War II Berlin between two diaristic excerpts putatively composed in 1930 and 1932–33, thereby enclosing his representative fictional microcosm within a comparatively nonteleological, pseudofactual discourse. One effect of this device is to historicize the text's fictional claims and to locate Sally Bowles and the other boardinghouse characters within the perceptual framework of a specified consciousness. The fiction does not self-evidently represent the social tensions of prefascist Berlin from an Archimedean vantage point; it is the product of a subjectivity that is itself implicated in these tensions. Another effect is to indicate the terrifying alterations taking place during the historical period spanned by the fictional stories: the Isherwood who watches the anti-Semitic persecutions and street battles on the eve of Hitler's rise to power discerns a fatalistic trajectory only partially visible in the fictional narratives.

But the ego cogitans who both authors and narrates *Goodbye to Berlin* is a self who is practicing the strategy of self-effacement and insisting on the diarist's prerogative to offer only fragmentary remarks on the world passing before his eyes. "I am a camera," he states in 1930, "with its shutter open, quite passive, recording not thinking. . . . Some day all this will have to be developed, carefully printed, fixed."[9] Writing in 1932–33, he concludes, "Even now I can't altogether believe that any of this has really happened." Such passivity is quite different from the detached consciousness recorded in the earlier pseudofactual novel. When H.F. and Jack Wilton take the world as their object, they do not hesitate to formulate analyses and judgments of it—even if these are put into relief by the framing strategy of the text. Isherwood's "camera eye," by contrast, hesitates to offer explanatory accounts of the phemonena that come before his

---

[9]Christopher Isherwood, *Goodbye to Berlin* (New York: Random House, 1939), 13. The passage quoted below appears on p. 317.

open lens. As a result, his work does not project the forceful autonomy of personality that would enable the reader to ironize the ideological perspective of his pronouncements, even though that perspective emerges as a patently subjective intervention in historical
process. In a peculiar combination of assertion and passivity, the documentary effect authorizes moral and political impotence.

In *You Can't Go Home Again*, Thomas Wolfe presents a fiction narrated by a still more self-conscious authorial presence. His autobiographical hero, George Webber, is himself depicted as being obsessed
with the problematics of autobiographical mimesis. Pondering the
difficulties accompanying an effective transformation of life into fiction, Webber declares that the weakness of his previous work was
that it was "not autobiographical enough." He exclaims, "[I must]
use myself to the top of my bent . . . use everything I have . . . milk
the udder dry, squeeze the last drop, until there is nothing left. And if
I use myself as a character . . . withhold nothing, try to see and paint
myself as I am—the bad along with the good, the shoddy alongside
of the true—just as I must try to see and draw every other character."[10] This fictional protagonist's dilemma clearly mirrors the discursive activity of his creator, who also attempts to use subjectivity as
a means of exploring a totalized range of human experience. Webber
announces, "I'm looking for a way . . . I think it may be something
like what people vaguely mean when they speak of fiction. . . . Not
the facts, you understand—not just the record of my life—but something truer than the facts—something distilled out of my experience
and transmitted into a form of universal application." Where other
modernist fictional autobiographers attribute the artist's prophetic interpretive stance to a privileged particularity with which the reader is
not permitted fuller identification, Wolfe posits in his ego cogitans a
stubborn embodiment of typicality, "a form of universal application." A strongly democratic and romantic impulse distinguishes
Wolfe's delineation of the artist. Interestingly, however, this typicality rests upon a notion of representation far removed from the premises of nineteenth-century realism. Where the bourgeois hero lays
claim to universality on the basis of a specified position in the social

[10]Thomas Wolfe, *You Can't Go Home Again* (New York: Harper, 1940), 385–86. I quote
below from pp. 386–87. For a discussion of the hybrid generic nature of Wolfe's fiction, see
Richard Kennedy, "Thomas Wolfe's Fiction: The Question of Genre," in *Thomas Wolfe and
the Glass of Time*, ed. Paschal Reeves (Athens: University of Georgia Press, 1971), 1–44.

formation, Webber insists upon an intersubjective essence that is "truer than the facts," one that transcends concretion in the historical moment.

Despite their many differences in outlook and sensibility, these heroes of fictional autobiography share their alienation from the very historical process that invests them with immediacy. In *Ulysses*, Stephen frankly sees history as a nightmare from which he is trying to awake. For Stein, the Great War is principally an uncomfortable gap between two phases of the modernist movement in the arts. For Miller, history is defined as "the women I've known . . . like a chain I've forged out of my own misery."[11] Social relations threaten to strip him of all identity, leaving him in the narcissistic "dead center" of a "constant flux" where "you slowly rot, slowly crumble to pieces, get dispersed again. Only your name remains." Webber, witnessing a Jew being seized by the Gestapo, seeks not to probe the roots of National Socialism (much less to interfere in the arrest) but to comprehend "the atavistic yearnings in himself." He concludes, "The dark ancestral cave, the womb from which mankind emerged into the light, forever pulls us back."[12] Isherwood's "camera eye" responds to the mounting oppression of prefascist Berlin by assimilating its metropolitan alienation to his own dispersed ego: "Berlin is a skeleton which aches in the cold; it is my own skeleton aching. I feel in my bones the sharp ache of the frost in the girders of the overhead railway, in the ironwork of balconies, in bridges, in tramlines, lampstandards, latrines. The iron throbs and shrinks, the stone and the bricks ache dully, the plaster is numb."[13] Whether the artist-hero of modernist fictional autobiography encounters the horror of contemporary history by evasion, denial, or self-flagellation, the effect is similar: the referent may be an object of cognition, but the knowledge that it yields is either transhistorical or ahistorical.

The modernist fictional autobiography thus reproduces features of both pseudofactual and realistic fiction, but it produces a synthesis qualitatively different from either. The text abandons both the mendacious sense of the real (which posits a subject undetermined by its object) and the privileged omniscience of realism (which posits an object undetermined by its subject). Instead, its generic contract asks the

[11]Miller, 287.
[12]Wolfe, 706.
[13]Isherwood, 287.

reader to consign the task of interpretation to the artist-hero who, as the central ego cogitans, produces cognition of historical actuality by proclaiming its alienation from that actuality. The documentary invocation of a residual sense of the real guarantees the authenticity of a self who discovers essence and identity apart from any historical concretion. The sense of the real in the pseudofactual novel mediated the exploratory energy of an emergent bourgeois subject. The residual sense of the real in the modernist fictional autobiography, by contrast, mediates the tenuous epistemological stance of a subject who attempts to combat the reification of an alien realm of fact by denying the relevance of this realm of fact to the task of interpreting and judging social reality. The text asserts the supremacy of the realm of the aesthetic, but it denies this realm any further propositional power. It should be clear that there are important connections between this peculiar valorization of impotence and the nonassertive theories of mimesis formulated by twentieth-century literary theorists.

The Metahistorical Novel

Where the fictional autobiography foregrounds the discursive operations of a transcendental subjectivity, the metahistorical novel (as I shall call it) directly confronts the problem of historical process. In contradistinction to the nineteenth-century historical novel, however, it abandons altogether the project of representing historical specificity, positing instead that recurrence constitutes the essence of historical movement. The metahistorical novel continues to invoke a number of the representational conventions of earlier historical fiction, but it no longer assumes that historical actuality constitutes a self-evident object of cognition. The artist-hero of fictional autobiography resurfaces here as the creative historian, who, as part of the text's referent, insistently calls attention to the ideological abstractions that mediate the text's reconcretization of that referent. The text submits Taine's "little significant fact" to critical scrutiny, for the documentary apparatus now directs attention to the process by which the little fact acquires its significance.

In Virginia Woolf's *Orlando*, documentary materials "testify" not to the validity of the text's interpretation of historical process but rather to the necessity of forging an aesthetic that will transcend that process altogether. Thus the references to Addison, Swift, and Pope function very differently than do the analogous appearances of Marlborough and Swift in *Henry Esmond*. Where Thackeray introduced his world-historical characters to delineate—and to validate his delineation of—the moral (or immoral) features of Esmond's environment, Woolf draws in the great artists of past ages in order to affirm the power of mimesis in synthesizing the fragmentary nature of lived time:

> The most successful practitioners of the art of life . . . somehow contrive to synchronize the sixty or seventy different times which beat simultaneously in every normal system so that when eleven strikes, all the rest chime in unison, and the present is neither a violent disruption nor completely forgotten in the past. . . . Indeed it is a difficult business —this time-keeping; nothing more quickly disorders it than contact with any of the arts.[14]

The text's playful presentation of itself as a "biography," moreover, reinforces its implication that fictionality constitutes a privileged mode of cognition. When "Orlando" and "Louise" appear in the index alongside "Victoria, Queen" and "Tennyson, the late Lord," and pictures of Vita Sackville-West are juxtaposed with Renaissance and eighteenth-century portraits of Orlando the ambassador and the gentleman, it becomes clear that "contact with . . . the arts" has triumphantly asserted its victory over the clock of linear historical time.

In one sense, *Orlando* could be said to embody the final flowering of nineteenth-century progressivism. The protagonist's historical alterations in style and ethos illustrate the Hegelian principle of concretion; the text's play with changing typicalities signals its easy assimilation of the historical novel's convention of representative characterization. But the present, rather than seeming to be the logical product of the historial dialectic represented in the novel, possesses a "terror," a "nondescript character." And Orlando is above all a quick-change artist: her/his alterations in personality articulate merely alterations in phenomenon; her/his essence is that of the writer, which remains unchanged over the centuries. It is no accident, then, that the text's resolution occurs with Orlando's completion of

---

[14]Virginia Woolf, *Orlando: A Biography* (New York: Harcourt, Brace, 1928), 305–6. I quote below from p. 322.

the poem "The Oak Tree," which, like its referent in nature, has experienced a slow and consistent growth over the centuries. Typicality, in *Orlando*, involves the valorization of a new type—the artist—conceived apart from his or her embodiment of a changing essence in the social formation; resolution signifies not the working out of a dynamis embedded in the materials of the plot but the affirmation of aesthetic completeness. Historical particulars thus function to corroborate a conception of essence fundamentally alien to Hegelian concretion. Despite their conventional cameo appearances, Woolf's world-historical figures in *Orlando* have far less in common with Thackeray's Great Men than they do with E. M. Forster's great novelists of the past, who are pictured in *Aspects of the Novel* as being "seated together in a room, a circular room, a sort of British Museum reading-room—all writing their novels simultaneously."[15]

In Robert Penn Warren's *All the King's Men*, by contrast, documentary particulars are more insistently grounded in a localized reality, and Warren clearly intends the reader to perceive a close resemblance between his Willie Stark and the historical Huey Long. Yet Warren's extended historical parallel ultimately implies the universality and recurrence of unchanging ethical choices. For, in recognizing Huey Long in Willie Stark, the reader perceives essential human qualities that transcend any given historical concretion; the veiled historical reference functions not to anchor the work in a verifiable historical actuality so much as to abstract the prototype itself from history. As Warren has noted of the novel,

> I do not mean to imply that there was no connection between Governor Stark and Senator Long. Certainly it was the career of Long and the atmosphere of Louisiana that suggested the play that was to become the novel. But suggestion does not mean identity. . . . I did have some notions about the phenomenon of which Long was but one example, and I tried to put some of these notions into my book. . . . The book, however, was never intended to be a book about politics. Politics merely provided the framework story in which the deeper concerns, whatever their final significance, might work themselves out.[16]

[15]E. M. Forster, *Aspects of the Novel* (1927; New York: Harcourt, Brace & World, Harvest, n.d.), 9.

[16]Robert Penn Warren, quoted in Russel B. Nye, "History and Literature: Branches of the Same Tree," in *Essays on History and Literature*, ed. Robert Bremner (Columbus: Ohio State University Press, 1966), 151. See also Robert Penn Warren, "*All the King's Men*: The

The shadowy presence of an actual historical model behind the fictional portraiture produces an undeniably powerful confluence of narrative elements; the text's resolution is rendered inevitable by both its represented dynamis and its external reference to the actual assassination of Huey Long. But even if "politics" are merely an epiphenomenal feature of social organization, never equivalent to "final significance," the dense tissue of documentary references cannot help signaling precisely the historical concretion that the tale must transcend if it is to represent its "deeper concerns."

In its replication of its referent, *All the King's Men* asserts that essence is transhistorical; in its manner of telling its story, the novel implies that historical reconstruction is a matter of intuition and hypothesis, aspiring more toward coherence than toward determinacy. Jack Burden, the narrator, is a historian whose intellectual and moral development implies a trenchant critique of positivism. His progression—from a dispassionate graduate student unsuccessfully attempting to garner facts about Cass Mastern to an ethically committed detective successfully piecing together information that establishes the guilt of his own father—is clearly presented as the triumph of a superior philosophical method. Yet this development in methodology is offset by the parallel that Burden discovers in the substance of his two inquiries; presumably, Cass Mastern's implication in the cruelties of slavery in the nineteenth century is ethically equivalent to Judge Irwin's shady business dealings in the twentieth. While probing the difficult relation between fact and meaning, then, Jack Burden ends up bypassing appearance—which is merely historical—to get at a timeless ethical essence. His final decision (to "go into the convulsion of the world, out of history into history and the awful responsibility of Time")[17] takes the novel not into the crucible of protofascist populism in the Louisiana of Huey Long but into that of a curiously abstract and ahistorical *condition humaine*. Warren's relativistic conception of the process of historical reconstruction thus converges with his implication that the story he is telling is simultaneously real and invented. Essence consists in metaphysical equivalence; differ-

---

Matrix of Experience," *Yale Review*, 53 (December 1963): 161–67. Warren states, "The [dialectic between myself and 'Huey'] was . . . far less important, in the end, than that deeper and darker dialectic for which the images and actions of a novel are only language." Louisiana, he continues, was less crucial than "my acquaintance with another country . . . even more fantastic than was Louisiana under the consulship of Huey" (167).

[17]Robert Penn Warren, *All the King's Men* (New York: Harcourt, Brace, 1946), 464.

ences in historical specificity are merely variants upon an opaque and unchanging facticity.

William Faulkner's *Absalom, Absalom!* is perhaps the prototypical modernist historical novel. In its representation of the pre- and post-Civil War South, the text invokes a contract in some ways similar to that accompanying the realistic historical novel. Sutpen is a type carrying a powerful generalized reference, and through Sutpen's interactions with the microcosm of fictional characters surrounding him, Faulkner conveys a series of judgments upon the course of Southern history. Yet Faulkner subordinates this historically specific representation to an informing cyclical pattern: the novel's extended network of allusions to Greek tragedy and the Old Testament points to repeating patterns of parental rejection, fratricide, and revenge throughout Western history and legend. The concreteness of Faulkner's projections of the historical specificity of Sutpen's tale is thus countered by an insistence upon mythic recurrence; as in *Orlando* and *All the King's Men*, historical parallels primarily serve to minimize the importance of the novel's embeddedness in a particular time and place.

Faulkner's treatment of the problem of documentary validation reinforces his premise that historical process transcends comprehension or purposive agency. The historical record is revealed to be discrepant and confusing: the appended "chronicle" of the Sutpen dynasty contains notable inconsistencies, and even the headstones in the Sutpen family burial ground yield information conflicting with presumably reliable sources.[18] Moreover, Mr. Compson, who plays the role of the positivist historian, proves unable to discover in his documents the "chemical formula" that will yield up the meaning of the Sutpen myth. "You bring [the letters] together in the proportions called for," he complains, "but nothing happens."[19] Given the capacity and intractability of "the facts," then, Quentin's and Shreve's narrative is ultimately valued above that of Miss Rosa or his father, not because it is more objective (all equally play out the teller's fantasies), but because it openly asserts its own patently subjective nature. Ob-

---

[18]Gerald Langford, *Faulkner's Revision of "Absalom, Absalom!" A Collation of the Manuscript and the Published Book* (Austin: University of Texas Press, 1971), 11–12. For much of this discussion of Faulkner's historiographical method, I am indebted to an unpublished essay by my colleague Harriet Gilliam entitled "Overpassing to Love: Phenomenological Truth in *Absalom, Absalom!*" (Northwestern University, 1976).

[19]William Faulkner, *Absalom, Absalom!* (1936; New York: Random House/Vintage, 1964), 101.

sessed with the problem of reconstructing a mythic past that possesses greater concreteness and vitality than the "cold, New England dark" of the abstract present, Quentin willingly invents crucial "facts" —such as the conversation where Bon reveals to Henry that they are brothers—in order to penetrate to the essence of the Sutpen tragedy. His criterion for validity in historical reconstruction is, finally, internal or imaginative coherence rather than external correspondence; he makes no claim that the patterns he uncovers inhere within the object of his inquiry. In one sense, *Absalom, Absalom!* renders a reconcretization of history; in another sense, its insistent focus on the procedures of ideological abstraction queries the very reality of that history. To tell the truth about Thomas Sutpen is to question whether he ever existed.

Clearly the metahistorical novel sets out to refute the empiricist illusion of neutral subjectivity and the positivist illusion of neutral objectivity, as well as the complacent liberal progressivism that these illusions sustain. It brings in documentary "facts" only to question their ontological status rather than to assume a priori their value as registers to truth. It is questionable, however, whether the metahistorical novel actually frees itself from the positivist paradigm that it takes as its adversary. Comte, we will recall, despaired of discovering the "inmost causes" of the "phenomena" that he studied so exhaustively; Mill posited a fundamental dualism between "facts" and the "essence . . . the real mode of production, of any fact." In the metahistorical novel, this dualism is not eradicated but instead intensified. Not only are the "inmost causes" more remote than ever, but the "little significant fact" assumes a chimerical quality. Narration is still undertaken from the vantage point of a transcendental subjectivity, although no longer that of the author, standing outside the analogous configuration, but of a character, haunted by the problem of penetrating the opaque historical world of which he is now a represented part. The present is the product of historical processes, but its peculiar unreality is not a historical problem. As Lukács remarks in *History and Class Consciousness*, "The unexplained and inexplicable facticity of bourgeois existence as it is here and now acquires the patina of an eternal law of nature."[20]

[20]Georg Lukács, *History and Class Consciousness: Studies in Marxist Dialectics*, trans. Rodney Livingstone (Cambridge: MIT Press, 1971), 157. The locus classicus of Lukács's attack on modernism remains "The Ideology of Modernism," in *The Meaning of Contemporary*

Radical Modernism: The Examples of Brecht and Dos Passos

The fictional autobiographies and metahistorical novels we have examined could be said to contain a symptomatic critique of reification. Certain modernist texts, however, offer an intentional challenge to fetishized ideological abstractions, not through their denial of the possibility of concrete totalization per se, but through their construction of a critical totalization, one that purports to render determinate explanations and judgments while foregrounding the political nature of their own epistemological frameworks. The politics of these texts are ineluctably radical: they can engage in their acts of critical totalization precisely because they view reification as a problem and as a product of capitalism, and they can also view their own critical perspectives as the articulation of a class outlook, rather than as an isolated protest. This leftist modernism was expressed in a variety of mimetic genres, from the theater of Meyerhold to the cinema of Eisenstein. For the purposes of our discussion here, its most significant theorist is Bertolt Brecht; its most significant documentary practitioner, John Dos Passos.[21]

Brecht polemicized both against the representational strategies of bourgeois realism and against the aesthetic theory of Lukács, which prescribed a return to typicality and totalization as the cure for the maladies of both naturalism and modernism. Plots constructed

---

Realism, trans. John Mander and Necke Mander (London: Merlin, 1962). Lukács's description of "concrete typicality" and "abstract particularity" in this essay is highly relevant to the preceding discussions of both fictional autobiographies and metahistorical novels. Throughout "The Ideology of Modernism," however, Lukács frequently succumbs to nostalgia for a bourgeois realism that is, by his own logic, irrecoverable. See above, Chapter 3, n. 11.

[21]The link between Dos Passos and Brecht is probably best understood in their discovery of a common ancestor in cubism as well as in their common admiration for Eisenstein. For a discussion of the politically radical implications of cubism, see Lunn, 48–54. For the argument that all modernism—even the fascist modernism of Wyndham Lewis—constitutes a rejection of reification, see Fredric Jameson, *Fables of Aggression: Wyndham Lewis, the Modernist as Fascist* (Berkeley: University of California Press, 1979). For example: "Modernism not only reflects and reinforces [the] fragmentation and commodification of the psyche as its basic precondition, but . . . the various modernisms all seek to overcome that reification as well, by the exploration of a new Utopian and libidinal experience of the various sealed realms or compartments to which they are condemned, but which they also reinvent" (14). Jameson's argument here is based on the Althusserian premise that literature undermines ideology.

around the exemplary careers of typical individuals might have
proven adequate to represent the configuration of social relations in
the progressive era of the bourgeoisie, Brecht remarked, but they had
little value in the present. "Those close interactions between human
beings in struggle were the competitive struggles of developing capitalism," he commented. "But time flows on, and if it did not it
would be a bad prospect for those who do not sit at the golden ta-
ble."[22] As a result,

> It is absolutely false . . . it leads nowhere, it is not worth the writer's
> while, to simplify his problems so much that the immense, compli-
> cated, actual life-process of human beings in the age of the final struggle
> between the bourgeois and the proletarian class, is reduced to a "plot,"
> setting, or background for the creation of great individuals. Individuals
> should not occupy much more space in books and, above all not an-
> other space, than in reality.

Altered mimetic strategies were needed to encompass and interpret
the altered nature of social reality in the era of monopoly capitalism:
"Methods become exhausted; stimuli no longer work. New problems appear and demand new methods. Reality changes; in order
to represent it, modes of representation must change." Brecht thus
argued strenuously against the ideological premises of bourgeois
dramatic realism, which, he claimed, substituted recognition for cognition, catharsis for inquiry, and resolution for the sharpening of contradictions. "Realism," Brecht declared (interestingly, he retained the
term), consists in the enactment of an essentially Leninist epistemology: "discovering the causal complexes of society / unmasking the
prevailing view of things as the view of those who rule it / writing
from the standpoint of the class which offers the broadest solutions
for the pressing difficulties in which human society is caught / em-
phasizing the element of development / making possible the concrete, and making possible abstraction from it." In Brecht's aesthetic,
concrete and abstract are not coterminous with one another; the concrete, indeed, is made possible only by freeing it from the reified abstractions by which it is confined. Neither, however, are concrete

---

[22]Bertolt Brecht, "Against Georg Lukács," trans. Stuart Hood, *New Left Review*, 84
(March–April 1974): 47. The passages quoted below are from pp. 47, 51, 40, 51, 44, and
47.

and abstract ontologically separate. They are dialectically related, and the essence of representing this dialectical relation is not objectivism but partisanship.

Brecht posed a theory of representation that could harness the epistemological self-consciousness of the modernist program to a revolutionary political praxis. He was passionate in his indictment of the ideological presuppositions coded into typicality, totalization, and resolution; he mocked the specious projection of neutrality and self-evidence in the traditional realistic text. Even the most radical mimetic representation, Brecht argued, could not present its rendition of reality as self-evident: in order to mobilize the critical awareness of the audience—a crucial element in the promotion of communist consciousness—the text must produce cognition by altering conventional habits of perception. Yet Brecht also sharply criticized those avante-garde artists who indulged in "an almost unbearable narrowing of perspective" and therefore "merely freed themselves from grammar, not from capitalism." His "alienation effect" sought instead to use defamiliarization as a way of producing revolutionary cognition of the referent. Lukács's fetishization of the productive forces tended to equate representation with the re-presentation of contradictions already defined and determined in their primary and secondary relations by the configuration of the productive forces and the class struggle. Conceiving of literary production as one of the "social forces of production," Brecht broke decisively with Lukács's productive forces determinism when he stressed the role of representation in shattering the synecdochic equation of the totality of society with one of its parts. For Brecht, Lukács's theory of typicality served merely to legitimate those conceptions of the "normative" that reinforced the hegemony of the capitalist class. The solution, Brecht wryly remarked, lay "not in the good old days, but in the bad new ones."

I do not wish to argue that Dos Passos was following Brecht's advice when he wrote U.S.A. Most of Brecht's theorizing postdated the trilogy and was in any case published only after a delay of many years. Dos Passos's letters and journals reveal no signs that he even knew of the German playwright's existence. Moreover, Brecht's openly communist politics would have been quite distasteful to the American author, who, even at his most radical, never abandoned his allegiance to "our storybook democracy." Nonetheless, Dos Passos's project in *U.S.A.* constitutes, in my view, the most successful, sustained instance of Brechtian realism—"making possible the concrete, and making possible abstraction from it"—in modernist prose fiction.

Dos Passos managed, first, to retain much of the generalizing and interpretive force of the nineteenth-century historical novel without falling into its characteristic fetishization of the "representative" bourgeois hero or of the transcendental vantage point of the author. Accordingly, the totalization afforded by *U.S.A.* is not self-evident but critical. No single individual in all of *U.S.A.* is taken to typify the complex interconnection of historical forces in the early decades of the twentieth century; as a group, the fictional characters project in microcosm the central contradictions shaping American life. The word-mongering empire of J. Ward Moorehouse functions as a cohering center around which many of the characters move. But it cannot furnish a hegemonic principle of structural unity, and Moorehouse himself is a shadowy parody of the typical tycoon. The intersecting lives of the characters thus fail to produce a fully overdetermining representation. Mac is lost in Mexico; Joe Williams and Daughter die and leave no appreciable mark on the lives of the others; Mary French drifts toward an uncertain future on the fringes of the left. Although they are grouped into a concretely historical microcosm, these characters do not constitute an analogous configuration transparently rendering the conflicts and tendencies of the historical moment. Class contradiction shapes the fictional plot of *U.S.A.* but it demands cognition, not recognition; types are represented in mutual relations that settle many questions but leave others unresolved. Yet these unresolved questions do not point towards the routine modernist conclusion that history involves either objective determinism or subjective indeterminacy; rather, they simply remind the reader that concretion is always richer and more various than any conceptual abstraction that would claim correspondence with it.

Second, the documentary elements in *U.S.A.* reinforce this projection of a critical totalization. The historical events and cultural trends referred to in the newsreels provide data validating the text's implicit generalizations about the various material and ideological abstractions shaping the lives of Americans in the early twentieth century. But Dos Passos locates the foundation of personal and social experience in the class struggle without posing his data as a posteriori empirical corroboration; many newsreel fragments resist ready assimilation into any of the patterns of judgment accompanying the different characters' lives. The references to the Florida land boom clearly contextualize the tragic arc of Charley Anderson's destiny; the documentary references to the Hall-Mills murder trial suggest the voyeuristic sensationalism of the mass culture in which Margo Dowling will achieve her apotheosis. But the many references to scandals, strikes, and society gossip that remain unincorporated into any specific thematic matrix point to a realm of historical event that exists—and signifies—beyond the interpretive configuration of the text. The contradictions informing the referent are at once equivalent to and greater than their representation in discourse, since the "known object" can only approximate, but never fully delineate, the "real object."

The short biographies also function simultaneously to reinforce and highlight Dos Passos's dialectical view of the relation between evidence and abstraction. These sketches reassert the subordinate status of the world-historical hero inherited from classical historical fiction: emphatically, it is the Eleanor Stoddards and the Joe Williamses who, in their largely unconscious pursuit of self-interest, make history. Yet Dos Passos's world-historical heroes and villains also possess a being apart from their validation of the text's ideological perspective. On the one hand, Henry Ford's institutionalization of the assembly line intervenes directly in Charley Anderson's career; Ford's decision to extract cash payments from his dealers in February 1921 precipitates the financial crisis in Charley's family. Ford here is not simply a concretion of the Hegelian World Spirit; he is, even more than the world-historical heroes of Cooper and Tolstoy, a figure whose actual deeds have direct impact upon the historical process represented in the text. On the other hand, Ford also inhabits the historical reality that surrounds the mimetic microcosm; the fictional stories come to a halt around 1928, but we are told that in 1932 Ford ordered his guards to machine-gun unemployed workers demanding jobs at his Dearborn plant.[23] The world of Henry Ford thus inter-

---

[23]For more on the manipulation of fictional time in *U.S.A.*, see my "From *U.S.A.* to *Ragtime*: Notes on the Forms of Historical Consciousness in Modern Fiction," *American Literature*, 50 (March 1978): 85–105, and "The Treatment of Time in *The Big Money*: An Examination of Ideology and Literary Form," *Modern Fiction Studies*, 26 (Autumn 1980): 447–67.

sects and overlaps with the world of the fiction, but the two are never asserted to be one and the same. Ford helps to ground the novel in a verifiable actuality, but his peculiar intractability as a character warns the reader that fictional analogy and reconcretization cannot presume to encompass or exhaust the totality of the referent.

The use of the Camera Eye, however, most decisively signals Dos Passos's departure from the ideological premises of nineteenth-century realism and demonstrates his affinity with a Brechtian program. In some ways the Camera Eye bears a genetic relation to the ego cogitans recorded in both the pseudofactual novel and the fictional autobiography; indeed Dos Passos often expressed his admiration for both Defoe and Joyce, especially the Joyce of *Portrait*. But Defoe's protagonists routinely take for granted the relation between perception and cognition; even when their vantage point is ironized by the author, a particular ideological formulation is foregrounded, not the intrinsically ideological nature of all discourse. By contrast, the Camera Eye, as modernist artist-hero, is painfully aware of his own preconceptions, and he continually scrutinizes the "upsidedown image on the retina,"[24] a phrase surely intended to echo Marx's and Engels's famous description of ideological thought in *The German Ideology*. But where the hero of modernist fictional autobiography ordinarily assimilates historical actualities to the dimensions of a problematized self-consciousness, Dos Passos's Camera Eye struggles to bring both his experience and his writing into alignment with historical processes objectively existing beyond the bounds of consciousness. Moving from a stance of Joycean spectatorship to one of engaged partisanship ("all right we are two nations"), the Camera Eye grapples with the historical process that shapes his own shaping of American history. Consciously confronting his own tendencies toward aestheticism and privatization, he repudiates a stance of transcendental subjectivity and acknowledges his own embeddedness in the reality he describes; at the same time, he retains the option to delineate, interpret, and judge.

Partisanship, for Dos Passos, means a political stance in material reality, rather than an admission of the intrinsic—and equivalent—

[24]John Dos Passos, *The Big Money* (New York: Modern Library, 1937), 196. The passage quoted below is from p. 462.

subjectivity of all angles of perception. Totalization is undertaken from a position involving neither specious neutrality nor solipsism but rather explicit grounding in the social contradictions of the historical moment. Dos Passos's praxis as author is inseparable from his view of history as the praxis of class struggle, which molds both inner states of consciousness and external historical events. At the trilogy's moment of climax, then, it is significant that subjective and objective realities, previously kept separate in the different segments of the narrative, are joined. Mary French's singing of the Internationale when she is arrested at the protest rally for Sacco and Vanzetti blends into the newsreel that follows the fictional narration, and Vanzetti's prison meditations are then excerpted in the midst of the Camera Eye's impassioned thoughts on the bankruptcy of the American judiciary. While both Isherwood and Dos Passos use the term "camera eye" to designate a privileged authorial lens, there is a crucial difference in the functions of these alter egos. Isherwood's affirms the transcendental vantage point of a subjectivity that cannot locate its own anguish in dialectical relation to its causes; Dos Passos's delineates the abandonment of detached subjectivity as a result of political activity affirming the necessarily social essence of individuality.

While asserting the primacy of a radical politics and epistemology in *U.S.A.*, we cannot say that the text is in any sense free of ideological contradiction. On the contrary, Dos Pasos repudiated many features of liberal ideology and mimetic practice, but his work also bears certain traces of the reification it exposes. The text's structural separation of public from private experience, while enabling Dos Passos to avoid the ideological effect of positing either the cast of fictional characters or the author's own subjectivity as exhaustively representative, also runs the risk of hypostasizing the personal and the historical as separate realms of experience. The text also proposes only an incomplete rendition of the process whereby the informing authorial consciousness has reached its stance of committed partisanship. The Camera Eye's apocalyptic recognition of class warfare emerges from a minimum of directly represented experience; it is significant that the Camera Eye disappears for over three hundred pages before its sudden appearance in the midst of the movement to save Sacco and Vanzetti. Accordingly, the Camera Eye's achievement of historical insight seems like a Joycean epiphany; even the text's powerful structural conjunction of fiction, newsreel, and autobiography in the Sacco and Vanzetti episode effects a certain mystification of historical process, although it also persuasively draws together the text's various strands of narration and commentary. Despite its powerful implied critique of empiricism and positivism, then, *U.S.A.* retains a privileged autonomy for the consciousness of its artist-hero. The text reproduces a certain fetishization of subjectivity, even as it describes truthfully the social and historical forces producing the isolation and alienation that lead to such subjectivity.

The Assault on Positivism in Philosophy and Historiography

The contradictory blend of protest and acquiescence that character-izes the modernist documentary novel's response to reification receives its full theoretical articulation in the reaction to positivism in much contemporaneous philosophy and historiography. As H. Stuart Hughes has pointed out, early twentieth-century theorists pursued various paths, but they were generally united in their antipathy to, and yet their curious reliance upon, the nineteenth-century philophical heritage that they variously termed "mechanism," "rationalism," "materialism," or "intellectualism."[25] We shall now consider certain paradigmatic conceptual abstractions that guide a range of early twentieth-century philosophers and historians. As we survey modernist thinkers as diverse as Bergson and Husserl, Spengler and Collingwood, I shall suggest correlations between their principal theses and the abstractions shaping the fictional reconcretizations we have just examined. I am not arguing, of course, that Woolf was directly influenced by Bergson (though this may have been the case), or Faulkner by Husserl. My concern is with mediation rather than with influence as such. My goal is to outline the recurring features of conceptual abstraction in key texts of the modernist epoch, in order to link these features plausibly to the "real abstraction" from which they arise.

[25]See H. Stuart Hughes, "The Decade of the 1890s: The Revolt against Positivism," in his *Consciousness and Society: The Reorientation of European Social Thought, 1890–1930* (New York: Knopf, 1958), 33–66.

Transcendental Conceptions of Time
and Essence in Modernist Philosophy

Henri Bergson's attempt to relate relativity theory to the problem of temporal perception and experience constituted a critical response to the positivist objectification of time and matter in the natural and physical sciences. For Bergson, both "empiricism" and "rationalism" had isolated the perceiving self within arbitrary boundaries that leave it confronted only with "empty space." A "true empiricism" he urged, "is one which purposes to keep as near to the original itself as possible, to probe more deeply into its life, and by a kind of spiritual *auscultation*, to feel its soul palpitate; and this true empiricism is the true metaphysics."[26] The key to this "true metaphysics," Bergson believed, was a renewed perception of time. Dissatisfied with the abstract conception of chronology inherited from Newtonian mechanics, Bergson proposed a radical distinction between *simultanéité*, or clock time, and *durée*, or experienced time: "We . . . call two external flows that occupy the same duration "simultaneous" because they both depend upon the duration of a like third, our own; this duration is ours only when our consciousness is concerned with us alone, but it becomes equally theirs when our attention embraces the three flows in a single indivisible act."[27] "Why must we speak of an inert matter into which life and consciousness would be inserted as in a frame?" he asked. "By what right do we put the inert first?"[28] He urged, "Let us become accustomed to see all things *sub specie durationis*: immediately in our galvanized perception what is taut becomes relaxed, what is dormant awakens, what is dead comes to life again."[29] The recovery of multiple temporal perspectives "in a single indivisible act" promises to revive the deadened isolation of reified consciousness, which is otherwise confined to itself alone.

Bergson's exploration of the epistemological implications he saw in relativity theory was clearly meant to liberate the subject from the old trap of Cartesian dualism. His favoring of durée over simultanéité

[26]Henri Bergson, *The Creative Mind*, trans. Mabelle L. Andison (New York: Philosophical Library, 1946), 206.

[27]Bergson, *Duration and Simultaneity: With Reference to Einstein's Theory*, trans. Leon Jakobson (Indianapolis: Bobbs-Merrill, 1965), 52.

[28]Bergson, *The Creative Mind*, 108.

[29]Bergson, *Duration and Simultaneity*, ix.

can be seen, however, as substituting a "metaphysics of temporality" (the phrase is Horkheimer's) for the positivist metaphysics of objectivity.[30] Bergson absolutized existential time as thoroughly as the positivists had absolutized the abstract time of Newtonian mechanics and—for all his celebration of the subject's newfound freedom—defined a new determinism. "It is time which is happening," he declared, "and, more than that, which causes everything to happen."[31] Moreover, the phenomena caught up in the flow of time become less real than time itself: "*There are changes, but there are underneath the change no things which change: change has no need of a support.*"[32] Bergson's attack on empiricism and rationalism, then, amounted to an attack on any analytical system that would presume to discern principles of order in facticity: "Disorder is simply the order we are not looking for." The joys of experienceing life sub specie durationis are available only to the metaphysical soul; otherwise life is condemned to the positivist realm of the inert, which will always "come first."

Where Bergson carefully avoided any rigorous systemization of the lessons he drew from his intuitive explorations of the realm of durée, Hans Vaihinger, in *The Philosophy of "As If,"* attempted to found a neo-Kantian theory of knowledge upon his critique of positivism. Curiously, however, he harnessed positivism itself in this critique, referring to his own theoretical stance as, alternately, "positivist idealism" and "idealistic positivism."[33] Conceding that "objective" reality is ruled by "an absolute, unchangeable necessity," Vaihinger grafted onto the positivist conception of a brute reality regulated by unswerving laws a neo-Kantian formulation of the inaccessibility of the "thing-in-itself"—a formulation that would, presumably, liber-

---

[30]Max Horkheimer, "Zu Bergsons Metaphysik der Zeit" (1934), quoted in Martin Jay, *The Dialectical Imagination: A History of the Frankfurt School and the Institute for Social Research, 1923–50* (Boston: Little, Brown, 1973), 51.

[31]Bergson, *Duration and Simultaneity*, x.

[32]Bergson, *The Creative Mind*, 173. I quote below from p. 116.

[33]Hans Vaihinger, *The Philosophy of "As If": A System of the Theoretical, Practical, and Religious Fictions of Mankind*, trans. C. K. Ogden (New York: Harcourt, Brace, 1925), 58–59. The quotations below are from pp. lvii and viii. Although Vaihinger is a relatively obscure figure of the modernist period, his philosophical formula, Hughes argues, "came the closest to providing social thought with the highly flexible criterion of investigation it required: his notion of a fiction in science was approximately identical to Weber's 'ideal type.' But Vaihinger's work remained unknown for the greater part of his academic life" (Hughes, 110). Vaihinger completed the first edition of *The Philosphy of "As If"* in 1877, but it was first published in German in 1911.

ate the ego cogitans from the constraints of a correspondence theory of knowledge. The world of ideas, he declared, is a "network of fictions" that claim explanatory power only on the level of abstraction. Indeed, Vaihinger could barely disguise his contempt for the realm of the concrete: "What we usually term reality consists of our sensational contents which press forcibly upon us with greater or lesser irresistibility and as 'given' can generally not be avoided."

Vaihinger's description of the relation of thought to actuality thus reveals an alienation of essence from phenomenon even more pronounced than that articulated by Comte or Mill. Materiality is impenetrable, opaque, and ruled by laws that can be reliably quantified but never fully understood; the subject can ultimately know only its own heuristic fictions and is in fact further implicated in the separation of appearance and essence that it seeks to overcome. Vaihinger attempted to avoid the fully idealist implications of his formulation by offering a central distinction between "hypotheses" and "fictions," the former being "natural" and "probable," the latter merely providing a dispensable intellectual scaffolding. But this strategic distinction was virtually impossible to maintain in practice. Presumably directed against the epistemological hegemony of the crude positivist equation of perception with cognition, Vaihinger's theory in fact codified the unknowability of the thing-in-itself as a necessary feature of all explanatory enterprises. Indeed, Vaihinger maintained, truth is not even a necessary criterion of the value of a "fiction," which might be demonstrably false but still possess "great practical importance." His theory of "as if," intended to free philosophy from the trammels of a reductionist materialism, ended up fetishizing the "unchangeable, absolute necessity" of brute facticity by rejecting the only potential virtue of positivism—namely, its insistence upon a world beyond consciousness that philosophy was to understand and interpret.

Husserl's project of redefining essence by means of "phenomenological reduction" also constituted an attack upon the positivist fetishization of the "little significant fact." "Individual Being of every kind is, to speak quite generally, '*accidental.*' It is so-and-so, but essentially it could be other than it is."[34] Such accidental facticity is limited, however, because it is "correlative to a *necessity* which does not carry

---

[34]Edmund Husserl, *Ideas: General Introduction to a Pure Phenomenology* (1913), trans. W. R. Boyce Gibson (London: Allen & Unwin, 1931), 53. I quote below from pp. 54, 55, 57, and 150.

the mere actuality-status of a valid rule of connexion obtaining between spatio-temporal facts, but has the character of *essential necessity*, and therewith a relation to *essential universality*. In order to grasp this "essential universality," "*empirical or individual intuition*" must be "transformed into *essential insight*," since "*just as the datum of individual or empirical intuition is an individual object, so the datum of essential intuition is a pure essence.*"

But, as with Vaihinger, "fact" and "truth" therefore come to inhabit mutually incompatible realms. "*The positing of essence,*" declares Husserl, "*does not imply any positing of individual existence whatsoever; pure essential truths do not make the slightest assertion concerning facts.*" Accordingly, the subject who seeks to understand essences reduces facts to the status of "exemplars." All merely factitious data occupy equivalent status, and, finally, "absolute consciousness" is the "residuum after the nullifying of the world." The ego cogitans who, in the formulation of Descartes, at least insisted upon the embeddedness of the subject in historical actuality, is now endowed with an absolutized trancendental status. For Husserl, Descartes's cardinal error was to anchor the subject in "absolute evidence" and to treat it as a "primary, indubitably existing *bit of the world.*"[35] While phenomenology certainly did not base itself in transcendental presuppositions (Husserl emphatically denied the charge of "subjective idealism"),[36] it led to such presuppositions, as Marcuse points out, for identity, in isolation from facticity, becomes the source of cognition.[37]

It should be apparent that many of the assumptions guiding these philosophical rejections of positivism also shaped the representational strategy of the modernist documentary novel in both its modes. Orlando's peculiarly relativized process of aging, for example, is a kind of mimetic projection of the Bergsonian opposition between durée and simultanéité. On the more obvious level of plot, Orlando's time-traveling suggests Bergson's notion that "there are changes, but . . . underneath the change no things which change." More significantly, however, Orlando's very identity derives from her/his implicit repudiation of the rational quantification of the clock of linear

[35]Husserl, *Formal and Transcendental Logic*, trans. Dorion Cairns (The Hague: Nijhoff, 1969), 227.

[36]Husserl, *Ideas*, 168.

[37]See Herbert Marcuse, "The Concept of Essence," in *Negations: Essays in Critical Theory*, trans. Jeremy J. Shapiro (Boston: Beacon, 1968), 55–58.

historical time and endorsement of a view of history in which all moments of time are simultaneously present: beyond the achievement of "The Oak Tree," it is, as in Bergson's ontology, "time which is happening, and which causes everything to happen." Even Woolf's parody of biography suggests a Bergsonian alienation from any explanatory scheme that would purport to affix identity by a measurable diachronism. *Orlando*'s play with its own status as a historical document thus ironizes not simply the linear conception of history but also the explanatory claims of any discourse presuming to invoke "inert matter" as a "frame" for comprehending "life and consciousness."[38]

Similarly, Vaihinger's postulation of a realm of "absolute, unchangeable necessity" and of the intrinsic fictionality of all explanatory abstractions bears a distinct similarity to the epistemology guiding *Goodbye to Berlin*. Like Vaihinger's maker of fictions, Isherwood's "camera eye" inhabits an opaque historical world (a "'given' that cannot be avoided") that leads him to postpone the time when all this will have to be developed, carefully printed, fixed." The privileged status of the artist thus hinges upon the provisional nature of any propositional schemes that he would impose upon the raw facticity of historical actuality. "'Christopher Isherwood,'" Isherwood tells us in his preface, "is a convenient ventriloquist's dummy, nothing more."[39] His statements about prefascist Berlin are thus to be taken as fictive hypotheses; even when he describes the mounting vigilante terror in Berlin, he "can't altogether believe that any of this has really happened."

In addition, Husserl's notion that facts are mere "exemplars" articulates a conception of phenomenological interchangeability that surfaces frequently in modernist fictions—whether in Stein's conjunction of the subjectivities of herself and Alice B. Toklas, in Faulkner's undifferentiated blending of the voices of Quentin and Shreve, or in Warren's suggestion of transhistorical ethical parallelism in the crimes of Cass Mastern and Judge Irwin. In these texts, indeed, the Husser-

---

[38]While I am not arguing that any of the philosphers mentioned here directly influenced any of the novelists in question, a case can be made for Bergson's influence on Woolf. See James Hafley, *The Glass Roof: Virginia Woolf as Novelist* (Berkeley: University of California Press, 1954), 43–44. See also, however, J. W. Graham, "A Negative Note on Bergson and Virginia Woolf," *Essays in Criticism*, 6 (June 1956): 70–74.

[39]Isherwood, 7.

lian equivalence of factitious objects of perception even implies an equivalence in the subjects of perception: "*Whatever belongs to the essence of the individual can also belong to another individual.*" In their abandonment of a historically based typicality that would mediate between the individual and the social, Stein, Faulkner, and Warren portray historical agents who partake of both a unique particularity and a collective being that supersedes individual identity altogether. Husserl's description of all empirical data as "facts of consciousness" also illuminates the treatment of documentary particulars in these mimetic texts. Quentin can undertake his bold imaginative extrapolations because all the data available to him are, it seems, equally verifiable and fallible: the "essential universality" of the Sutpen story is therefore unrelated to the "connection obtaining between spatio-temporal facts" and, indeed, need not make "the slightest assertion concerning the facts."[40]

Relativism and Determinism in Modernist Historiography

Historians and philosophers of history in the early decades of the twentieth century also participated in a critical reassessment of the positivist heritage—in particular, they took as their target the objectivist pretensions of "scientific history." Alfred Bushnell Hart voiced the new skepticism when he declared in 1899 that "the analogy of the natural sciences may be pushed too far. . . . Facts as facts, however carefully selected, scientific treatment in itself, however necessary for the ascertainment of truth, are no more history than recruits arranged in battalions are an army.[41] Pursuing the methodological implications of this insight, some modernist historiographers became relativists, engaging in a self-conscious reflection upon their own epistemological assumptions and proclaiming the limitations of their conclusions. Others, going in the opposite direction, proposed grand

[40]For the argument that Faulkner historicizes his referent and defetishizes the specious objectivity of the "reified reader," see Carolyn Porter, *Seeing and Being: The Plight of the Participant Observer in Emerson, James, Adams, and Faulkner* (Middletown: Wesleyan University Press, 1981), 241–76.

[41]Alfred Bushnell Hart, "Imagination in History," *American Historical Review*, 15 (January 1910): 234, 236–37. For more on the shifts in American historiography early in the twentieth century, see *History*, by John Higham, with Leonard Krieger and Felix Gilbert (Englewood Cliffs: Prentice-Hall, 1965), 87–131.

schemes of historical development that turned speculative history away from the task of scientific description and toward the goal of philosophical meditation. While the relativist and the speculative historians wrote very different kinds of narratives, they each rejected a heritage that they saw as linear and progressive in its conception of historical process and as positivist in its assumptions about historical inquiry.

Croce was to modernist historiography what Hegel had been to the historiography of the previous century. Launching a broadside against the methodological and philosophical presuppositions of the positivist historians, Croce declared that scientific method was intrinsically antithetical to the enterprise of the historian; historical reconstruction, he argued, is a "spiritual act." Science, for Croce, could yield only an "external" perception of data, whereas history necessitated an "internal" comprehension, an imaginative reenactment of the motives of historical agents. The historian's own subjectivity was therefore the key to effective historical narration; the scientific method could produce only dead history, or "chronicle," whereas the intuitive intervention of the historian produced "living" history, necessarily written from the standpoint of the present. "The deed of which history is told," stipulated Croce, "must vibrate in the soul of the historian."[42] If the scientific method violated the creative nature of historical discourse, however, the attempt to write comprehensive or speculative philosophies of history of the Hegelian sort was, for Croce, equally bankrupt. Because of the inherently inventive and provisional nature of historical reconstruction, the historian could never hope to generate totalizing explanatory systems, which were simply "metaphysical constructs" invoking a superficially empirical methodology. The historian, declared Croce, is limited to exploring only "proximate causes."

In the hands of Croce, then, the Hegelian conception of history as the unfolding of reason underwent a crucial transformation. Croce retained the idealist aspects of Hegel's formulation:

> The spirit itself is history, maker of history at every moment of its existence, and also the result of all anterior history. Thus the spirit bears with it all its history, which coincides with itself. . . . The spirit, so to

---

[42]Benedetto Croce, *History: Its Theory and Practice*, trans. Douglas Ainslie (New York: Russell & Russell, 1960), 12. I quote below from pp. 65 and 25.

speak, lives upon its own history without those external things called narratives and documents; but those external things are instruments that it makes for itself, acts prepatory to that internal vital evocation in whose process they are resolved.

Croce abandoned the Hegelian requirement that Spirit is manifested only in its concretions, asserting instead that history is thought, an "internal vital evocation," to which the "facts" of history stand in merely an illustrative relation. Hegelian totalization could therefore be, for Croce, only a hubristic venture, for there were no empirical standards for evaluating the relative adequacy of any causal analysis of past events. Croce explicitly repudiated relativism and irrationalism (he continually dissociated his project from that of Bergson, to which it was often linked), but his theory logically implied the subjective idealism that it claimed to disdain. His formulation of the process of historical reconstruction required that the historian rely centrally upon intuition—what he called the "lightning-flash" of insight. Aprioristic imagination thus emerged as the ultimate source of historical knowledge; as in Husserlian phemonenology, identity furnished the basis of cognition, and historical discourse became an "act of faith."

Croce's contemporaries in the United States, the "New Historians," were confronting their positivist heritage in a somewhat less hostile manner, but they eventually endorsed a relativistic stance that was readily compatible with Crocean idealism. James Harvey Robinson, author of the seminal *The New History*, mounted an assault on the followers of Ranke. "What onlookers call 'impartial history' and the professionals call 'objectivity,'" he quipped, "is merely history without an object."[43] Yet Robinson also denigrated the tradition of novelistic narration exemplified by Bancroft and favored some of the "scientific" aspirations that Croce deplored. The historian "is at liberty to use only his scientific imagination, which is quite different from a literary imagination," he declared. Charles Beard, whose *An Economic Interpretation of the Constitution of the United States* exemplifies the achievement of the New History at its most rigorous, answered Robinson's call for a history that would be both "present-minded" and "scientific." In this study, Beard called explicit attention to his

[43]James Harvey Robinson, *The New History* (1912; New York: Free Press, 1965), xxi. The quoted passage below appears on p. 52.

own methodological procedures. In his preface to the 1913 edition, Beard distinguished his own work from the three dominant historio-graphical traditions in the United States—the romantic nationalism of Bancroft, the chauvinsim of the racialist historians, and the neu-tralist pretensions of the scientific historians.[44] Yet Beard did not re-strict himself to a Crocean exploration of "proximate causes." In his exhaustively documented study of the economic interests of the Founding Fathers, he offered a compelling analysis of the class nature of the Constitution that retains its influence to this day. Like Dos Passos's *U.S.A.*, Beard's study defamiliarizes the course of American history, submitting it to a subversive critique that is itself aware of its own ideological premises. It is perhaps no accident that Dos Passos was a great admirer of Beard.

While the New Historians corrected the errors of scientific history in important ways, they hardly disowned all its guiding assumptions. Beard declared that his highly partisan stance in *An Economic Interpre-tation* was "coldly neutral"; Robinson celebrated the liberation of his-tory from its "long servitude to philosophy."[45] The New Historians did not wish to resolve the contradiction between "science-minded-ness" and "present-mindedness" by positing that historical truth can be both objective and partisan at the same time: a Brechtian theory of discourse and a Leninist theory of politics were alien to their liberal temperament. By the 1930s, they had abandoned their objectivist posture and had come to endorse Croce's notion that all history is "contemporary history." Thus, Beard, who became Croce's most ar-dent apostle and popularizer on this side of the Atlantic, remarked in his 1935 preface to *An Economic Interpretation* that his study was "merely what it professes to be—a version, not the absolute truth —of history." It "does not 'explain' the Constitution," he conceded. "It does not exclude other explanations deemed more satisfactory to the explainers."[46]

[44]Charles Beard, *An Economic Interpretation of the Constitution of the United States* (1913; New York: Macmillan, 1944), 1–4. I quote below from p. ix.

[45]Robinson, 99.

[46]Beard, ix. For the later Beard, Robinsonian "present-mindedness" came to mean rela-tivism, not relevance. "The pallor of waning time, if not of death," he lamented in the 1930s, "rests upon the latest volume of history, fresh from the roaring press." Quoted in Richard Hofstadter, *The Progressive Historians: Turner, Beard, Parrington* (New York: Ran-dom House, 1968), 308. For more on the changes in Beard's view of history, see Hofstadter, 304–17.

From the explicit relativism of the later Beard it was only a step to the acknowledged idealism of R. G. Collingwood, the most important British practitioner of Crocean historiography. Collingwood asserted, like Croce, that history is the "reenactment" of past experience," requiring imaginative empathy and identification on the part of the historian. History therefore comprises—in his famous phrase —an immense "web of imaginative construction,"[47] in which not merely the lacunae and the connections, but the "fixed points" themselves, are determined by an essentially autonomous cognitive procedure. The historian, said Collingwood, builds up a "picture of the past, the product of his own *a priori* imagination, that has to justify the sources used in its own construction." In Collingwood's hands, Croce's conception of history as "internal vital evocation" received its fullest theoretical articulation. The criterion for validity in historical discourse is, emphatically, coherence rather than correspondence; like the Husserlian subject, the Collingwoodian historian posits identity (that is, reference to subjective insight) as the source of knowledge and seeks from facticity only secondary corroboration. In Collingwood's philosophy of history, the attack on positivism comes full circle, and we meet again Comte's despair of ever knowing the "inmost causes of phenomena."

While in the early decades of the century analytical philosophers of history were moving toward a narrowing and a qualification of the historian's explanatory claims, speculative philosphers of history were launching the attack upon positivism from another direction. Spengler exemplified the most conservative tendency in this ideological opposition, for his attack upon scientific history was, fundamentally and explicitly, an attack upon rationalism as such. Indeed, Spengler resisted primarily the residually progressive aspect of positivism—its insistence upon the possible objectivity and determinacy of knowledge and upon the uses of empiricism in historical reconstruction. Rejecting the search for causal uniformity, laws, and "measurability" in history, Spengler declared that "*causality has nothing whatever to do with Time. . . . Real history is heavy with fate but free of laws.*"[48] The historian thus explicitly repudiates the regulative

[47]R. G. Collingwood, *The Idea of History* (1946; New York: Oxford University Press, 1956), 242. I quote below from p. 245.

[48]Oswald Spengler, *The Decline of the West: Form and Actuality* (1918), trans. Charles Francis Atkinson (New York: Knopf, 1926), 120, 118.

principle of reason in favor of an irrationalist vitalism: "Only the insight that can penetrate into the metaphysical is capable of experiencing in data *symbols* of that which happened, and so of elevating an Incident into a Destiny. . . . *Life* is the alpha and omega, and life has no system, no programme, no rationality; it exists for itself and through itself, and the profound order in which it realizes itself can only be intuited and felt—and then perhaps described." Spengler's charged fatalism thus coexisted with a peculiar methodological relativisim: determinism in the sphere of events is clearly linked with indeterminacy in the sphere of contemplation.

Spengler may have denigrated the "scientific" or "empirical" method, but he asserted nonetheless that history does indeed realize itself in a "profound order." He called for a "morphology of world history" that would discover the essence of historical movement in cyclical recurrence and in the appearance of "contemporaneous" phenomena in separate ages. Spengler thus associated "fate" with the rise and fall of peoples and nations. In his disturbingly Europocentric view of the "great" civilizations and his glorification of great autocrats and military leaders, Spengler reasserted the teleological nationalism of many historians in the century before—with the difference that national destiny, in Spengler's hands, is a grim proposition indeed, divested of the enlightenment association of progress with reason and democracy that had energized the pronouncements of a Michelet and even a Bancroft. "The genuine Internationale," he declared, "is imperialism."[49] Spengler thus proclaimed the irrelevance of scientific method at the same time that he invested his own vitalistic philosophy with a fatalistic authority. This charged combination of irrationalism with apocalyptic nationalism accounts for the easy assimilation of the major tenets of Spenglerian thought to Nazi ideology.

Spengler articulates an overtly reactionary version of the modernist critique of positivism. But even liberal speculative historians like Arnold J. Toynbee and H. G. Wells reached comparable conclusions. Toynbee insistently differentiated his own Anglo-American "empiricism" from Spengler's Germanic idealism and proclaimed hope where Spengler saw only decline. He argued that the study of his-

---

[49]Quoted in Georg Lukács, *The Destruction of Reason*, trans. Peter Palmer (Atlantic Highlands, N.J.: Humanities, 1981), 464.

tory demonstrates the succession of rising and falling civilizations, whereby each one experiences a similar pattern of "rally and rout," "challenge and response." He claimed that release from cyclical recurrence was possible, however, not by the working out of a progressive principle in human affairs, but by a repetition of the divine intervention first illustrated in the coming of Christ. "Inasmuch as it cannot be supposed that God's nature is less constant than man's," he hypothesized, "we may and must pray that the reprieve which God has granted to our society once will not be refused it we ask for it again in a humble spirit and with a contrite heart."[50] Wells, in the 1921 edition of his *An Outline of History*, sadly concluded that "there has been a slipping off of ancient restraints; a real *decivilization* of men's minds." He prophetically noted, "New falsities may arise and hold men in some unrighteous and fated scheme of order for a time, before they collapse amidst the misery and slaughter of generations."[51] Despite his liberal faith in progress, Wells, like Toynbee, ultimately placed his hopes for world salvation in the religious spirit: "Religious emotion —stripped of corruptions and freed from its last priestly entanglements—may presently blow through life again like a great wind, bursting the doors and flinging open the shutters of the individual life and making many things possible and easy that in these present days of exhaustion seem almost too difficult to desire." While Well's vision of a collectivist future "flinging open the shutters of the individual life" has little in common with Spengler's grim conclusion about the "genuine Internationale," he, like Toynbee, appears to have abandoned the Hegelian notion that change is generated by contradictions internal to the historical process itself. All three look to a telos beyond human agency or scientific formulation.

It should be apparent that many of the conceptions of historical process and inquiry guiding analytical and speculative historiography furnish the epistemological premises to modernist documentary fiction. Faulkner's Quentin Compson in *Absalom, Absalom!* can be seen as a prototype of the Collingwoodian historian, for he boldly constructs a "web of imaginative construction" in his "*a priori* imagination" and evaluates the explanatory power of facts on the basis of dis-

---

[50]Arnold J. Toynbee, *A Study of History*, reprinted in *Theories of History*, ed. Patrick Gardiner (New York: Free Press, 1959), 205.

[51]H. G. Wells, *The Outline of History: Being a Plain History of Life and Mankind*, 3d ed. (New York: Macmillan, 1921), 1089, 1100.

cursive coherence rather than referential correspondence. In his futile attempt to wrest a meaning from the accumulated data about Cass Mastern, Warren's Jack Burden dramatizes the dilemma of a historian trained in the positivist method; his intuitionist discovery of patterns of historical recurrence—personalized instances of "rally and rout," as it were—is treated as the discovery of a more adequate method of historical inquiry. Thomas Wolfe's attribution of fascist violence to an unconquerable atavism embedded in all of humanity represents a horrified liberal's surrender to the primitive irrationalism that Spengler celebrates with hearty gloom. The extreme alienation and despair of Isherwood's camera eye bear an affinity to the disillusionment voiced by Wells at the termination of his tour of world history. Even Orlando's succession of historical reincarnations blends into a cyclical pattern similar to those described by Spengler or Toynbee: her/his diachronic roles are hardly identical in appearance, but they constitute a "morphology" signaling a synchronic essence. Historians and novelists alike reject the use of empiricist documentation to support linear theories of historical development which the events of the early twentieth century seemed to belie. In so doing, however, they relinquish the search for a determinate interpretation that would enable them to see their own reified present as the product of concrete historical developments. Their crisis is the crisis of liberalism in the era of monopoly capitalism.

The "Problem of Commodities" in the Modernist Era

The modernist era spanned the period when capital underwent the transition from its competitive to its monopolist phase. Because competition forced it constantly to modernize its technological base, capital became increasingly concentrated in its fixed component (raw materials, machinery, and overhead), as opposed to its variable component (wages). This process—designated by Marx as the "increase in the organic composition of capital"—resulted in a number of important changes in capital's social role. Sohn-Rethel states,

> Firms where . . . part of the cost is high in relation to the direct costs, in the main of materials and wages which vary according to the volume of output, cannot easily respond to the market regulatives of social economy controlling the play of the law of value. When demand recedes and

prices tend to slump, production should be cut down and supplies be diminished. But heavy overheads will cause unit costs to rise with lessened output, and we obtain the contradiction that adaptation of supplies to receding demands forces the cost to rise when prices fall. In other words the rising organic composition of capital makes production increasingly inadaptable to the market regulatives. The reaction to the contradiction on the part of the firms affected can only be to force them, as a matter of life and death, to try to obtain control of the movements of the market. This is how they become "monopolists."[52]

Where capitalists formerly had adapted production more or less to the demands of the market and had expanded or contracted their labor pool as they chose, now they were compelled to keep their plant functioning at all times in order to offset the tendency toward a falling rate of profit that accompanied their large-scale investment in fixed capital. As a result, the imperatives of production and consumption and the imperatives of exchange entered into a highly contradictory and often antagonistic relationship, in which the second nature of commodities (as embodiments of abstract labor) stood in open opposition to their first nature (as use values embodying concrete labor). Two central consequences of this development—one highly visible, one more covert—are of importance to our inquiry here.

Imperialism

The more palpable effect of the movement toward monopolism was the growing necessity to open up new markets and resume colonial expansion—in other words, imperialism. The last quarter of the nineteenth century witnessed apparently uncontrollable cycles of boom and bust, in which the limited markets of the industrialized nations were unable to absorb the flow of commodities produced by the rapidly expanding industrial base. Imperialism was the necessary solution to the economic and social dislocations generated by this development. Lenin, in his *Imperialism: The Highest Stage of Capitalism*, quoted Cecil Rhodes's frank admission of the "importance of imperialism":

[52]Sohn-Rethel, *Intellectual and Manual Labor: A Critique of Epistemology*, trans. Martin Sohn-Rethel (Atlantic Highlands, N.J.: Humanities, 1978), 144–45.

I was in the East End of London yesterday and attended a meeting of the
unemployed. I listened to the wild speeches, which were just a cry for
"bread, bread!" and on my way home I pondered over the scene and I
became more than ever convinced of the importance of imperialism. . . .
My cherished idea is a solution for the social problem, i.e., in order to
save the 40,000,000 inhabitants of the United Kingdom from a bloody
civil war, we colonial statesmen must acquire new lands to settle the
surplus population, to provide new markets for the goods produced in
the factories and mines. The Empire, as I have always said, is a bread
and butter question. It you want to avoid civil war, you must become
imperialists.[53]

Imperialist expansion did postpone civil war—at least in the Western
nations—and it temporarily offset the worst of the periodic crises in
overproduction. The state intervened more unabashedly than before
in the affairs of capital, and cartels were formed to control the vagar-
ies of the market. These measures, however, could only delay the inevitable consequences of sharpened interimperialist rivalry. As Lenin
pointed out, these cartels would inevitably collapse, involving the
monopolists in a war to partition the markets and resources of the
globe. The spiraling of presumably enlightened nations toward the
Great War and the unprecedented carnage and horror of the combat
thus resulted from the inevitable contradictions within both production and exchange in the monopolist era.

To Lenin, who saw the "problem of commodities" at the root of
early twentieth-century historical developments, the causes of the
Great War were transparent. In his preface to the 1917 edition of *Imperialism*, he noted the prophetic character of the analysis of imperialism he had published the year before and urged that "unless the question of the economic essence of imperialism is studied, it will be
impossible to understand and appraise modern war and modern politics." But to Western bourgeois intellectuals reared on evolutionary
liberalism in what Dos Passos called the "peaceful afterglow of the
nineteenth century," Lenin's answer was by no means apparent. Taking the organization of production based upon the sale and purchase
of labor power as a self-evident premise, a metaphysical axiom, bourgeois intellectuals generally failed to penetrate the opacity of the com-

[53]Quoted in Lenin, *Imperialism: The Highest Stage of Capitalism*, in *Collected Works*, trans.
George H. Hanna, ed. Robert Daglish (Moscow: Progress, 1967), 22:256–57. I quote below from p. 194.

modity form or to question the legitimacy of the exchange of wages
for labor power—hence their tendency to reify the very phenomenon
of reification. In the time of Adam Smith, Marx noted, "the interior
of the commodity" was only partially penetrated by the contradiction
between use value and exchange value, concrete and abstract labor.[54]
One hundred years later, however, the visibility of production processes in the object of production had been blurred, for the entire
economy was organized around the commodification of wage labor.

As the normative self-evidence of the market economy gave way
to uncontrollable cycles of boom and decline, therefore, bourgeois
intellectuals experienced a crisis in ideology. Instead of attempting
to penetrate the opacity of the social relations of production, they
tended to resort to causal explanations that presupposed the legitimacy (or at least the fixity) of the mode of production that was caus-
ing the uncontrollable—and seemingly irrational—course of modern
history. A phenomenon that was political to the core assumed the status of an epistemological dilemma. The pressures of urbanization and
economic depression appeared to signal the automatism of industrialization and technology per se, rather than the historically specific organization of the social relations of production necessitated by finance
capital. And subjectivity was advanced to supply the locus of meaning that social reality lacked. Husserl proclaimed, "There are only
two escapes from the crisis of European existence: the downfall of
Europe in its estrangement from its own rational sense of life, its fall
into hostility and into barbarity; or the rebirth of Europe from the
spirit of philosophy through a heroism of reason that overcomes naturalism once and for all."[55] The postulation of a heroic, reasonable
self transcending the naturalistic nightmare of fragmentation and
chaos was thus an ideological mediation of monopoly capital's increased need to subordinate the entire social synthesis to the imperatives of the exchange relation.

In the context of this crisis in self-evidence, the Great War appeared
to corroborate either the uncontrollable cyclicality or simply the
unpredictability of historical processes. Where the French Revolution

[54]Marx, *Grundrisse: Foundations of the Critique of Political Economy*, trans. Martin Nicolaus
(New York: Random House/Vintage, 1973), 169.
[55]Edmund Husserl, *The Crisis of European Sciences and Transcendental Phenomenology*
(1954), trans. David Carr (Evanston: Northwestern University Press, 1970), 299.

and the Napoleonic wars had shattered the ahistorical abstractions of Nature and Providence and had signaled the power of the masses in making history, the Great War signaled the omnipotence of History over the acts of individual participants and once again appeared to subordinate history to Nature—only this time to a Nature constituted by an odd admixture of indeterminacy and determinism, contingency and fatality. Confronted with the imperialistic consequences of the "problem of commodities" in its most naked form, most novelists, philosophers, and historians took the commodity itself as an aprioristic foundation rather than as an object of analysis. As Lukács remarked in *History and Class Consciousness*, bourgeois society, "unable to comprehend [its] reality and [its] origin . . . as the product of the same subject [i.e., capital] that has 'created' the comprehended totality of knowledge," will espouse an "ultimate point of view, decisive for the whole of its thought, . . . of immediacy."[56] The contradictory response to reification in modernist thought thus articulates not any failure of nerve or intellect but the inadequate ideological premises upon which this response was founded. The assault upon fetishism and objectification was carried out with the artillery of conceptual abstractions that took as axiomatic the second nature of the commodity form.

Taylorism

The growth of imperialism was the most obvious result of the increase in the organic composition of capital, but equally significant consequences were manifested in the process of production itself. Capital was compelled to engage in a greater degree of exploitation of the work force and, consequently, to exercise a greater degree of control over production. When the capitalist had invested so great a proportion of his financial resources in machinery and overhead, he could not afford to let his plant be underutilized through the inefficient use of variable capital; not simply a greater or lesser amount of profit but his very survival as a capitalist depended upon his ability to extract maximum productivity from his laborers. Earlier phases of capitalist development had witnessed the subjugation of the proletariat as a class to the autonomism of capital and the harnessing of pro-

---

[56]Lukács, *History and Class Consciousness*, 156.

duction to the machine. But only in the era of monopoly capital did the entire labor process become segmented and quantified in accordance with the dictates of Taylorism, or "scientific management"; labor did not merely confront and direct, but was actually incorporated into, the functioning of the machine. With production fragmented into components measurable by stopwatches and slide rules, human labor became, as Sohn-Rethel puts it, "directly adaptable and could be inserted or transferred into [the machinery] without any difficulty of conversion."[57]

In the era of Taylorism and flow production, then, the split between mental and manual labor entered into the arena of production itself, and reification emerged as a self-evident feature of both the labor process and the social relations of production.[58] Braverman notes,

> Both in order to ensure management control and to cheapen the worker, conception and execution must be rendered separate spheres of work, and for this purpose the study of work processes must be reserved to management and kept from the workers, to whom its results are communicated only in the form of simplified job tasks governed by simplified instructions which it is thenceforth their duty to follow unthinkingly and without comprehension of the underlying technical reasoning or data. . . . In the setting of antagonistic social relations, of alienated labor, hand and brain become not just separated, but divided and hostile, and the human unity of hand and brain turns into its opposite, something less than human. . . .
>
> The separation of hand and brain . . . is inherent in the [capitalist] mode of production from its beginnings, and it develops, under capitalist management, throughout the history of capitalism, but it is only during the past century that the scale of production, the resources made available to the modern corporation by the rapid accumulation of capital, and the conceptual apparatus and trained personnel have become available to institutionalize this separation in a systematic and formal fashion.[59]

[57]Sohn-Rethel, 155.

[58]For the alternate view that reification is attributable mainly to the shift toward production for Department II (consumer goods), and hence derives principally from the realm of consumption, see Michael Spindler, *American Literature and Social Change: William Dean Howells to Arthur Miller* (Bloomington: Indiana University Press, 1983), esp. 97–120.

[59]Harry Braverman, *Labor and Monopoly Capital: The Degradation of Work in the Twentieth Century* (New York: Monthly Review, 1974), 118, 125–26.

It is arguable whether Taylorism represented a qualitative alteration in capitalist forces of production or simply a tremendous quantitative expansion of the reifying tendencies noted by Marx. In either case, however, it involved a new level of abstraction in production relations. Now, from the perspective of both the capitalist and of the worker, the telos of production in its first nature (that is, the production of use values) became entirely subordinated to its second nature telos (that is, the production of surplus value). The residual quality of labor that Marx specified as distinctly human—that is, that "at the end of every labour process, we get a result that already existed in the imagination of the labourer at its commencement"—was finally eradicated.[60] The worker was increasingly dependent upon the capitalist, for not only the equipment and raw materials but also every aspect of engineering and planning were the property of the capitalist. "The power of capital is magnified in monopoly capitalism," Sohn-Rethel remarks, "because in the size of the modern system the workers are more powerless than they ever have been since slavery, owing to the minuteness of each individual contribution."[61] Accordingly, the "fair exchange" of wages for labor power gained in legitimacy, or least in apparent naturalness, for the worker was divested of the capacity to plan production or even to control the machine to which labor was attached.

Reification and Representation

It is interesting to speculate about the ways in which the conceptual abstractions guiding the characteristic representational strategies of the modernist documentary novel mediate the distinctive form of the exchange relation in the era of imperialist war and Taylorism. The modernist postulation of autonomous subjectivity, for example, can be seen as articulating the full divorce of mental from manual labor in the production process. In one sense, of course, the modernist text's empyrean positioning of a transcendental subject simply signifies an increased implication in the fetishistic epistemological paradigms that had been fostered by capitalist production in its earlier phases. In the modernist novel, however, the transcendental subject is fully tran-

[60]Marx, *Capital: A Critique of Political Economy*, ed. Frederick Engels, trans. Samuel Moore and Edward Aveling (New York: International, 1967), 1:178.
[61]Sohn-Rethel, 158.

scendentalized, for the res extensa cannot provide a locus of significance or value in which the ego cogitans may meaningfully define itself. The ego cogitans now constitutes a dualism: an authentic self that discovers identity apart from production, history, and social relations, and a public self that merely plays a role in the social collectivity. As George Simmel noted in his *The Philosophy of Money*, in a society characterized by universal commodity exchange and the universal commodification of labor power, "every material content of life" becomes "more and more material and impersonal so that the non-reifiable remnant may become all the more personal and all the more indisputably the property of the person."[62] The modernist novel's abandonment of typicality and totalization thus reveals a disenchantment not only with realism's epistemological naivete but also with the notion that any social definition of individuality can successfully embody the intersection of personal and extrapersonal realities. The isolation of the perceiving self is now a priori: Santayana's "private little rivulet" of personal experience is separated from the "vast cosmic flood" of history by the severence of conception from execution, of abstract from concrete, right within the process of production itself.

If the perceiving self takes as a premise not merely its separation but also its ontological isolation from the object of perception, it follows that the subject's attempts to account for that object will be correspondingly divested of power. The artist-hero's proclamation of the inadequacy of his discourse to explain specific historical phenomena can be seen as further testimony to the pervasiveness of the second nature abstraction at the material base of consciousness. To offer a determinate account of causality is, implicitly, to associate oneself with a degrading positivist rationalism that subsumes discourse to the province of exchange: if the use value of labor power to capital is the expansion of surplus value and if the use value of reason is the more efficient quantification and control of production, then the use value of mimesis will be its lack of use. This conclusion does not represent a concession to the theoretical position (for which the foundation is laid in the modernist period) that modernist documentary novels actually lack cognitive power: the very affirmation of indeterminacy

---

[62]Georg Simmel, *The Philosophy of Money*, quoted in Lukács, *History and Class Consciousness*, 156-57.

and impotence is itself a proposition carrying assertive force. A ventriloquist's dummy does, after all, express the ventriloquist's words, even if the authorial self appears committed to a mysterious silence. Nonetheless, the modernist novel's elevation of aesthetic sensibility over instrumental reason constitutes a capitulation to the monopolist divorce of conception from execution, since it relegates the protest against reification to a fictional realm that denies its own explanatory relation to its referent.

One response to reification in modernist fiction is to valorize the apparently nonpropositional operations of the transcendental subject; another response is to propose an undifferentiated equivalence of subjectivities. By divorcing thought from practice, Taylorism enforces a series of equivalences—between the various products of abstract labor, between humans and machines. This abstraction of particularities in the realm of production manifests itself in the modernist documentary novel's paradoxical treatment of narratorial identity: the text celebrates the uniqueness of the autonomous self whose identity is the source of insight, but it also proclaims the peculiar interchangeability of this self with alternate subjectivities. Ironically, the subsumption of commodities to the abstraction of their second nature effects the abstraction of the very subject who presumes to hold itself apart from the dehumanization it beholds. Henry Miller's "women I have known"—as women, of course, easily objectified as abstractions—blur in his attempts at recall; Cass Mastern and Judge Irwin signal, by their Spenglerian "contemporaneity," the accidental nature of their individual historical concretions; Quentin and Shreve treat all empirical data as equally valuable and fallible. But the Gertrude Stein who is valorized as a prophet of revolutionary modes of perception also blends imperceptibly into Alice B. Toklas; Quentin and Shreve lose their individual articulation and merge into a single undifferentiated Faulknerian voice. The Husserlian subject who finds the source of cognition in identity, once divested of the social contextualization that would provide a concrete historical definition of self, is finally assimilated to the very undifferentiated abstraction to which it sets itself in opposition.

Finally, the kinds of documentation that appear in modernist fiction can be understood as mediations—at once critical and concessionary—of the dominant form of the exchange abstraction in the monopolist era. The pseudofactual ambience surrounding the fictional autobiography testifies to the isolation of the perceiving subject: the sense of the real anchors the subject's discourse in a felt historicity while avoiding the sorts of authorial judgments that would imply—indeed, necessitate—the subject's contextualization in social experience. Hence the significance of Isherwood's decision to frame the fictional parts of *Goodbye to Berlin* within the documentary frame of a personal diary. The camera eye ruminating in isolation provides an insight into the terrors of the metropolis that the character featured in the fictions cannot hope to signal through his analogizing role. Yet by virtue of their very historicity, the protagonists of modernist fictional autobiography are denied the capacity fully to enforce their views upon the reader. The peculiar rhetorical status of Stephen's aesthetic, for example, derives not merely from the questionable worth of the aesthetic itself but also from the etiolated interpretive force of the fiction in which it is presented. Where the eighteenth-century sense of the real projected a hesitant empiricism, its counterpart in the modernist fictional autobiography denies the epistemological premises of empiricism altogether, since the abstracting activity of the subject now possesses only an incidental relation to the realm of the concrete. In the pseudofactual novel, the foregrounding and ironizing of the perceiving subject's discourse reflected the configuration of a society in which capital only partially controlled the labor process. In the modernist fictional autobiography, the position of the ego cognitans is valorized, but as a locus of sensibility rather than as one of comprehension: capital is the social subject, and individual perceiving subjects question their ability to propose cognition on the basis of the empirical data they perceive.

The uses of documentation in the metahistorical novel can also be seen as signaling the mediation of reification in the "real abstraction." Where the realistic historical novel introduced empirical data to corroborate its thematic statements, the metahistorical novel brings in historical documentation to highlight the provisional and indeterminate nature of historical knowledge. Jack Burden thus is initially hampered by his objectivist desire to "know" Cass Mastern through "facts" rather than intuitive identification. Quentin and Shreve, despite their superior imaginative synthesis, finally produce a version of the Sutpen story that is only a superior "fiction," in Vaihinger's sense of the word. The realm of historical concretion is related only incidentally to the abstractions by which historical processes can be described. The introduction of historical data in the metahistorical novel thus serves to dislocate, rather than to reinforce, the reader's perception of the protagonist as a synecdochic type. Orlando is defined as a consciousness who discovers in aesthetic production a stability and continuity of ego denied by the fluid and peripheral nature of her/his particular historical incarnations. The Hegelian dialectic between abstraction and concretion that undergirded the representational strategy of the realistic historical novel has collapsed. Abstraction now supersedes a fragmented concretion, just as the telos of production as conception is severed from its execution as practical activity. Telling the truth becomes difficult indeed when the teller sees all particular truths as variants on an undifferentiated facticity and sees the activity of telling itself as a praxis lacking a determinate subject.

In most documentary fiction of the nineteenth and early twentieth centuries, reification enables a new level of totalization, but it also pressures that totalization toward increasing autonomy and ahistoricity. The documentary novel invokes facts to buttress its propositional claims, but these facts become more and more incidental to the general truths that the text asserts. Abstraction is a curious phenomenon, however, for it is constituted by a contradiction between empirically based synthesis and fragmentation, between explanatory adequacy and opacity. The documentary novel routinely exemplifies this contradiction, and its varying and conflicting claims to assertive power can thus be seen as signaling divergent tendencies within reification itself. When the text does not simply take abstraction as an epistemological premise but instead treats it as an epistemological (and political) problem (as in U.S.A.), the contradictory nature of abstraction is foregrounded, and empiricism becomes a means rather than a barrier to the representation of social reality. Ordinarily such oppositional texts are the exception rather than the rule. When a group of writers find themselves confronting abstraction in a particularly intrusive form, however, they generally cannot avoid its contradictory implications, and they together constitute an adversarial tradition that formulates and practices distinct conventions for asserting mimetic truth. Racism constitutes one such form of abstraction, and Afro-

American documentary novelists one such group of writers. In the closing chapter of this book, we shall consider the Afro-American documentary novel as an oppositional tradition that uses empiricism as a weapon against the abstractions that empiricism ordinarily validates.

8

The Afro-American
Documentary Novel

Just as one sees when one walks into a medical research laboratory jars of alcohol containing abnormally large or distorted portions of the human body, just so did I see and feel that the conditions of life under which Negroes are forced to live in America contain the embryonic emotional prefiguration of how a large part of the body politic would react under stress.

—Richard Wright

In the preceding chapters, I have set forth a model describing the principal changes in the documentary novel over the past three centuries and relating these changes to fundamental shifts in the mode of production. In this closing chapter, I shall treat a body of fiction, the Afro-American documentary novel, that invites me to test and reformulate—though not basically alter—my theoretical model. In my discussions of pseudofactual, historical, and modernist documentary fiction, I have suggested that writers choose modes of documentary corroboration that both articulate and confirm existing types of abstraction, both economic and conceptual—that, in short, writers reinforce dominant ideology. In my discussion of the Afro-American documentary novel, however, I shall argue that specific social and historical circumstances can set writers in opposition to dominant ideology. The generic contract accompanying most Afro-American documentary novels is situated in social circumstances that affect in far-reaching ways the procedures by which reality enters the fictional text. Even as writers use familiar strategies of fictional representation, they call into question various of the ideological premises routinely associated with these strategies of representation. Accordingly, the

conceptual abstractions shaping the process of fiction-making reproduce but also query the "real abstraction" that the text represents.

The Afro-American documentary novel continues to adopt the familiar representational strategies of realistic and modernist documentary fiction, but it introduces documentation in ways that subvert
rather than reinforce certain aspects of bourgeois hegemony.[1] In the
Afro-American documentary novel, the two main types of documentary validation—veracious and verifying—are characteristically
blended. The effect of this documentary synthesis is a powerful
historicizing of the referent. Novels in the realistic mode project additional assurances that they tell a truth to which the author directly
attests, and novels written in the modernist mode—both fictional
autobiographies and metahistorical fictions—insistently remind us
that their referents are historically specific. In the hands of the Afro-
American realistic novelist, the text's claim to typicality ordinarily
takes on oppositional force, for the bourgeois hero's status as a representative of the key contradictions informing historical actuality is replaced by the Afro-American protagonist, who clearly possesses no
favored status in the mind of the implied (usually white) reader. The
empiricist claims of realism are therefore challenged even as they are
employed: documentation functions not to authenticate an interpretation of reality that the reader is assumed to share but to probe certain
assumptions—about race, history, social order—that the reader
might hold to be self-evident. Similarly, the pseudofactual projection
of a veracious voice takes on a distinctly adversarial quality in much
Afro-American documentary fiction, since the reader's attention is
continually focused upon the historical conditions that render its
authenticating presence an apparent necessity. The text's flouting of
nonfictional discourse carries added significance when the reader is
led to question whether the text's putative factual model could ever
have been composed. The generic contract of the Afro-American
documentary novel in its various modes is thus characterized by—to
recall Rabinowitz's useful terms—a cautious amount of "assumption" and a considerable amount of "assertion." The proliferation of
documentary materials testifies to the text's denial of an ideological a

[1]It will be noted that, in the discussion that follows, I have cited a few white authors—
that is, Stowe, Tourgée, and Fast. I have included these writers because they directly confront the problem of racism and its representation, which is my central concern here. I do
not mean to imply that they become honorary Afro-Americans by virtue of this fact.

priori and to its insistence that its reconcretized analogous configuration does indeed correspond to a real historical referent.

The reasons for the documentary overdetermination of much Afro-American fiction are apparent: racism denies full subjectivity to the black protagonist and full authority to the black author, so any text affirming such a subjectivity or such an authority necessarily requires the reader to engage in a (willing or unwilling) abolition of disbelief. The Afro-American documentary novel is vehement in its assertion of propositionality. I am not saying, of course, that the text therefore possesses an ideology-transcending propositional force. Recalling the Leninist conception of ideology as partisan discourse outlined in Chapter 4, I contend that the procedures of analogous configuration and ideological abstraction are as embedded in counter-hegemonic mimetic works as they are in texts that project propositions assimilable to dominant systems of belief. Both racism and anti-racism, in other words, constitute ideological positions. Nor am I claiming that Afro-American documentary novels are in any sense contradiction-free; indeed, they frequently incorporate some aspect of dominant ideology as a secondary—at times, even, a primary—aspect of ideological contradiction. I am simply asserting that, as a group, these documentary works are distinguished from the broader Anglo-American tradition by their persistent—and intentional—foregrounding of contradiction in the referent. They continually point to the disjunction between theory and practice in American democracy; their own representational contradictions and constraints express limitations upon "representation" in social reality. In both realistic and modernist works of Afro-American fiction, then, documentary validation calls attention to the epistemological relation between generalization and evidence, even as the texts purport to tell the truth about a reality that has too frequently been misrepresented or simply ignored. It is this insistent stress upon contradiction, rather than any supersession of contradiction, that enables us to speak of Afro-American documentary fiction as an adversarial tradition.

Racism, Empiricism, and Representation

In order to grasp the significance of the testimonial strategies peculiar to Afro-American documentary fiction, it is necessary to establish the essential features of American racism as a social and historical phenomenon and to examine its relation to the epistemological and political paradigms accompanying the growth of American capitalism. Racism is situated, I shall argue, in both the superstructure and the base of society; it denotes attitudes and cultural practices, and it also denotes economic activities and political imperatives. The empirical mode of thought has thus historically provided an important buttress to racist theory and practice, and democratic theories of popular representation have posed no insuperable barriers to the institutional operations of racism, either before or after the abolition of chattel slavery. Racism is a quintessential mode of abstraction, embodying both the imperatives of the real abstraction in capitalist society, as well as the conceptual formulations of human essence and potential to which this real abstraction gives rise.

Racism and Empiricism

Precapitalist social formations had numerous ways of reinforcing and justifying social hierarchy, to be sure, and slavery flourished for thousands of years before the coming of capitalism. Racism as such is a creation of the capitalist epoch, however, originating in the colonial activities of mercantile capitalism. "At first the Spaniards and Portuguese just took over whatever kingdoms they could, and looted them," Richard Popkin notes. "Then, when they were challenged, racial theories were worked out to justify the conquest and rape of America, and later the enslavement of Africa."[2] As Indians died off by the tens of thousands in the gold and silver mines of the New World, racial theorizing abandoned its "ideal speculations about the curious diversities of mankind" and took on increased practical importance. The ensuing dispute over the morality of slavery occurred mainly in the domain of theology. When the more humanistic arguments of De Las Casas and De la Vera Cruz lost out to those of Sepulveda, however, it is significant that the latter invoked nature as well as religion to justify the Spaniards' enslavement of the Indians. "Because of the gravity of their sins," declared Sepulveda, and "be-

[2]Richard Popkin, "The Philosophical Bases of Modern Racism," in *Philosophy and the Civilizing Arts*, ed. Craig Walton and John P. Anton (Athens: Ohio University Press, 1974), 128.

cause of the rudeness of their heathen and barbarous natures," the Indians were obliged "to serve those of more elevated natures, such as the Spaniards possess."[3] As recent research into the history of slavery has shown, this sort of argument was distinctly characteristic of the emerging capitalist epoch. Various kinds of ethnocentrism and religious doctrine provided ideological justification to earlier forms of bondage, but the biological notion of race first supplements and later supplants these as colonial expansion makes it possible to enslave masses of peoples of color.[4]

When capitalism shifted from its mercantile to its manufacturing and then to its industrial phase, the African slave trade figured prominently in the primitive accumulation of capital.[5] "It was a common saying," Eric Williams remarks, "that several of the principal streets of Liverpool had been marked out by the chains, and the walls of the houses cemented by the blood, of the African slaves."[6] The labor power that yielded up surplus value may therefore have been purchased from white proletarians, but the capital that enabled the construction of the factories and mills was largely drawn from the exploitation of slave labor. As Marx noted,

> The discovery of gold and silver in America, the extirpation, enslavement and entombment in mines of the aboriginal population, the beginning of the conquest and looting of the East Indies, the turning of Africa into a warren for the commercial hunting of black-skins, signalised the

[3]Gaines de Sepulveda, cited in Oliver C. Cox, *Caste, Class, and Race: A Study in Social Dynamics* (New York: Monthly Review, 1959), 334.

[4]For more on the relation of slavery to different ideological paradigms, including modern notions of race, see David Brion Davis, *The Problem of Slavery in Western Culture* (Ithaca: Cornell University Press, 1964), and William McKee Evans, "From the Land of Canaan to the Land of Guinea: The Strange Odyssey of the 'Sons of Ham,'" *American Historical Review*, 85 (February 1980): 15–43.

[5]There is a heated debate among scholars of slavery about the precise nature of the relation between the institution of chattel slavery in the Americas and the political economies of merchant and industrial capitalism. Williams argues that slavery was crucial to the primitive accumulation needed for industrialization and that merchant capital actively aided in this process. Elizabeth Fox-Genovese and Eugene Genovese, by contrast, agree that "the slaveholders arose on the foundations of merchant capitalism," but they argue that merchant capital was a "parasitic" and "passive" phenomenon that actually impeded the development of industrial capitalism. See *Fruits of Merchant Capital: Slavery and Bourgeois Property in the Rise and Expansion of Capitalism* (New York: Oxford University Press, 1983), 15–16 and passim.

[6]Eric Williams, *Capitalism and Slavery* (1944; New York: Capricorn, 1966), 63.

rosy dawn of the era of capitalist production. These idyllic proceedings are the chief momenta of primitive accumulation.[7]

As capital modernized its methods of exploitation, the grounds of the arguments justifying bondage on the basis of race were unabashedly shifted from the Bible to biology. In the seventeenth century the term "African" denoted merely geographical origin, similar to "Irish" or "Scottish"; in the eighteenth, it came to denote physical traits and racial essence.[8] Various Enlightenment thinkers produced elaborate taxonomies linking "higher" and "lower" racial types to various environmental determinants. Linnaeus, for example, decided that the climate had produced in Africans an "indolent, negligent" nature that was "governed by caprice," and in Europeans an "acute and inventive" nature that was "governed by laws."[9] Hume, who claimed that he was applying "the experimental method of reasoning to moral subjects," proclaimed that "there never was a civilized nation of any complexion other than white."[10] On the basis of this incontrovertible evidence—gleaned, it would seem, from an "experiment" performed in his own "reasoning" mind—Hume concluded that "such a uniform and constant difference could not happen in so many countries and ages, if nature had not made an original distinction betwixt these breeds of men." George Fredrickson has shown that in the eighteenth century such blatantly racist pronouncements were generally adduced to justify an essentially paternalistic view of race relations. The more "acute" were the keepers of the "indolent." Even the mechanistic materialism of the environmentalist theories of race provided a kind of safety valve: presumably changes in climate would produce changes in phenotype, since these were not coded into the genes.[11]

[7]Marx, *Capital: A Critique of Political Economy*, ed. Frederick Engels, trans. Samuel Moore and Edward Aveling (New York: International, 1967), 1:751.

[8]See Lerone Bennett, *The Shaping of Black America* (Chicago: Johnson, 1975), and Gary Nash, *Red, White, and Black: The Peoples of Early America* (Englewood Cliffs: Prentice-Hall, 1974).

[9]Linnaeus (Karl von Linné), *A General System of Nature through the Three Grand Kingdoms of Animals, Vegetables, and Minerals* (1758; London, 1806), 1: "Mammalia. Order I, Primates."

[10]David Hume, "Of National Characters," in *The Philosophical Works*, ed. T. H. Greer and T. H. Grose (London, 1882), 3:252n.

[11]George Fredrickson, *The Black Image in the White Mind: The Debate on Afro-American Character and Destiny, 1817–1914* (New York: Harper & Row, 1971), chap. 3, passim.

Europeans developed the initial justifications for modern racism. In the United States, however, racist practice gained the surest foothold and biological theories of racial difference received the fullest articulation; the compulsion of African slave labor provided the foundation of fortunes accumulated in the American colonies. Originally utilizing the labor of both black and white indentured servants, the planters found it difficult to control their workers in a territory where labor was in such great demand. "The Americas presented entrepreneurs not only with their greatest opportunities," remarks William McKee Evens, "but also with their most acute problem: how to persuade people to work for bare subsistence in mines and on plantations located in a country of 'open resources,' where there was an abundance of land often free for the taking? How could entrepreneurs control other people's impulse to 'get ahead' in a land of boundless opportunity?"[12] The plantation owners went a long way toward solving this problem when they designated for permanent servitude one segment of the work force that was readily identifiable on the basis of color. Not only did this measure guarantee them a supply of controllable labor, but it also blunted the edge of white rebellion. White servants, apprentices and laborers had to be taught that blacks were not their natural allies (as Lerone Bennett has pointed out, it took one hundred years of legislation, religious exhortation, and corporal punishment to get the message across),[13] but once taught, these whites could prove a valuable buffer for the plantation class. Even though North American chattel slavery was an anachronism and an anomaly, then, for many decades it was compatible with the growth of capitalism in the United States and in fact became increasingly implicated in the global market of the nineteenth century. As H. Bruce Franklin notes, slavery successfully changed "from a predominantly small-scale, quasi-domestic institution appended to hand-tool farming and manufacturing" into the productive base of "an expanding agricultural economy, utilizing machinery to process the harvested crops and pouring vast quantities of agricultural raw materials, principally cotton, into developing capitalist industry in the Northern states and England."[14]

[12]Evans, 42.

[13]Bennett, 61–80.

[14]H. Bruce Franklin, "Animal Farm Unbound; or, What the *Narrative of the Life of Frederick Douglass, An American Slave,* Reveals about American Literature," *New Letters,* 43 (April 1977): 31–32.

Practice

With the expansion of slavery to the vast cotton plantations of what was then the Southwest, the planters abandoned their earlier stance of protective paternalism and invoked more aggressive arguments of biological superiority. Thomas Jefferson, whose *Notes on the State of Virginia* exemplifies the transitional phase between patriarchal and biological theories of race, declared, "I advance it therefore as a suspicion only, that the blacks, whether originally a distinct race, or made distinct by time and circumstances, are inferior to whites in the endowments both of body and mind."[15] The founders of the new pseudosciences of ethnology and craniology were not so hesitant in their proclamations, particularly when slavery apologists were faced with the threat of abolition. The famous biologist Louis Agassiz endorsed a polygenetic theory of human development, holding that blacks had a racial origin wholly separate from that of whites. George Gliddon, in his *Crania Americana* and *Crania Aegyptica*, "proved" by means of skull measurements that the ancient Egyptians had been white and that Caucasians had a demonstrably larger cranial capacity than Africans. Josiah Nott, who explicitly set forth the connection between racist pseudoscience and the cause of the plantation holders, said that "ethnology" was really "niggerology." Samuel Cartwright diagnosed the slave's tendency to run away as "drapetomania." When skull measurements and charts of genetic origin could be adduced as empirical evidence, how could anyone question whether the enslaved Africans were suited for their condition?

By the mid-nineteenth century, the anomalous features of American chattel slavery proved incompatible with modern industrial capitalism, and the Civil War ensued. But when, after Emancipation, the entire national economy came under the sway of Northern business, racism remained central to the expansion of capital and the control of the work force. For decades, Black laborers were restricted to sharecropping, domestic labor, and the most menial industrial jobs; whatever multiracial movements of resistance arose among rank and file farmers and wage laborers were viciously suppressed.[16] Contemporary studies of the economics of racism reveal that even in the aftermath of the Civil Rights movement, the further exploitation of racial minorities continues to yield high profits, to hold down the

[15]Thomas Jefferson, *Notes on the State of Virginia* (Baltimore: Pechin, 1800), 155.
[16]See C. Vann Woodward, *The Strange Career of Jim Crow,* 3d rev. ed. (New York: Oxford University Press, 1974).

wages of whites, and above all to create social and political divisions that seriously impair the possibility of united working-class opposition to monopoly capital.[17] Evans has commented,

> Wherever color prejudice has been reinforced by the profit motive, wherever relations with the blacks have been conditioned not only by face to face contact but also by the pressure of distant and impersonal markets, white prejudices have taken on such an immediacy, a consistency, a neurotic intensity that a number of scholars have understandably mistaken this attitude for an "irrational" psychological phenomenon, rather than a discrete historical one.[18]

Furthermore, ethnology and skull measuring have passed into the archives of myth, but contemporary racist ideology, invoking the "data" of IQ tests, continues to cloak itself in the mantle of empiricism. In short, racism is systematically integral to the social relations of capitalism and cannot be examined as a sociological or psychological phenomenon without attention to its foundation in the production and exchange for profit. It should be argued that, rather than being an unfortunate stain upon the record of bourgeois liberalism, racism has furnished a—if not *the*—principal means by which the American ruling class has gained and maintained its position of dominance.

Racism and Representation

Racism enjoys a paradoxical relation to the basic premises of bourgeois theories of representation. It would appear that a social system founded upon the principle that all men are created equal could only with difficulty enforce practices and espouse theories aiming at the systematic subjugation of entire portions of the human species. Surely, it would seem, the Homo economicus is sufficiently abstract to allow for variations in pigmentation of the skin. Bourgeois political theory has proven quite resourceful in confronting this dilemma, however. Locke, for example, held that "the NATURAL liberty of man is to be free from any superior power on earth, and not to be under the will or legislative authority of man, but to have only the law of nature for his rule."[19] He also contended, however, that, if a man has

---

[17]See, for example, Victor Perlo, *The Economics of Racism U.S.A.: The Roots of Black Inequality* (New York: International, 1975).

[18]Evans, 43.

[19]Locke, *An Essay Concerning the True Original Extent and End of Civil Government* (1690),

"by his own fault forfeited his own life by some act that deserves death, he to whom he has forfeited it may . . . make use of him in his own service." Such positions may not seem compatible with the mass enslavement of Africans, who were, surely, hardly accountable for heinous crimes deserving death. In his capacity as drafter of the constitution of the Carolinas, however, Locke produced a theory that would justify the peculiar relation of freedom to unfreedom in the colonies. Popkin observes that Locke

> saw the Indians and Africans as failing to mix their labors with the land, and thus failing to create property as an extension of their persons. Hence they had no property as their natural right due to their own failings. They also had properly lost their liberty "by some Act that deserves Death" (presumably opposing the Europeans) and hence could be enslaved. Their lands were wastelands. The Europeans were therefore justified in turning them into property and enslaving the resistors.[20]

Apparently the Homo economicus did not enter into the social contract on an equal basis with all comers; certain assumptions about property, nationality, and social custom were a prerequisite to participation in the contract—and, when it became necessary, these could very conveniently be linked with race.

The republican egalitarianism of the colonial ideologists could therefore readily encompass the institution of slavery; it is, indeed, one of the ironies accompanying the contradictions of American history that colonial democratic political platforms took as their operational premise the forced bondage of Africans. As Edmund Morgan has argued, it is no accident that Virginia, which had outstripped the other colonies in extending property rights to former indentured servants and in color-coding the division of labor, articulated the most radically democratic platform for independence:

> Aristocrats would more easily preach equality in a slave society than in a free one. Slaves did not become unruly mobs, because their owners would see to it that they had no chance to. . . . [Slavery] was . . . the so-

in *The English Philosophers from Bacon to Mill,* ed. Edwin A. Burtt (New York: Modern Library, 1939), 409. The passage quoted below is from p. 410.
    [20]Popkin, 133.

lution to one of society's most serious problems, the problem of the poor. Virginians could outdo English republicans as well as Northeast ones, partly because they had solved the problem: they had achieved a society in which most of the poor were enslaved.[21]

Democracy for some necessitated bondage for others. Doctor Johnson should not have been so shocked when he exclaimed, "How is it that we hear the loudest yelps for liberty among the drivers of negroes?"[22]

Even since the Civil War, racism has continued to justify limitations on representation, and biological theories of inequality have proven especially suited to the democratic form of the state prevalent in the capitalist era. In precapitalist social formations, rulers adduced such overtly idealist justifications as church doctrine or the chain of being to legitimate their own positions of hegemony. In the capitalist era, however, the realities of economic compulsion are masked by the "freedom" of the marketplace, and inequality in social relations is obscured by "equality" before the law. In order to account for the ensuing contradiction between economic hierarchy and political democracy, capitalist apologists have been compelled to resort to causal accounts that would locate an individual's—or a group's—failure to succeed in intrinsic physical essences, rather than in the structural inequities of capital itself.

Racist ideology thus constitutes a logical extension and refinement of the conceptual abstractions embedded in classical bourgeois epistemology and political theory: in invoking "factual" validation, racist ideology points to the entrapment of empiricism within the apriorism of its unexamined social presuppositions. Where Locke and Hobbes take nature as a metaphysical point of departure, ignoring the historical process that leads the Homo economicus to be constituted by property as an emblem of human essence, racist theory develops the implications of this attribution of social position to an inborn nature. The notion that some people are "other" is indeed the epitome of objectification, revealing how one person's (really, one group's) selfhood hinges upon the abolition of another's humanity. Racism offers a self-fulfilling prophecy: a people's position within the social forma-

---

[21]Edmund S. Morgan, *American Slavery, American Freedom: The Ordeal of Colonial Virginia* (New York: Norton, 1975), 380–81.
[22]Quoted in Davis, 3.

tion is construed to be founded in that people's nature, and "data" from that nature are then offered as proof of their suitability for their condition. People become things—literally so, when commodified as slaves—and the conceptual paradigms describing their nature posit their necessary status as objects rather than subjects of historical process.

Documentation in Afro-American Realism

If racism reduces the subject to an exemplar of a degraded collectivity, antiracism proclaims the integrity of both the individual and the group. Indeed, individual identity cannot be secured without a formulation and a defense of group identity. As William Fischer notes,

> Whereas the traditional expectation of the novel reader is, in general, the representation of one or a few characters whose unique personal qualities are gradually revealed in an extended fictional dramatization —the concept of the *bildungsroman* is the critical basis for this expectation—the most striking Afro-American [novels] place the emphasis upon a representative man, one whose singular identity is less important to the author's purpose than the protagonist's representative or composite identity.[23]

In Afro-American realism, this conception of "the protagonist's representative or composite identity" produces two traits that distinguish Afro-American texts from the mainstream tradition. First, the postulation of typicality assumes a subversive quality: instead of confirming, analogous configuration disputes deep-seated assumptions about the nature of the social totality and who is eligible to represent it. Second, the text frequently assumes a picaresque quality, for its goal of rendering an encyclopedic portraiture of its referent comes into conflict with realism's tendency to resolve and defuse the contradictions informing its referent. The episodic format of the fugitive slave narrative thus enjoys an enduring popularity in novels from Martin Delany's *Blake* to Ralph Ellison's *Invisible Man*. Totalization involves a recognition of the irreconcilability of some of the text's

---

[23]William C. Fischer, "The Aggregate Man in Jean Toomer's *Cane*," *Studies in the Novel*, 3 (Summer 1971): 7.

represented conflicts, and resolution is achieved when such irreconcilability has been exhaustively depicted.

Abolitionist Documentary Fiction

Abolitionist novelists invoked the generic contract of the realistic novel for expressly political purposes: the typical hero was intended to stand at the center of social forces representing the key issues facing the abolitionist movement. For example, William Wells Brown, the first Afro-American novelist, centered the plot of *Clotel; or, The President's Daughter* around the fate of the supposed slave daughter of Thomas Jefferson and introduced a range of characters who encapsule different types of slave experience. Although Brown ascribed some heroic features to his dark-skinned male protagonist, he gave central significance to the tragic figure of his female mulatto, indicating his own preoccupation with the particular oppression suffered by the light-skinned offspring of slave owners. Harriet Beecher Stowe, in *Uncle Tom's Cabin; or, Life among the Lowly,* delineated a vast social canvas also intended to encompass the entire institution of slavery, from its most benign case in the St. Clare household to its most brutal enactment on the plantation of Simon Legree. Her designation of Uncle Tom as a typical protagonist articulated her belief that the cause of the slaves was best represented by a hero combining stoical dignity with Christian forbearance. Directing realistic typicality and comprehensiveness toward more radical ends than either Brown or Stowe, Martin Delany, in *Blake; or, The Huts of America,* took his hero on a tour of the Southern states and Cuba to outline for the reader the seething unrest of the antebellum South. In contrast with Stowe's Uncle Tom, Delany's rebellious hero, Blake/Henry, stubbornly rejects passive stereotypes in his claim to typical status. Indeed, Blake/Henry was constructed in explicit contradistinction to Stowe's portraits of blacks; as one critic has noted, Delany openly "resented Mrs. Stowe's prominence as an interpreter of the Afro-American slave experience to both whites and blacks," and he offered the fate of his protagonist as "the antithesis to Mrs. Stowe's picture of . . . slave docility, Christian endurance and Liberia as the destination of the successful fugitive slave."[24]

[24]Floyd J. Miller, introduction to Martin Delany, *Blake; or, The Huts of America* (Boston: Beacon, 1970), xx.

Where most contemporaneous works of realistic social criticism (for example, *Bleak House*) invoked generic contracts hinging upon straightforward fictional representation, the abolitionist novelists routinely underlined their claims to truthful representation by including corroborative materials that testify to the texts' verifiability. By appending this apparatus, the abolitionist novelists were not simply aping the practice of Scott or Cooper, nor were they mobilizing conventions of pseudofactual truth-telling from the century before. Rather, they were grafting onto their novels a convention peculiar to the slave narrative, namely, the practice of prefacing the accounts of escaped slaves with testimonials to the texts' accuracy as portraits of the evils of slavery. Thus, Lydia Maria Child began Linda Brent's *Incidents in the Life of a Slave Girl* with the assurance that the author of the following autobiography "is personally known to me, and her conversation and manners inspire me with confidence. . . . Those who know her will not be disposed to doubt her veracity, though some incidents in her story are more romantic than fiction."[25] Wendell Phillips declared that Frederick Douglass's *Narrative of the Life of an American Slave, Written by Himself* gives "a fair specimen of the whole truth," representing "no incidental aggravations, no individual ills, but such as must mingle always and necessarily with the lot of every slave."[26] Stowe was invoking this kind of authority when, in her preface to the European edition of *Uncle Tom's Cabin,* she responded to attacks on the book's accuracy:

> It has been said that the representations of this book are exaggerations! and oh would that this were true! Would that this book were indeed a fiction, and not a close wrought mosaic of facts! but that it is not a fiction the proofs lie bleeding in thousands of hearts—they have been attested and confirmed by thousands of witnesses in the slave states; they have been endorsed by slaveholders themselves! with express reference to this book.[27]

[25]Lydia Maria Child, preface to Linda Brent, *Incidents in the Life of a Slave Girl,* ed. Lydia Maria Child (1861; New York: Harcourt Brace Jovanovich, 1973), xi.

[26]Wendell Phillips, preface to Frederick Douglass, *Narrative of the Life of Frederick Douglass, An American Slave, Written by Himself,* ed. Benjamin Quarles (Cambridge: Belknap Press of Harvard University Press, 1960), 18–19.

[27]Harriet Beecher Stowe, *Uncle Tom's Cabin; or, Life among the Lowly,* ed. John A. Woods (1852; Oxford: Oxford University Press, 1965), lxi. For more on Stowe's sources—especially her use of Josiah Henson's autobiography—see Robin Winks's preface to *Four Fugitive Slave Narratives* (Reading: Addison-Wesley, 1969).

In addition, in 1853 Stowe published a collection of documentary materials entitled "A Key to Uncle Tom's Cabin . . . . Presenting the
Original Facts and Documents Upon Which the Story Is Founded,"
in which she made available to the reader the "mosaic of facts" that
validated the truth-telling claims of her narrative. Apparently Stowe
felt that analogous configuration alone could not convey the text's
propositions. If the novel could not assume full powers of generalization, the author would introduce the empirical materials that would
ground its assertions in a reality to which the reader would be compelled to give assent.

Delany rejected such a testimonial procedure in *Blake,* which asserts its analogous configuration with a good deal more confidence.
Nonetheless, he conceded something to the reader's presumed need
for verification when he sprinkled the text with footnotes testifying
to the sociological accuracy—at times, indeed, to the exact historical
truth—of the incidents recorded in the text. Thus, one note informs
the reader that the footnoted episode describes "a real incident which
took place between a slave and a free black."[28] Another note states
that a presumably fictional character "had really $2,000 in gold, se-
curely hid away unknown to any person but his wife, until showing
it to the writer." The effect of Delany's notes is to anchor the text's
propositions in an actuality that is vouched for by personal testimony. To be sure, this mode of authentication somewhat resembles
that practiced by Cooper in *The Pioneers.* But Cooper, who comes
from the landholding family that gave its name to Cooperstown, is in
a position very different from Delany's when he declares that his account of Judge Temple's (William Cooper's) beneficence is "literally
true." Cooper provides a private assurance, but it carries public resonance; Delany, by contrast, speaks from a position of anonymity
when he assaults the legitimacy of William Cooper's Southern ana-
logues. He must validate the very facts that would validate his novel's
generalized assertions about brutalities in the antebellum South.

Brown's mode of documentation highlighted the problems that
Delany kept literally to the margins of his text. In the first edition of
Clotel, Brown prefaced the text with a lengthy "Narrative of the Life
and Escape of William Wells Brown," in which the author not only
cited book reviews testifying to the favorable reception of his previ-

---

[28]Delany, 85, 84.

ously published slave autobiography but also related a number of factual episodes that reappear in the fictional tale that immediately follows. The result is a curious sort of déjà vu: the text provides the reader with the raw materials utilized in its own construction, and the correspondence of mimesis to historical actuality is unmistakably assured. Brown's documentary materials thus constantly signal the author's need to guarantee the credibility of his description of slave life. "I have personally participated in many of these scenes," Brown solemnly attests. "Some of the narratives I have derived from other sources; many from the lips of those who, like myself, have run away from the land of bondage."[29] Brown's claim—omitted in later editions of the novel—that Jefferson was indeed the father of Clotel thus takes shape as a charge possessing more than typical appropriateness; the reader is led to query the possible historicity of the assertion, since so many of the tale's propositions carry the ring of authority.[30]

Abolitionist novels also reveal their indebtedness to the model of the fugitive slave narrative by their frequent replication of its segmented and rambling structure, which conveyed the text's indictment of slavery by the unrelenting accumulation of its vignettes. The rather sprawling plot sequence of *Uncle Tom's Cabin* enabled a many-fronted assault upon the institution of slavery; what the novel lost in tightness of plot and character development it recovered in the breadth of its social survey. *Blake,* which features an even more disjunctive story line, surveyed quite a remarkable number of locales, from Mississippi to Arkansas to Cuba. *Clotel* illustrates the extent to which the abolitionist documentary novelist utilized the picaresque structure of the slave autobiography more than the standard plot structures of realism. In the novel's final revised version, published after the Civil War *(Clotelle; or, The Coloured Heroine),* Brown decided to rescue Clotelle from Clotel's tragic suicide, appending instead four final chapters that take his preserved heroine through the Civil War and deposit her in a Freedman's School, where she happily

---

[29]William Wells Brown, *Clotel; or, The President's Daughter: A Narrative of Slave Life in the United States* (1853; New York: Arno, 1969), 244.

[30]For more on Brown's allegations concerning Jefferson and on the different versions of *Clotel,* see W. Edward Farrison, "Clotel, Thomas Jefferson, and Sally Hemings," *College Language Association Journal,* 17 (December 1973): 147–74; W. Edward Farrison, *William Wells Brown, Author and Reformer* (Chicago: University of Chicago Press, 1969); and J. Noel Heermance, *William Wells Brown and Clotelle: A Portrait of the Artist in the First Negro Novel* (Hamden, Conn.: Archon, 1969).

presides as an "Angel of Mercy." Clearly, Clotelle's life was intended to encompass as broad a range of significant social experience as possible. When this experience needed to be altered in accordance with historical changes in the text's referent, Brown felt no qualms about tailoring his narrative to suit new ideological requirements. One version's tragic trajectory was another version's path to comic fulfillment; Aristotelian *dynamis* was less important than externally directed social commentary.

The unremittingly episodic structure of most abolitionist documentary novels reveals something about the premises of the generic contract that the abolitionist author invoked. The hero's destiny was intended to illustrate social trends and conflicts, but it was not conceived as a synecdochic reconciliation of these trends and conflicts. Rather, in the frequent arbitrariness of its conclusion, the abolitionist novel proposed that the conditions for formal completeness and closure were dictated by extratextual as well as textual considerations: the text's attempt to construct an analogy to the historical world was constrained by the very intensity of the contradictions informing that world. These contradictions urgently required mimetic representation, yet they tested the limits of realism; the explanatory requirements of totalization found themselves at odds with the conventional gravitation toward resolution.[31] The text could not project a concretion of the Hegelian World Spirit when such a concretion had not occurred in historical actuality: the very real limitations upon resolution in the referent carried structural consequences for the strategy of representation. Realism takes as its referent the fate of a bourgeois hero whose career encapsules the arc of national destiny; even when that career calls into question the integrity of that destiny, the generic contract assumes their representational equivalence. Clearly such a generic contract would be invoked only ambivalently by abolitionist novelists, who were treating both a historical experience that belied the most fundamental principles espoused in bourgeois political theory and a people whose very existence in the nation was acknowledged by the legal designation of "three-fifths."

---

[31]The extant text of *Blake* is incomplete; the closing chapters, which presumably follow the rebellion to its termination, have yet to be discovered. This circumstance does not alter my argument, however; no imaginable resolution could alter the essentially picaresque structure of the novel, which achieves a sense of fullness primarily through the additive accumulation of rhetorically powerful episodes.

While some works of abolitionist documentary fiction exhibit at times a tenuous control over their extensive testimonial apparatus, Herman Melville's "Benito Cereno" exemplifies the powerful rhetorical effects that were possible for the writer working with heavily overdetermined documentary materials.[32] Based upon the actual memoir of one Captain Amasa Delano, who encountered off the coast of Chile a slave ship that had been commandeered by bondsmen in revolt, Melville's microcosmic fictional representation presents a trio of characters who together set forth the central ideological and political contradictions informing a society based upon slavery. Thus Delano—alternately confused, condescending, and frightened— stands forth as an exemplar of the Northern liberal racist whose imagination cannot admit the selfhood, much less the typicality, of the captured Africans. The decadent Cereno, with his pale mien and artificially stiffened scabbard, typifies the self-pitying Southern aristocrat, who is ultimately destroyed by his own irrational fear of the abstracted specter of "the Negro." The inscrutable Babo, whose unusually large skull implicitly refutes the craniological arguments to which the naive Delano half-consciously subscribes, emerges as both the object and the subject of racist abstraction: deprived of a voice in

[32]The determination of Melville's stance on racism and slavery in "Benito Cereno" has occasioned extensive controversy. For the argument that Melville adopts a racist perspective, see Sidney Kaplan, "Homer, Melville, and the American National Sin: The Meaning of 'Benito Cereno,'" *Journal of Negro History,* 41 (October 1956): 311–38, and 42 (January 1957): 11–37. For the opposing argument, see Sterling Stuckey and Joshua Leslie, "Babo —The Negro as Hero," forthcoming, and Carolyn K. Karcher, *Shadow over the Promised Land: Slavery and Violence in Melville's America* (Baton Rouge: Louisiana State University Press, 1980). Stuckey and Leslie have recently recovered from a Chilean archive further documents relating to the historical incident upon which Melville's tale was based. Some of these letters and court transcripts reveal that, in response to the Africans' takeover of the *Tryal* (the *San Dominick* in "Benito Cereno"), greater security precautions were legislated on all Spanish slave ships. Others contain the quite significant information that Amasa Delano agreed to rescue the *Tryal* from the Africans only after Cereno promised him half the value of the ship's cargo and that Cereno subsequently reneged on his end of the deal. Only after a bitter controversy, in which members of the crew of the *Perseverance (Bachelor's Delight)* testified to the brutality—and financial desperation—of their captain, did Delano finally secure some compensation, although not all that he had demanded. It is interesting to speculate about the way in which Melville may have used these materials in his characterizations of the Spanish and Yankee captains; it is certainly possible that he saw the documents, since he clearly had access to the trial transcript. An excerpted version of these documents is forthcoming in *Modern Philology,* with a preface by Stuckey and Leslie. For further evidence that Melville satirizes racist pseudoscience in "Benito Cereno," see also his short story, "The 'Gees," in *Great Short Works of Herman Melville* (New York: Harper & Row, 1966), 355–61.

the narration, he nonetheless controls the majority of the action and emphatically represents an explosive potentiality. As a parable prophetically prefiguring the historical conflicts of the 1850s, "Benito Cereno" incorporates its characters into an analogous configuration inviting determinate evaluation; Melville's tale may be based upon the first-person account of Delano, but it transforms this raw material into an interpretive fiction requiring decisive judgment on the part of the reader.

Melville invited scrutiny of the evidence by which dominant ideology justifies itself, moreover, by appending to the main portion of his narrative a detailed testimony derived in large part from the actual transcript of the rebels' trial; a posteriori, the mimetic representation is grounded in an empirically specified historical reality. This documentary material does not simply corroborate the text's status as a replication of real historical events, however; it also provides a satiric commentary upon the very pretense of legal—and empirical— neutrality, since the testimony accepted by the court is, of course, that of Benito Cereno. The authenticating voice of the corroborative apparatus designs the official version of the "facts" that will constitute the historical record; the self-evidence of the data proclaims not the legitimacy but the savagery of the Africans' revolt. Melville's use of corroborative materials not only reinforces the felt historicity of the referent (as in the works of Stowe, Delany, and Brown) but also shows how empiricism reconstructs that referent for political purposes. His tale is true, but not neutrally so; to tell Babo's story is not to tell Benito Cereno's story, much less that of Captain Delano.

Afro-American Documentary Realism since the Civil War

In treating Reconstruction and the new forms of racism that followed in its wake, documentary novelists continued to make use of an extensive testimonial apparatus. In A Fool's Errand, for example, Albion Tourgée adopted an anonymous posture and presented his radical account of the attack upon Reconstruction as the discourse of a quixotic fool. He ironically declared in his preface, "The one merit which the story claims is that of honest, uncompromising truthfulness of portraiture. Its pictures are from life. And even in this which he boasts as a virtue may be found, perhaps, the greatest folly yet committed by ONE OF THE FOOLS."[33] Faced with the barrage of criticism that greeted the first edition of the novel, Tourgée included in subsequent editions a lengthy appendix entitled "The Invisible Empire." Here, citing eyewitness accounts and the records of senatorial investigations, he meticulously corroborated his historical allegations about the Ku Klux Klan's plot to undermine Reconstruction. Perhaps significantly, in these later editions Tourgée cast aside the mantle of anonymity and acknowledged his authorship; the full irony of his self-designation as "one of the fools" who supported Reconstruction was reinforced by his careful documentation of the forces of reaction aligned in opposition. He apparently felt comfortable with claiming authorship only when his novel presented itself as more than a generalized interpretive commentary. Where in most realistic fictions, as we have seen, the sense of the real is incompatible with the strategy of realism, here verifiability underlines rather than undermines the text's attempt to tell the truth.

Frances Harper, less bent upon either political education or precise verification than was Tourgée, included a note at the end of her *Iola Leroy* in which she reinforced the moral of her Civil War romance:

> From the threads of fact and fiction I have woven a story whose mission will not be in vain if it awakens in the hearts of our countrymen a stronger sense of justice and a more Christlike humanity in behalf of those whom the fortunes of war threw homeless, ignorant and poor upon the threshold of a new era. Nor will it be in vain if it inspire the children of those upon whose brows God has poured the chrism of that new era to determine that they will embrace every opportunity, devote every faculty, and use every power God has given them to rise in the scale of character and condition, and to add their quota of good citizenship to the best welfare of the nation.[34]

Harper's decision to append this guarantee of truthfulness reveals a certain anxiety about the generic contract she has invoked. She in-

[33]Albion Tourgée, *A Fool's Errand,* ed. John Hope Franklin (Cambridge: Belknap, 1961), 6–7.

[34]Frances E. W. Harper, *Iola Leroy; or, Shadows Uplifted,* 2d ed. (1892; College Park, Md.: McGrath, 1969), 282. For more on authenticating devices in late nineteenth-century and early twentieth-century Afro-American fiction, see Arlene A. Elder, *The Hindered Hand: Cultural Implications of Early African-American Fiction* (Westport: Greenwood, 1978), esp. 41–43.

tends her story to convey highly moral generalizations, generalizations that will instruct both whites and blacks about their ethical responsibilities in the new era, yet she lacks confidence in the power of analogous configuration to persuade her readers of their duties— hence her hortatory use of the testimonial apparatus. Presumably her assurances that there are "threads of fact" in her fictive fabric will increase the probability that her readers will attend to her plea.

In *Hanover; or, The Persecution of the Lowly,* Jack Thorne (David Bryant Fulton) exposed the brutal racism that still prevailed nearly half a century after Stowe had subtitled her *Uncle Tom's Cabin* "Life among the Lowly." Thorne presented a fictionalized retelling of the Wilmington massacre of 1898 (when the entire black population of Wilmington, North Carolina, was attacked by racist vigilantes incited by local Democratic politicians) and added a battery of documentary materials. He first cited the Associated Press Market Report that gave the official version of the facts: "With the killing of the Negroes yesterday the backbone of the trouble seems to have been broken. The authors of the tragedy have gone to their homes and the mob has disbanded as if in contempt of the gangs of Negroes who still hang about in the black quarters growling and threatening the whites."[35] Taking issue with this description of the "authors of the tragedy," Thorne composed a prefatory protest:

> It has always been the rule with mobs to vilify their victims, assail their characters in the most shameful manner in justification of their murder. But an attack upon the character and integrity of the Negroes of Wilmington, in order to justify the massacre of November 10th, shall not go unchallenged. If what I write should raise a howl of protest and call another ex-Governor Northern to Boston to brand it as a lie, it is nevertheless a truthful statement of the causes that led up to the doings of the 10th of November, and although I shall fictitiously name some of the star actors in this tragedy and the shifters of the scenes, I can call them all by their names and point them out. It will be proven that the massacre of November 10th, 1898, had been carefully planned by the leading wealthy citizens of Wilmington.

Thorne's documentation serves an interesting function. On the one hand, *Hanover* is clearly a fiction, with its scenic dramatization and

---

[35]Jack Thorne, *Hanover; or, The Persecution of the Lowly* (New York: Arno, New York Times, 1969), 3. I quote below from p. 10.

psychological interiorization, and its factual apparatus reinforces the text's generalized status as a challenge to the Associated Press's "attack upon the character and integrity of the Negroes of Wilmington." On the other hand, Thorne proposes that his reconcretization is an unmediated replication of its referent: it is a "truthful statement." Thorne assigns a privileged veracious status to his mimetic representation because the journalism of the dominant class denies the truth: fictive discourse must step in to tell the truth when nonfictional discourse lies.

Sutton Griggs, also writing in the grim years of the Jim Crow era, explored the limits of documentary overdetermination in his *The Hindered Hand; or, The Reign of the Repressionist*. In his preface, he remarked that "in no part of the book has the author done violence to conditions as he has been permitted to view them";[36] in his "Notes for the Serious" at the end of the text, he cited the factual basis for various fictionalized characters and incidents. Like Tourgée, Griggs clearly felt it necessary to point out that his typical characters did indeed represent a broad range of experience, unknown as this experience may have been to most readers. In the third edition of the novel, moreover, Griggs went so far as to remove a debate between fictional characters and to append it instead as "A Hindering Hand, Supplementary to *The Hindered Hand:* A Review of the Anti-Negro Crusade of Mr. Thomas Dixon, Jr." In Griggs's eyes, no purely fictional representation could respond to the racist representations in *The Leopard's Spots* with sufficient polemical force; factual authentication was required. *The Hindered Hand* signals in both its referent and its strategy of representation the continuing pressure of many of the issues that had motivated the abolitionist novelists. Clearly the legal extension of certain aspects of "universal humanity" had hardly produced the sorts of social transformations that would permit a writer such as Griggs to project his generalized fictional assertions from a position of assumed ideological authority.

Subsequent realistic writers addressing the issues of slavery and racism have introduced documentary materials in a less intrusive manner, but they have continued to rely upon explicitly extratextual

---

[36]Sutton E. Griggs, *The Hindered Hand; or, The Reign of the Repressionist* (1905; Miami: Mnemosyne, 1969), 5. Also see *Imperium in Imperio*, in which Griggs uses a complicated testimonial apparatus to vouch for the truth of a rather implausible account of a black separatist movement.

proof and argument. Thus Howard Fast, in his depiction of multiracial unity during Reconstruction, attached a postscript attesting to his
novel's recovery of a past that had been deliberately erased from the
historical record: "There was not one Carwell in the south at that period, but a thousand, both larger and smaller," he declares. "When
the eight-year period of Negro and white freedom and cooperation in
the South was destroyed, it was destroyed completely. Not only
were material things wiped out and people slain, but the very memory was expunged."[37] Richard Wright had similar purposes in mind
when he attached authenticating prefaces to the naturalistic narratives
contained in *Uncle Tom's Children* and *Native Son*. He introduced the
second edition of *Uncle Tom's Children* with an autobiographical
sketch, "The Ethics of Living Jim Crow," in which he reinforced the
generalizing power of his fictional tales by anchoring their gruesome
events in the writer's own experience. He prefaced the second edition
of *Native Son* with an explanatory essay, "How Bigger Was Born,"
in which he argued that the character of Bigger Thomas was a composite of many youths the author himself had known and that it embodied a grim symbol of American social reality: "Just as one sees
when one walks into a medical research laboratory jars of alcohol
containing abnormally large or distorted portions of the human
body, just so did I see and feel that the conditions of life under which
Negroes are forced to live in America contain the embryonic emotional prefiguration of how a large part of the body politic would react under stress."[38] In positing Bigger as an "abnormally large" and
"distorted" native son, Wright thus highlights the contradictory ideological abstractions of American democracy: the very individuals to
whom it denies representation become, ironically, the synecdochic
representatives of its social essence. Even Margaret Walker's *Jubilee*,
which proffers its narrative largely as a transparently realistic replication of its referent, contains a brief preface informing the reader that
the text has its foundation in a verifiable historical actuality: "I have a
true photograph of my great-grandmother, who is the Vyry of this
tale," Walker remarks. "The picture was made approximately one
hundred years ago."[39] Documentation reminds us that the text is not
the product of a transcendental subjectivity standing outside or above

[37]Howard Fast, *Freedom Road* (New York: World, 1944), 262.
[38]Richard Wright, *Native Son* (New York: Harper & Row, 1940), xxi.
[39]Margaret Walker, *Jubilee* (Boston: Houghton Mifflin, 1966), x.

the historical process that constitutes the text's referent. It is based in family history; oral tradition provides the text with a determinate locus of narrative consciousness.

Modernism in the Afro-American Documentary Novel

A pronounced concern with extratextual verification and veracity also characterizes the Afro-American documentary novel when it enters the domains of modernism and postmodernism. Even as it participates in the relativism and skepticism characterizing many twentieth-century metahistorical novels and fictional autobiographies, the text doggedly insists upon its status as a purveyor of historically specific cognition.

The Afro-American Metahistorical Novel

The novels of John A. Williams project a peculiar blend of paranoia and prophecy that situates them in the strain of metahistorical modernism extending into the tradition of Pynchon and Barth. In *The Man Who Cried I Am*, Williams's Harry Ames—a barely disguised version of Richard Wright—is assassinated when he discovers an interimperialist plot to exterminate all the earth's people of color. In *Captain Blackman*, Williams's Orlandoesque protagonist participates in all the major military experiences of the United States Army, from the American Revolution through the Vietnam War to some nameless neocolonial war of the future in which blacks seize the arsenal and threaten genocidal retaliation. In both novels, history is guided by conspiratorial forces that threaten global holocaust: the free-floating anxiety of Isherwood and Wolfe has become a vision of global conspiracy. Also in both novels, a series of documentary devices enforces the notion that the history we have learned is a text constructed by nefarious powers. Williams's suggestion, in *The Man Who Cried I Am*, that Richard Wright was killed by the C.I.A. challenges the official account of his death; the novel's inclusion of thinly veiled counterparts to Martin Luther King, Malcolm X, and James Baldwin only intensifies its implication that the entire course of modern black history may have been misreported.[40] In *Captain Blackman*, Williams's prefacing of each of his hero's lives with quotations from such sources as the *New York Times*, the *Congressional Record*, and official military documents reveals the mendacity and double-dealing that masquerade as legitimacy. When Williams invents his own documents, (as when Captain Blackman receives a discharge signed by George Washington), the reader is thus forced to agree that Williams's lying is no worse than that of the powers that be. If one fiction is contained in the military archive, another will be set forth in the novel.

Williams clearly identifies with those who proclaim that reality is a fiction. His works cannot simply be dismissed as solipsistic, however, for they insist that their suspicions constitute a justifiable response to very concrete historical circumstances. The government plan for detention and genocide depicted in *The Man Who Cried I Am*, for instance, bears a chilling resemblance to certain actual provisions of the McCarren Act and of the Internal Security Act of 1950. As C. W. E. Bigsby notes,

> The suggestion that Harry Ames (Richard Wright) died at the hands of a C.I.A. assassin is, in a way, no more absurd than the black comedy of the events which followed President Kennedy's assassination. Those suspicious of the existence of a vast political and even cosmic conspiracy no longer seem so paranoid as once they did. To Williams, the conspiracy which the novel proposes as being responsible not only for Lumumba's death but also for the disproportionately high level of black casualties in Viet Nam, is at least as plausible as the public fictions advanced as explanations of those events.[41]

Pynchon's postal conspiracy in *The Crying of Lot 49* is ominous enough, but it lacks a specific historical referent. Williams's representation of a plan for massive racist suppression, by contrast, replicates features—perhaps not widely publicized—of a referent that is in some respects all too real.

In *Captain Blackman*, Williams's elaborate documentary apparatus invests his metahistorical prophecy with a strange aura of historicity.

[40]Williams has also set forth his theory that Wright was killed by the C.I.A. in *The Most Native of Native Sons: A Biography of Richard Wright* (Garden City: Doubleday, 1970).
[41]C. W. E. Bigsby, "Judgment Day Is Coming!" in *Black Fiction: New Studies in the Afro-American Novel since 1945*, ed. A. Robert Lee (New York: Barnes & Noble, 1980), 164.

The hero may undergo a Bergsonian asymmetrical aging, but his essence is anything but the transcendental subjectivity of a modernist artist-hero. If there is, to echo Woolf, a "terror" in the represented "present" of the novel's final scene, it by no means derives from the "nondescript character" of that present: the horror of historical process is real. If the novel's final scenario seems beyond plausibility, it is only a little less plausible than the novel's representation of the Tombolo massacre—a little-known episode in World War II when scores of black GI's were murdered by the American military in the Italian swamps. Williams's fictionalized account of the Tombolo massacre is followed by a reference to Eisenhower's letter to the Allied Expeditionary Forces, in which the commander in chief offers "colored troops who have had infantry training" the "opportunity to fight shoulder to shoulder" with white troops "to deliver the knockout blow" to the Germans.[42] Public documentation from the archives reverses the truth of what actually happened: the "fighting shoulder to shoulder" at Tombolo, rather than contributing to the defeat of fascism, revealed the fascist tendencies within the United States military itself. Thus, in both *The Man Who Cried I Am* and *Captain Blackman,* the closing prediction of genocide is given an aura of horrific possibility by the invocation of a factual apparatus that calls into question received versions of the historical record. Indeterminacy has a determinate adversary, and apocalyptic determinism is grounded in a historical trajectory that, it can be demonstrated, already characterizes the development of American history.

Ishmael Reed, in *Mumbo-Jumbo* and *Flight to Canada,* engages in a parodic play with narrative forms that have supposedly encoded the essential truths of Afro-American experience. In *Mumbo-Jumbo,* Reed asserts that Haitian folk rituals are at the heart of the major strands in modern American popular culture—a movement that he terms "Jes Grew," in an ironic sideswipe at Stowe's Topsy, who is presented in *Uncle Tom's Cabin* as a typical exemplar of black folk experience. Intersplicing his narrative with such materials as a photograph from Mark Sullivan's *Our Times,* an advertising poster from the Cotton Club, and, anachronistically, a photograph of Attorney General John Mitchell, Reed parodies historical chronicle by demonstrating that the evidence that can be used to validate one version of the past can be

---

[42]John A. Williams, *Captain Blackman* (Garden City: Doubleday, 1972), 273.

258

creatively rearranged to prove another. He even adduces what looks like documentary proof when, to substantiate his assertion that Woodrow Wilson was stricken down by an act of "Voo Doo vengeance," he footnotes as his source Robert K. Murray's *The Harding Era*—a book which, of course, makes no such claim.[43]

In *Flight to Canada,* Reed parodies the classical historical novel, inviting the reader to flout the very generic contract he has invoked. The world-historical heroes of cultural mythology receive a severe drubbing: Lincoln and Stowe, for example, enter the text not as a posteriori validation of the historical dialectic embodied in Raven Quickskill's career but as real impediments to the hero's aspiration to represent supposedly universal democratic ideals. Stowe emerges as a particularly villainous presence, for she pillages Uncle Robin's (Josiah Henson's) slave autobiography in her *Uncle Tom's Cabin* and thus strips him of "his story . . . his gris-gris . . . his Etheric Double."[44] The text's numerous anachronisms underline its critique of complacent liberal progressivism. When house slaves watch TV on waterbeds in the quarters and fugitive slaves travel by jet, the text's pretension to depict and resolve historically specific social contradictions is lampooned. The struggle for freedom may have been "resolved" in 1863, Reed implies, but clearly new forms of enslavement (to the commodity form, to the mass media) have emerged.

In both *Mumbo-Jumbo* and *Flight to Canada,* Reed attaches a specific historical urgency to the Collingwoodian enterprise, for the story that he would understand and reconstruct from within—even if he has to create his own "fixed points"—is nothing less than the historical experience of black Americans. In one sense Reed identifies clearly with the tradition of idealist historiography. In both novels, he valorizes "hoo doo" as a privileged discourse that can, through mystical insight, penetrate the opacity of a racist and consumerist culture. Moreover, he posits the radical indeterminacy of all historical discourse, including his own; Raven Quickskill muses, "Who is to say what is fact and what is fiction?" This proclivity toward a highly sub-

---

[43]Ishmael Reed, *Mumbo-Jumbo* (1972; New York: Avon, 1978), 167.

[44]Reed, *Flight to Canada* (New York: Random House, 1976), 8. The statements quoted below are from pp. 7 and 89. For an indication of how easily Reed can be assimilated to the postmodernist celebration of self-conscious textuality, see Frank McConnell's treatment of Raven Quickskill as an artist-hero in "Ishmael Reed's Fiction," in *Black Fiction,* ed. Lee, 145–47.

jectivist epistemology accompanies an often dubious critique of the content of historical process: chattel slavery somehow becomes a Husserlian equivalent to consumer fetishism, and freedom becomes abstracted as, again in Raven Quickskill's words, a "state of mind." Reed's ideological stance differs from that of much contemporary writing, however, in his insistence upon the specifically historical assertive power of discourse. He would not pose a cultural alternative to *Our Times* if he did not think Sullivan's chronicle had significant powers of misrepresentation; he would not direct such ire toward Stowe if he did not think that she in some way distorted a referent existing beyond the borders of *Uncle Tom's Cabin*. In his novels, Reed invokes a generic contract similar to that accompanying Barth's mirthful lampoon in *The Sot-Weed Factor*. The difference is, however, that, as "poet," he does not wonder "whether the Course of Human History Is Progress, a Drama, a Retrogression, a Cycle, an Undulation, a Vortex, a Right-or-Left-Handed Spiral, a Mere Continuum, or What Have You."[45] Rather, he asks the reader to anchor the text's analogous configuration in a historical actuality that requires determinate judgment, even if it evades determinate codification. History is never simply "What Have You," if only because it has the power to destroy.

Afro-American Fictional Autobiography

Just as the metahistorical novel retains a connection to concrete and specific historicity in the hands of Afro-American practitioners, the fictional autobiography retains a power of generalized interpretation and commentary. Where much modernist fictional autobiography, as we have seen, repudiates its roots in nineteenth-century realism, invoking a sense of the real that evades controlled evaluation and judgment, the Afro-American fictional autobiography typically projects a veracious narrative voice, but it mobilizes its sense of unmediated historicity to reinforce the text's larger claims about the historical world in which this veracious voice is situated. The speaker does not simply become a character in a first-person realistic narration; on the contrary, as in the pseudofactual novel of the eighteenth century, the text projects a discrepancy between its speaking voice as

---

[45]John Barth, *The Sot-Weed Factor* (Garden City: Doubleday, 1960), 718.

an agent and as an object of perception. The character is only partially incorporated into the text's representation of events, for his or her voice asserts an authority superseding that of the absent author. This irony is directed, however, not toward fissures and contradictions in the ideological discourse of a given speaker but toward the social and discursive practices that would deprive the speaking voice of its claim to typicality—that would, in effect, reduce it to either stereotypicality or anonymity. The Afro-American fictional autobiography asserts a critical totalization of historical actuality; its pseudofactual posture primarily serves to reinforce the felt presence of a subject refusing objectification within the paradigms of racist ideology.

James Weldon Johnson's *The Autobiography of an Ex-Coloured Man* poses a complex and contradictory overdetermination of historicist claims, for the text purports to represent a voice that is at once actual, anonymous, and typical. It proposes itself as the true confession of a light-skinned artist-hero who has made the decision to pass for white but finally concludes bitterly that, like the biblical Esau, he may have sold his birthright for a mess of pottage. Johnson so effectively simulated the "double consciousness" of a member of the "talented tenth" that, when the work first appeared under a pseudonym, it was widely accepted as a genuinely factual document. "Even after Johnson revealed his identity," Robert Bone remarks, "he was so beset by readers who thought it was the story of his life that he was forced to write a real autobiography in self-defense."[46] Indeed, Johnson himself made the interesting assertion that the text, while wholly invented, was to be seen as a "human document," rather than as a "piece of fiction."[47] Instead of ironizing the text's generalized claims, however, this pseudofactual posture greatly enhanced the text's interpretation and judgment of American society, since the speaker's derogatory assessment of the cost of whiteness becomes the dominant ideological perspective that guides the text's entire commentary on social reality. The hero's veracious insistence upon his anonymity reinforces the veiled threat contained in his discourse: no

[46]Robert Bone, *The Negro Novel in America* (New Haven: Yale University Press, 1958), 46.

[47]James Weldon Johnson to Carl Van Vechten, March 25, 1925. The statement quoted below is from Johnson to Carl Van Doren, December 28, 1922, in Eugene Levy, *James Weldon Johnson: Black Leader, Black Voice* (Chicago: University of Chicago Press, 1973), 132, 128–29.

doubt the notion that this speaker might be enjoying the status of the very whiteness he scorned—including even marital prerogatives—disturbed the equanimity of a number of readers when the novel appeared in 1912. At the same time, the hero's stubborn assertion that he has no name places his pseudomemoir in ironic juxtaposition with the entire tradition of the fugitive slave autobiography, which celebrated the subject's emergence from anonymity to membership in universal humanity.

The Autobiography of an Ex-Coloured Man thus grafts a compelling sense of the real onto the broader propositional assertions of realism. John's nameless hero is, like Ellison's invisible man four decades later, a figure whose very anonymity constitutes not an idiosyncratic destiny but a composite experience. Accordingly, the situations that the hero encounters render a microcosmic depiction of early twentieth century racist practices and beliefs: the forms of picaresque and bildungsroman intersect. Yet the hero's rejection of the role of the tragic mulatto reveals the radicalism of his claim to composite status: if he does not represent a type comfortably familiar to the conventions of assimilationist fiction, whom does he then represent? Could there be substantial numbers of equally cynical black men, secretly implanted in the bosom of white society? I propose that the text's implication of a new typicality, one refusing equation with conventional sterotypes, accounts for the ambiguous generic reception of the *Autobiography*. The contradictions in the text's representational strategy thus direct attention toward contradictions in the referent: the nameless hero is difficult (at least for many contemporaneous white readers) to grant as a type precisely because of the real limitations placed upon the recognition of such types in social reality. The sense of the real thus operates to foreground the text's problematic relation to the representational claims of realism; if recognition cannot be assumed, then cognition must be highlighted. The artist-hero's insistence upon the integrity of his own voice opposes the discursive and social conventions that would not permit this voice recognition as an interpretive presence.

Published a good sixty years after Johnson's cynical mock autobiography, Ernest Gaines's *The Autobiography of Miss Jane Pittman* invokes a generic contract that reflects a cautious optimism: the protagonist can and does claim a universal selfhood. This proposition is asserted, however, not through the projection of a transparent realism but through the simulation of a transcribed oral history. Although the text is classed as a novel in the Library of Congress and carries Gaines's name on its title page, it contains a preface in which a nameless editor claims that the text consists of a series of taped interviews that he has simply condensed and selected. Since this "editor" is not definitively identified with Gaines, Miss Jane herself enjoys the status of a possible real person, rather than of a patently fictional construct. This editorial posture is not entirely a ruse, either: *Miss Jane Pittman* is indeed based to a large extent upon the oral accounts of former slaves similar to Miss Jane, for the novel owes much to Gaines's own childhood on a Southern plantation during the Depression, when he listened to the lengthy stories about slavery told by elders of his grandparents' generation.[48] As in *Jubilee,* this invocation of the authenticating apparatus of oral history has the effect of enhancing the protagonist's status as an active historical subject. The documentary procedures that would rescue the protagonist from anonymity also assure her typicality.

Nonetheless, *Miss Jane Pittman* is primarily a mimetic work designed to project a composite portrait of an aged former slave. As the editor obliquely indicates in his preface, "others" filled in the hiatuses in Miss Jane's narrative, and they deserve inclusion in his acknowledgments, since "this is not only Miss Jane's autobiography, it is theirs as well."[49] Through the blended voices that attest to the historicity of a single individual, Gaines thus manages to convey much of the totalization ordinarily accompanying realism; the self is, emphatically, a type, and consciousness is, emphatically, a social phenomenon. Indeed, Gaines's careful orchestration of realistic and pseudofactual representational strategies enables him to incorporate into his text the lengthy saga of Mary Agnes and Tee Bob (an interracial couple meeting a predictable Southern Gothic end), without violating the pseudofactual posture that frames the text. In certain structural respects, this miniature parable of racial tragedy resembles the interpolated narratives about Thomas and John in *A Journal of the Plague Year* and of Henry and Bon in *Absalom, Absalom!* But the three interpolated narratives perform very different formal and ideological func-

[48]Ruth Laney, "A Conversation with Ernest Gaines," *Southern Review,* n.s. 10 (1974): 1–14.
[49]Ernest J. Gaines, *The Autobiography of Miss Jane Pittman* (New York: Dial, 1971), x. The statement quoted below is from p. 192.

tions. In *Journal,* the fictional account of Thomas and John's escape from London is incorporated into the text's memoiristic frame and enhances H. F.'s authority as a presumed witness to the plague. In *Absalom, Absalom!* the imagined interactions of Henry and Bon assume the status of Collingwoodian constructed "facts," and they reinforce the authority of Quentin and Shreve as practitioners of an idealist historiographical method. In *Miss Jane Pittman,* the tale of Mary Agnes and Tee Bob augments the authority of Miss Jane as a composite type privileged to witness, interpret, and even dramatize the experience of subjectivities exterior to her own. Sitting with Jules Raynard, the white lawyer, after their joint reconstruction of the final episode of the story, Miss Jane reports:

> "But ain't this specalatin?" I said.
> "It would be specalatin if two white people was sitting here talking," Jules Raynard said. . . .
> "But it's us?" I said.
> "And that makes it gospel truth," he said.

Miss Jane's claim to typicality clearly hinges upon her status as a collective historical subject, which enables her to articulate "gospel truth" where others may be only "speculatin." The final meaning of the Mary Jane/Tee Bob episode may be a matter of conjecture, but it is not radically indeterminate, and Miss Jane is, by virtue of her social and historical situation, the most reliable teller of its probable truth.

Conclusion

The preceding analysis of the uses of documentation in Afro-American fiction shows that empiricism does not always function in the same way when it is incorporated into fiction's claim to render cognition. Most writers working in the realistic tradition have assumed a good deal of ideological congruence between their own beliefs and those held by their readers; accordingly, extratextual corroboration serves to validate these beliefs a posteriori. Most writers working in the modernist tradition, by contrast, have been hostile toward the neutralist pretensions of realism, but they have responded by postulating a radical indeterminacy: accordingly, their invocation of documentary materials has asserted the prophetic (but impotent) status of the artist-hero and has enhanced the view of history as a realm of alien and undifferentiated facticity. Writers grappling with the phenomenon of racism, however, have started from quite different premises. Realistic writers have had to confront the ignorance of much of their audience—and the skepticism of some of it—regarding the text's presumption to be rendering a generalized portraiture of its referent. Indeed, empirical "proof" often seemed to rest with the opposition. Empiricism thus serves for these writers as both antagonist and polemical ally: they do not abandon empirical documentation as a means of conveying cognition but instead use it in ways that will disturb fixed assumptions and augment the text's propositional claims. Similarly, modernist writers addressing the issue of racism have altered the conventions of the fictional autobiography and the metahistorical novel in significant ways, for they have directed their hostility to empiricism toward a critique of the specific ideologies that empiricism routinely sustains. If there is an incomprehensible destiny guiding historical processes, its strangeness and irrationality are concretized in practices that would either subjugate or marginalize an entire group of historical subjects. And if historical knowledge seems radically indeterminate, its explanation is the vested interest that the powers who formulate and disseminate historical information have in distortion and obfuscation. In the hands of the Afro-American documentary novelist, then, the invocation of an extratextual reality does not constitute a pretension to unmediated propositionality. Rather, it foregrounds the relation between evidence and generalization and calls attention to the ideological nature of any discourse—itself included—purporting to represent reality.

The Afro-American documentary novel, by virtue of its privileged—or, one might say, embattled—social and historical situation, highlights the definitive features of documentary mimesis. Indeed, it focuses attention on the strategies of representation and reference commonly used in nondocumentary fiction as well. In closing, I shall reexamine the theoretical theses set forth in Part 1 in the light of my readings of Afro-American documentary fiction.

First, the Afro-American documentary novel reveals that fictional representation entails a social contract between author and reader and that this contract is an intrinsically historical phenomenon. The empiricist overdetermination accompanying *Clotel* points to William Wells Brown's uneasiness about his audience's ability to accept the novel's incidents as valid generalizations about the conditions of chattel slavery; the strongly felt autobiographical presence in *The Autobiography of an Ex-Coloured Man* reveals James Weldon Johnson's desire to convince his audience that the novel's protagonist is both a plausible social type and an authentic artist-hero. My point is not simply that these novels address issues of contemporaneous concern. I am arguing, rather, that the very decision to read these novels as works of fiction involves a series of other decisions that are constitutively historical and ideological. To read *Clotel* as a realistic novel is to participate in many assumptions about typicality and representation—political as well as artistic—that are definitively characteristic of the mid-nineteenth century. To read *The Autobiography of an Ex-Coloured Man* as a fictional autobiography is to ground modernist conceptions of the artist's relation to reality in the particular context of Jim Crow racism. As works of fiction, these novels mobilize conventions of abstraction and reconcretization that are historically specific, and their acts of mimesis cannot be fully understood without reference to the contracts they proffer to their readers.

Second, the foregoing analysis of the Afro-American documentary novel demonstrates that the problem of reference is central to the act of mimetic communication. The documentary novel, it is true, exhibits what might be called an "anxiety of reference": as a genre, it is preoccupied with convincing its readers that its reconcretized particulars of character and event have close links with the original concrete entities to which the text refers. Thus Melville's incorporation of the transcript of the Africans' trial into "Benito Cereno" assures the reader that his tale of rebellion and revenge is not a speculative flight of fancy. Wright's prefacing of *Native Son* with the sketch "How Bigger Was Born" requires the reader to recognize that Bigger's apparent deviance contains a trenchant commentary on everyday realities. But the documentary novel's distinctive concern with verifiable reference should not be taken as a concession that the text would lack referential power if it did not assert its particular links with actual persons and events. Rather, the invocation of a documentary apparatus operates to guarantee that the generalizing powers of fiction do indeed have applicability to the particulars the text contains. Rather than implying that fiction ordinarily lacks the capacity to assert a view of the world, the use of documentation suggests that a particular character or episode, presumably so terrifying or abnormal, recreates essential features of the world inhabited by the reader. Documentation thus testifies not only to the reality of a specific cluster of represented materials but also to the formidable referential power of fiction.

Finally, the very empiricist overdetermination of much Afro-American documentary fiction affirms that, as a mode of cognition, fiction possesses a distinct and separate status. The documentary novel approaches the frontier between fictional and nonfictional discourse, but it does not transgress or blur that borderline. Sutton Griggs appends his "Notes for the Serious" to *The Hindered Hand* not to turn his novel into an undifferentiated amalgam of mimesis and sociological commentary but to underline the generalized portraiture of race relations that his fictional tale projects. Even Ishmael Reed, whose protagonist explicitly asks where fiction leaves off and fact begins, brings Lincoln and Stowe into the domain of the novel not to suggest that they are fictional constructs but to validate his parodic commentary on liberal conceptions of progress. From the most meticulous naturalism to the most far-flung fantasy, fiction renders knowledge of the world by means of analogous configuration. As we have seen, factual particulars may enter the text in a variety of ways to suit a variety of ends, but they frame and highlight the text's generalized propositions. The documentary novel's insistence that it has a particular truth to tell thus reinforces rather than undermines fiction's distinct status as a means of telling the truth.

Index

Index

Index

Library of Congress Cataloging-in-Publication Data

Foley, Barbara, 1948–
  Telling the truth.

  Includes index.
  1. American fiction—20th century—History and criticism. 2. Nonfiction
novel. 3. Marxist criticism. 4. Historical fiction, American. I. Title.
PS374.N6F58 1986   813'.081'09   85-48198
ISBN 0-8014-1877-1 (alk. paper)